Living
in the
Woods
in a Tree

Remembering Blaze Foley

Living
in the
Woods
in a Tree
Remembering Blaze Foley

by Sybil Rosen

Number 2 in the North Texas Lives of Musicians Series

University of North Texas Press

Denton, Texas

10 9 8 7 6 5 4 3 2 1

Permissions:
University of North Texas Press
P.O. Box 311336
Denton, TX 76203-1336

The paper used in this book meets the minimum requirements of the American National Standard for Permanence of Paper for Printed Library Materials, z39.48.1984. Binding materials have been chosen for durability.

Library of Congress Cataloging-in-Publication Data

Rosen, Sybil.
    Living in the woods in a tree: remembering Blaze Foley / by Sybil Rosen.
        p. cm.—(North Texas lives of musicians series ; no. 2)
    ISBN 978-1-57441-250-5 (cloth : alk. paper)
        1. Foley, Blaze, 1949-1989. 2. Singers—United States—Biography. I. Title.
    ML420.F674.R67 2008
    782.42164092—dc22
    [B]

                                                                2008015456

Living in the Woods in a Tree: Remembering Blaze Foley is Number 2 in the North Texas Lives of Musicians Series

Cover Photo of Blaze Foley is used with the kind permission of C.P. Vaughn (www.cpvaugn. com).

Cover photo of Depty, author, and Sandra Jean in Udo, December 1975, by Michael Boyle.

Blaze Foley lyrics and letters are reprinted with
the kind permission of Texas Ghost Writers Music.

To
our tree house landlord
Zonko Joe Bucher
a phoenix rising

Contents

Illustrations

after page 122

1. Michael David Fuller
2. Mike at 8
3. Tex
4. The Banning Mill Ensemble
5. Depty and me
6. With Billy and Margery
7. Construction day
8. Atlanta airport
9. My parents
10. Grody Mike at the tree house
11. Backseat sleepers
12. Dog River
13. Hippies with puppies
14. Letter from Blaze
15. Self-portrait
16. Painting of Dep
17. Blaze Foley and the Beaver Valley Boy
18. Blaze in Houston
19. Close-up
20. Stacking hats in Georgia
21. Blaze's sister and mom
22. Hardin family
23. Berry family
24. Bird painting
25. Gravestone

Preface

Half a lifetime ago I was twenty-five years old and living in a tree house in rural Georgia with a country musician named Depty Dawg. It was, I would later write, "like falling out of a dream." How could I know then where our lives would take us?

In the course of our love affair Depty Dawg would reinvent himself as Blaze Foley—the enigmatic, outlaw singer/songwriter whose fatal shooting at the age of thirty-nine would insure his status as legend. I, too, would become a writer, only to spend the next couple of decades trying to put that time and that man into words. Stuffed into plays and shaped into idealized characters, he eluded my attempts to recapture his untamed spirit, as there was always something missing, some misplaced piece of our story I forgot to remember for a very long time.

Fourteen years after his death, I found that piece again and was compelled to go looking for the reasons why I'd lost so much of the memory of our love. They were harder to face than I could have imagined, and surprisingly easier to find; Blaze had left me clues along the way. Now, sitting down again, this time to tell the unvarnished truth, it, too, wants to become a story; it's inescapable I guess.

For the truth can be hard to recognize through a twenty-five-year-old lens. Translucent with age, veined with tiny fractures, the glass crinkles the borders of distant images, blurring certain moments and crystallizing others. I'm helpless to do anything but describe what I see and feel now, in the hope that these words will convey some of the fleeting sweetness we knew then.

Yet if memory is unreliable, what becomes of the past? Can it only be known through the present? At this moment I am fifty-two, a writer, single and childless. In the twenty-odd years since my life with Depty Dawg, I've known pleasure, jealousy, affection—though never again did I expect to find a heart in which my own could make a home. Over time I made up my mind: I would learn to long without suffering; I would make peace with being alone. Secretly, I used to dream that if I reached middle age with love still unmet, some man from my past would come back to claim me.

It never occurred to me that he might be dead.

Moonlight shinin' through the trees
Moonlight shinin' down on me
Lights the way for lovers in the dark
Moonbeams dance on rain-drenched trees
Sparkle for our eyes to see
Moonlight shine on down
And shine on me

Moonlight bathes the woods around
Paradise that we have found
Here among the trees and things we love
Shines on friends off far away
Brings us to another day
Moonlight shine on down
And shine on me

Layin' with the one I love
Lookin' at the moon above
Bein' where we really want to be
The autumn winds for now are still
The moon shines on
It always will
Moonlight shine on down
And shine on me

Moonlight Song by Depty Dawg, 1975

Part 1

Moonlight

1

Things I Can't Throw Away

T he dead have a long reach. And they can be patient. They wait till you are ready, and then they seep back into your heart and crack it open. They pour out of the tissue where you've hidden them away and insist on being known again.

Depty Dawg had come back without warning two months ago, in early September 2002. In eight short weeks I've gone from being a menopausal skeptic about love, to a hormone-drenched teenager who believes in ghosts, who waits at night for one to visit her. Where once I prided myself on self-knowledge—a contradiction at best—now I stumble blind through memory and grief, astonished to find myself jealous of rivals I never knew, for the heart of a man who's been dead thirteen years.

I can hardly remember who I was before. The one thing I'm certain of is that I was already mourning the latest dog in my life—a blond, sassy lab-and-Irish setter mix named Larue. She had been felled by cancer of the snout, cruel karma for a being who always followed her nose. In long rambles through the woods Larue had revealed to me events I might not have otherwise noticed: beavers swimming in a moonlit embrace, bear cubs high in the pines. Her sturdy presence had made it possible for me to live on my own for more than a decade and write. Often I'd thought of dedicating every word to her, since she'd given up so many hours when she could have been out rolling on a dead skunk, to snooze beside me on the floor while I sat at my computer, wrestling with the muse. At the end of July I had put her to sleep for the last time, and now my bones still ached for her big-barreled body and undiluted affection, the warp and woof of our life together.

Larue had been gone for five weeks when Depty Dawg showed up, first in the form of a note from an old friend in Georgia whom I hadn't spoken to in years. I didn't hesitate; I was ripe for distraction, and a voice from the past was calling. I emailed him back right away: "Hello, hello, hello, are you still Billy and do you still have a ponytail down your back?"

Billy's reply told me that he'd exchanged the ponytail for a beard. He was getting in touch after all these years to inform me of a documentary film about Blaze Foley who—unbeknownst to me in the years since his death in 1989—had become a posthumous country music legend. Apparently, Abraxas Productions, the film company out of Austin, Texas, had been looking for me for a long time. The filmmakers were too young to have known Blaze personally. But drawn to his moving music and tragic fate—not to mention a growing number of fans worldwide—they had started production six years ago with no clue that their roving subject had once been Depty Dawg with a tree house address. From the very first interview, they kept hearing about some woman Blaze had loved in Georgia, though the only name anyone could come up with then was "Little Sybil." Finally, this past summer, they had backtracked him to Whitesburg, the red-clay hamlet west of Atlanta where Depty Dawg and I had first met.

"By the end of filming," Billy wrote me, "they were desperate to find you. You were the inspiration for his song 'If I Could Only Fly' (is that not true)?"

True or not, Billy had been reticent to tell them our story. After all, no one in Whitesburg had heard from me in years, and maybe that was the way I preferred it. I'd never forgotten the tree house, but I rarely thought of Depty Dawg apart from it any more. If I did, it was always with the unquestioned assumption that he, like me, had assigned our time a vague negativity and moved on. The last time I'd seen him was in New York City, sometime in the early '80s; I couldn't even tell Billy the year now.

Intrigued, I got in touch with the filmmakers. They were willing to come to the Catskill Mountains in eastern New York where I'd made my home for the past three years—if I were willing to talk to them about Blaze or Depty or both. Somehow it made more sense to meet them halfway in Whitesburg, as so much of my time with Depty Dawg had taken place there. They think I have secrets to tell them; I know I have secrets to learn.

Since the arrival of Billy's note, I'd begun to feel like I'd entered a dream I'd been having for years, but couldn't recall until now. I went up to the attic to dig out a box labeled "Things I Can't Seem to Throw Away." It's not very big, nor is there very much in it, considering how much I've moved around in the last twenty-five years. Or the volume of clothing, jewelry, furniture, house wares, knickknacks and whatnots that have passed through my hands so far—all of them weightless, whatever their appearance. Try to grasp them and they float on through, like items on a spaceship freed from gravity or meaning, and so are soon forgotten. But some things will not let you forget them; no matter how hard you try to let them go, they insist on sticking around.

From the box I unearthed a stack of yellowing postcards and letters, post-marked 1976 and addressed to "Mrs. Little Sybil Rosendawg-Foley" of Austin, Texas. How long had it been since I'd thought about our hippie wedding on the back porch of a friend's cabin in Georgia? Or the book of Shakespeare Depty had given me our last Christmas together? Here, too, were drafts of plays I'd begun about him after we parted, both unfinished. Beneath the scripts I found this other Depty Dawg keepsake—housed in the same black paper sack for over twenty-five years, coiled like an unbroken brushstroke and glossy as the day he gave it to me in Chicago: his ponytail.

Online, I typed in the words "Blaze Foley." To my amazement, there were hundreds of links to his name. Websites devoted solely to the fallen legend, replete with photos, song lyrics, accolades, and eulogies, some exalting him as the Duct Tape Messiah, others as a poetic pain in the ass. His last live per-formance recorded a month before his death—as well as three tribute albums by fellow Texas musicians—had been released in Austin in the past decade. Tunes had been written about him too, including the late Townes Van Zandt's "Blaze's Blues" and Lucinda Williams' "Drunken Angel." And Van Zandt was said to have written "Marie," his woeful song about homelessness, with Blaze in mind.

This was all news to me.

The man pictured on my screen was not the one I'd known. This man was thicker-set, weighted by intractable sorrow, aged beyond his years. Described as a "homeless homebody, champion of the dispossessed, mystical maverick, outcast, hero, addict, saint"—none of these exactly contradicted the man I once knew. Yet all of them together could not sum him up.

Through every mention ran a palpable reverence for his talent as a song-writer. Most of all he was celebrated for "If I Could Only Fly." Willie Nelson and Merle Haggard had recorded the song on a duet album, *Seashores of Old Mexico*, released in the late '80s. Now I learned that Haggard had rerecorded it over ten years later on a solo album entitled *If I Could Only Fly*. He had sung the song at Tammy Wynette's memorial service, broadcast from the Grand Ole Opry on national TV. Until this moment I had no idea of the tune's popularity or reach, though I could still sing every word.

I'd first heard them on a blustery March day in Chicago in 1977. Dimly I could see Depty Dawg sitting on the bed in our drab apartment, twenty-seven years old and razor thin, hair long and dark around his face. He'd been on the road, but now he'd come home to play this new song for me. Tears slid down his face as he sang:

> I almost felt you touchin' me just now
> Wish I knew which way to turn and go
> I feel so good but then I feel so bad
> Wonder what I ought to do
> If I could only fly
> If I could only fly
> I'd bid this place good-bye
> To come and be with you
> But I can hardly stand
> Got nowhere to run
> Another sinkin' sun
> One more lonely night

Neither one of us could have predicted that, twenty-five years later, I'd be sitting in front of a computer in upstate New York reading how, in the last months of his life, Blaze Foley still cried when he sang these words.

2

The Mill

I was in love with Depty Dawg before I ever met him. Our collision would take place in Whitesburg in May of 1975, but by then I was already pretty much a goner.

I was twenty-four that spring. Three years had passed since I graduated from the University of North Carolina with a bachelor of fine arts in theater. College had been all about social development; my educational advance as a freshman was that I'd finally made out lying down. I'd matriculate to intercourse senior year.

After leaving the university, I had acted in dinner theater and summer stock, doing postgraduate work in complex sensual pleasures. Now it was April. A children's theater tour in North Carolina had just ended, and I was at my parents' home in Virginia, waiting for the next job or the next adventure, whichever came first.

Depty was twenty-five then. He'd landed in west Georgia the year before, singing for beers and tips in nightspots in Carroll County. No one really knew where Depty Dawg had come from—only that Buzzards Roost, a bluegrass band out of north Georgia, had given him the name. By now it was vestigial, left over from a time when he'd been heavy and wore a flat, broad hat like the buffoonish cartoon character from '50s TV.

He wasn't fat any more. He was long and lean, six-foot-three and handsome in a sharp-boned kind of way, and his name in some mouths around the county had been elevated to "Deputy." Recently Deputy had landed a choice gig at a new private bar in Whitesburg, The Banning Mill Dinner Club, set in the old yarn factory down on Snake Creek.

I was in Virginia when Depty Dawg began performing there. At the end of April, I received a letter from Jo, a former college classmate, asking me to come down to Georgia to help start a theater at Banning Mill. In her letter,

Jo described the artists already in residence: a warlock jeweler, the hippie woman who made batiks, a gifted Jewish guitarist and his bartending wife—plus a traveling troubadour named Deputy. The name attracted me instantly, as if the individual letters radiated a rugged, romantic light. Something was going to happen to me with this man—though whether I knew it or decided it at that moment, I couldn't really say. Only that I was already fantasizing about Deputy when I wrote Jo back and said yes.

Jo was a square-jawed Nordic beauty, versatile as a director and actress. After college, she and I had been roommates in a tidy Atlanta bungalow shared with two other actresses. Our house on Tenth Street was next door to a menagerie of male hookers. Their pimp was a large, pale woman who sat in the grass in a see-through robe with her legs apart and no underwear on, an enticement I never really understood, given the sexual preference of her customers. Every once in a while the old lady who lived in their cellar would come out and scream at the pimp; I never knew the reason for that either. Sometimes the old lady would show up at our door, naked and asking for a peanut butter sandwich.

Our household was tame by comparison. We were serious thespians looking for theater work in the area. In the fall of '74, the four of us had acted in a play in the basement of old, converted Banning Hill, forty miles west of the city. *The Killing of Sister George* by British playwright Frank Marcus was directed by an ex-Atlanta actor living in a teepee on Snake Creek. We wondered how the play would be received in rural Georgia, considering it was about four savage English dykes. The role of Childie, George's mentally-challenged girlfriend, required me to drink her bathwater and eat her cigar onstage. We'd not reckoned on the local hippie turnout; the play was an unqualified hit.

Two days before opening night, I got arrested for shoplifting at K-Mart. I needed a few props for Childie; at the time it seemed in character to steal them, no doubt taking method acting to an illegal madness. The security guard caught me with $4.85 worth of hot bobby pins, hair spray, and razor blades. He suggested I call my parents to bail me out, since at twenty-four I still looked young enough to play teenagers on stage. I refused, preferring incarceration.

At the police station I sobbed with humiliation before giving in giddily to the bizarre. In line to be fingerprinted, the woman beside me asked me what I'd done. Confessing to theft, I returned the question.

"I stabbed my husband in the butt with a potato peeler," she replied, not without pride. I didn't know that was a crime.

Brought into a room to be processed—a term usually reserved for cheese—I was photographed front and side, just like in the movies, and taken to be fingerprinted. A plain-clothed officer rolled my index finger over the ink.

"Do you have a telephone?" he queried in a blues man's contralto. "'Cause I'd certainly like to see you again."

"I'm a criminal!" I insisted. Not that it mattered; he'd probably taken the job to meet girls.

In the meantime Jo had found a bondsman, a middle-aged guy with greasy hair and brown teeth, to cover my $500 bail. He offered me a lift home after my dawn release.

"Thanks for the ride," I said as we pulled up to the house. "And the bail." I wasn't sure what one said to one's bondsman.

"No problem." Turning off the engine, he flashed a mottled smile. "Want to drop some acid?"

I demurred; it had been a long night. My crime spree had proved I was not cut out to be a bad girl. Except, as it happened, onstage at Banning Mill.

The Mill was a nouveau-rustic artist-colony bed-and-breakfast—the kind of cultural oxymoron only the '70s could produce. A wet club in a dry county, in that lay much of its appeal.

For over a century the three-story, brick-and-wood factory had sagged beside the thundering stream. Snake Creek slithered through the granite foothills of the Chattahoochee River, dropping sixty feet in two miles and picking up power galore. Churning out Confederate uniforms during the Civil War, the Mill had been earmarked for destruction by Union General Sherman on his scorched earth march across Georgia. Banning Mill had survived, so local lore still maintained, because the hell-bent Yankee couldn't find it.

That aura of enchanted seclusion had endured into the twentieth century. The creek's white rapids provided a dizzying backdrop that drowned out the rest of the world. When mill operations ended in 1971, a local banker's son recognized the Mill's aesthetic and recreational appeal. McGukin was a cherubic young man with soft red curls, braces on his teeth as a result of a bad auto accident, and an unmistakable gift for mismatched ornamentation. Nothing that decorated the Mill's restaurant and parlors went with anything else, a razzamatazz of homespun and chi-chi that could bring on stigmatisms. People loved it.

McGukin's genius not only provided guests with wild country close at hand—they also got to rub shoulders with the wild unwashed, hippie artisans at work and play. Resident artists lived on the top two floors. Weekenders could wander up to the large, third-story studio where Ben the jeweler welded metal, if he wasn't out in the creek, bare-chested, panning for gold. Or they could visit the batikist stirring vats of richly colored wax for the sensuous tapestries of goddesses and landscapes she hung over the Mill's crumbling walls. Musicians and actors occupied the smaller rooms on the second floor.

Jo's letter had explained that I, too, could live at the Mill for free, so long as I was willing to create my own work and living spaces. A fair trade for a Utopian ideal: bring Banning Mill back to life—which included being civil to its guests—in exchange for a place to live, a small stipend, and the chance to make theater in a psychedelic wilderness.

That May I drove down from Virginia in the '65 Plymouth Belvedere my father had co-signed the loan for. Ethyl was my first car, bought for $500, and already a relic of sorts. By the mid-70s, push-button gears had gone out of favor, in response to housewives' complaints that they were breaking their nails on the buttons.

North of Whitesburg, I turned off the highway onto the unpaved wagon road that led down to the dilapidated mill. Tall magnolias studded the leafy corridor with fragrant white blossoms, fringed brown by the late spring sun. Parking the car, I went in to find Jo. All I had with me were a few clothes, some stage knickknacks, and a slender black kitty named Meander. A vagabond for a number of years now, I'd learned to live lean.

The theater was on the second floor where a metal door facing the water shut out the roar of the creek. The first production of the newly formed Banning Mill Ensemble would be a pair of one-acts performed in the round. Jo and I would act in the curtain raiser, *The Master and the Apprentice* by R. Ball, to be directed by Leo, the teepee dweller who had staged *Sister George*. The second, longer offering—*The Bear* by Anton Chekhov—would have lumbering Leo as the oafish suitor to my equally ludicrous widow, and Jo would direct. We had only two weeks to get both plays on their feet.

The Mill was still being restored, board-by-board, brick-by-brick. McGukin had contracted Zonko Enterprises, a local carpentry outfit, to remodel the basement. Often we had to project our lines over the racket of the renovations, so we sometimes scheduled rehearsals in the late afternoons, once Zonko had knocked off for the day. Sometimes the crew would come by to watch us work.

Since his arrival in Carroll County, Depty Dawg, as many still called him, had become fast friends with Zonko's foreman. Kentucky-born Joe had a wit that sizzled, and an unrivaled devotion to dancing despite the flat feet that had kept him out of the draft. He and Dep had bonded over a mutual love of songwriter John Prine, radical politics, and hardcore carousing. At night, Depty Dawg sang with a band in the downstairs bar, but during the day he moonlighted for Zonko.

"I'm no Jesus, but I can pass," he remarked of his carpentry skills the afternoon we were, finally, formally introduced.

Hillbilly cadences gave his bashful manner a comic lilt. His lean figure was slouched, sweaty and dusty, against the wall of the theater where he and Zonko Joe were downing a cold six-pack.

Joe chortled. "Yeah, tell her about the time you painted Mrs. Lumpkin's curtains."

Depty blushed. "What I lack in sense, I make up for in zeal."

I could hardly meet his glance. From the beginning we would be shy with each other. And for me, since I'd already planned—if not our wedding, then at least our madcap elopement—there could be nothing casual in our encounters.

He had fulfilled my expectations of Deputy. His eyes were luminously blue and unerringly direct. So what if he wasn't exactly the Sundance Kid? He had the requisite cowboy boots, mustache, and pierced ear. And besides all that, he was funny and sweet, with a curious, listing limp.

But mostly there was the music. I'd never heard anyone sing the way he did, in a deep, resonant baritone, his heart laid open and bare. He performed familiar country standards: Hank Williams, Merle Travis, Chet Atkins, with a little John Prine and Kris Kristofferson thrown in, and a dash of bluegrass and gospel. Nothing of his own yet. A young, raw performer, he had an unmistakable purity, a depth of feeling revealed by an unadorned delivery.

Watching him perform, I sensed a vulnerability that drew me closer. During his break we found it impossible to make small talk. In an early, halting conversation, he told me that his given name had been Michael David Fuller, and that Mike Fuller had been fat. It wasn't difficult to feel the lonely kid this svelte young man still carried on his skin. I was drawn to that fat boy too. In high school I'd been a dark-haired, flat-chested Jewish island in a sea of blonde, stacked WASPs. I wasn't a wallflower; I was the wall. Gravitating toward the theater crowd, I'd felt at home with the self-proclaimed weirdoes, the ones who were different and unafraid.

Mike Fuller had found a measure of acceptance when he lost a hundred-and-fifty pounds—only a year or so ago, Depty Dawg informed me now. In that way he felt brand new, a slim blank page waiting to be written on.

I was curious. "How'd you lose all that weight?"

He smiled. "I was on Thorazine."

The remark was thrown out so casually, I didn't know how to respond. What did I know about Thorazine, except that it suggested madhouses and insanity? Perhaps he was trying to tell me something about the life he'd already lived; I wasn't sure and didn't pursue it. In time I put it out of my mind. He never mentioned it again.

It didn't matter. What mattered then was the musician before me. I wanted to be absorbed into that music. And I wanted to put my arms around the tender man it was coming from.

3

ħear ₥y Song

Years later, his music would bring him back. Though I'd distanced myself from his memory, my feet had never stopped responding to the melodies he taught me. Bluegrass, country, gospel, and swing—these were the rhythms I still claimed as my own. Yet all I had of Blaze's songs was a 45-rpm single of "If I Could Only Fly" released in 1978. It had to be at least twenty years since I'd listened to it. I told myself that was because nobody had record players any more.

Then, in early October, a month before my trip back to Georgia, the filmmakers sent me two Blaze Foley tribute albums, and his final performance, *Live at the Austin Outhouse*. My hands shook strangely as I took out the live CD.

With the first plunk of his guitar, the first vibration brought back the flat pad of his thumb against the strings, and then in a rush he came flooding into me—hands, hair, mouth. With piercing clarity I recalled the dark patch of hair on his chest, the warm fur of his belly. Through his voice, so suddenly close and familiar, he was in the room, and in my body too.

Love. My love.

Weeping, I sank to my knees. His return was more than a quality of memory, arrayed in thought and image. It had a shimmering, visceral substance, startling in its vividness and irresistible in its grip.

In a word, I was haunted.

From that moment on, Depty Dawg became utterly present, appearing in the morning before my eyes opened, bending over me, our bodies joined. I didn't know if he was phantom disguised as memory, or just the mind's insistent conjure. I didn't care. I'd been given back a piece of my life I didn't know was missing, reunited with a real love. It had to be, or else why would its return be affecting me so?

It shattered me to realize I'd buried him so deeply, he could remain un-visited for so long. Unable to staunch the crying jags, or the sense of loss that drove me to my knees, I wondered if I was depressed or possibly going mad. Truth is, I'd never mourned for him, not for Depty or Blaze, not for our break-up nor for his death. Now I'd been summoned, of that I was certain. Like a *dybbuk*, a wandering spirit, he'd come back to finish what was unfin-ished between us.

Larue's recent death became so enmeshed with this pent-up grief for Depty that at times I had to ask myself, *which dawg am I grieving for?* And now there's a third dog in this wagging tale: the big silver greyhound painted on the bus I'm boarding this morning to take me back to the tree house after an absence of twenty-six years. A thousand miles lie between New York and Georgia, and all I want to do now is travel them as quickly as I can, as if by do-ing so I can return time to its old familiar order, where past precedes present instead of inhabiting it.

I never intended to take the bus. But as I had no car, and no money for the train, the film company had sent me the means to rent a vehicle. Which I set out to do until, at the last moment, life conspired to relieve me of both my credit card *and* my drivers' license—and I ended up riding the dog. This unexpected twist to this unforeseen odyssey—emphasis on the *odd*—mirrors Blaze's exodus from Chicago after we parted there in 1977, as described in his song "Clay Pigeons":

> I'm goin' down to the Greyhound station
> Gonna get a ticket to ride
> Gonna find that lady with two or three kids
> And sit down by her side
> Ride till the sun comes up and down around me
> 'Bout two or three times
> Smokin' cigarettes in the last seat
> Try to hide my sorrow from the people I meet
> And get along with it all
> Go down where people say ya'll
> Sing a song with a friend
> Change the shape that I'm in
> Start playin' again

Call it karma, poetic justice, or coincidence, I've surrendered, if not to the inevitable, then at least to the absurd.

Rain is making silver slits on the bus' glass panes as I slide across the rough upholstery to sit by a window. I picture Depty Dawg crowding his large frame into these small seats, leaving Chicago and our life behind.

A young man, crowned in headphones, comes down the aisle and sits beside me. I smile and turn away, trying to hide my sorrow.

The bus leaves New York in a blur of fog and haloed lights, and my mind is traveling too, willing to go anywhere answers may hide. Say it is possible to unravel the past. How far back in time must I go to make my present circumstances make any sense at all?

By nightfall the bus has grown quiet, the only sounds the rumble of the engine and the ringing of cell phones. Up and down the aisle, passengers are holding whispered conversations with someone who isn't there. But that's no different from what I've been doing for weeks.

In the darkness I press Blaze's songs to my ear like seashells, hoping to receive some echo beyond sadness. His music has stunned me—not because it's so good, that does not surprise me. What I can't understand is how these songs could be around for so long and I'd never heard them. Who was he beseeching with this plea in "Oh Darlin'"?

> Nights are lonely so lonely
> All by myself all by myself
> Want you only want you only
> Nobody else nobody else
> Come back to me come back to me
> It's been too long it's been too long
> Got to soothe me come and soothe me
> Hear this song got to hear this song

Decades later, I am at last hearing his song. In this and others I feel his longing and regret. Without knowing a thing about them—when they were written, or for whom—they speak to me anyway. And the flip side of my regret is jealousy. Lyrics I once knew have been altered. In an early song, "Big Cheeseburgers and Good French Fries," Depty Dawg had written, *Got an angel of a woman with big brown eyes*. Somewhere down the years, those eyes became blue. When did he change them, and for what sweetheart? I know jealousy when it bites me, but these pangs are for a woman who was in his life lifetimes ago. They have nothing to do with the fact that I broke off with him, or that I had other loves after him. They are simply further proof that I am going out of my mind.

In his last live performance, Blaze dedicated "Picture Cards Can't Picture You" to a married mother he was clearly in love with. Remembering a note he once left me in Austin with that endearment in it, now the same words stung:

> Win or draw, no chance to lose
> Picture cards can't picture you
> But I can see like you are
> When I just close my eyes

My eyes open. It's nearly dawn, and I'm on a bus somewhere in the Shenandoah Valley. In another hour I'll be getting off in Roanoke to visit my parents' grave.

Out of the corner of my eye, I see my present seatmate's handsome profile, silhouetted against the opaline sky. I took the seat beside him in Washington, D.C., a black-skinned man with long hair in a white suit and orange shirt. The moment I sat down, he informed me that he has a gun in the fanny pack on his lap, that he is a federal marshal on (literally) busman's holiday. These days they're everywhere.

"We don't look like the guys in gray suits anymore," he told me. "But we're out there, don't you worry."

"Great," I reply. "You're either the best or the worst person to be sitting next to."

During the night, while I pretend to sleep, I listen to him calling frantically on his phone, looking for his wife. There was an emergency but at last he's found her, sitting up with an overdosed friend.

"I was panicked," he whispers into the phone. "'Where's my girl?' I asked myself. 'Where is my girl?'"

The longing in his voice winds around me in the dark. It's been seven years since my last lover. After so much time alone, I guess I can't help falling back in love with a ghost.

4

Stolen Hearts

O ur romance would not begin till Ben, the Mill jeweler, fell hard for a local girl, and was rumored to have kidnapped her. At the age of thirty-five, Ben claimed to be barred from seven counties in Georgia on account of being a warlock. Broad-chested and rangy, he had a mane of red-gold hair and a Viking sex appeal, cinched by a wide metal belt and the perpetual absence of a shirt. That spring he'd set his sights on Wanda, whose bleached blonde hair and cushion of baby fat made her look younger than her nineteen years.

One afternoon in late May, Ben took Wanda—by force it was said—up to his studio on the third floor. And all the men at the Mill, who at that fateful moment included Depty Dawg, decided it was their duty to climb the stairs and rescue her, while we women waited breathlessly at the bottom, wondering what the hell was going to happen next. From the third floor came a male voice crying, "He's got a gun!" and then all those brave knights came tumbling down, scattering every which way to whatever hiding place they could find. I fell in with Depty Dawg, he took my hand, and together we ran across the theater into the old stone millhouse, heading for a new, Zonko-built closet.

Depty whisked the door open and followed me inside, closing it behind us. There was no lock and nowhere to hide. We crouched and listened, the only sound our ragged breathing.

"Doesn't Ben date?" I whispered.

Depty grinned. "Warlocks don't date." When I giggled, he whispered, "Shhh. You wanna get shot?"

"No. But where'd he go?"

Dep shook his head. "That'll teach me to stand in the way of true love."

The Mill was perfectly still. We looked at each other. It was the first time we'd ever been alone, and neither of us was going anywhere.

Poetic license urges me to report that we made glorious love in the closet that day. Pledged to tell the truth (when I know it), I must confess that all we did was talk. Depty was too much a gentleman for anything else. Yet being unexpectedly thrown together like that gave us the chance to go beyond shyness.

We settled on the floor facing each other. I was aware of his legs close to mine, his eyes on my thin T-shirt, a jumpiness in my stomach.

I asked about his limp. He'd had polio as an infant, he told me. "I got the distinction of being the first person in Arkansas to be cured of it." That was why, as a kid, he'd never been able to run around much, or play sports.

"You hauled ass pretty good right then," I replied. For some reason my accent had just gone decidedly cornpone.

His laugh was a string of mirthful hiccups. "I always been something of an oddity."

I knew a thing or two about that. Growing up in a small Virginia mill town, I was also an odd duck.

Depty winked. "Ain't you of the Jewish distraction?"

I snickered. "I was the only Jewish kid in my entire elementary school. They used to invite me to the other classes for 'Show and Tell.'"

He frowned. "You're joking."

"Yes. But kids did ask to see my horns."

I told him how my father had designed the first split-level house in town, how people used to drive by to admire its pink-and-gray trim, while all I wanted was to live in a white-frame house, and go to one of those churches gospel poured out of, the same kind of music I'd heard pour out of him.

Turned out he'd grown up in a family of traveling gospel singers. The Fuller Family trio had gone from church to church, singing for their supper and a place to stay.

He described their performances. "Mother'd tap her foot and play the ukulele and Daddy'd sit out in the station wagon and drink Ripple. Then he'd sell all the canned goods we'd earned for another bottle."

"Were you Baptist? It's hard to keep you Gentiles straight."

He laughed. "Grandpa was a Pentecostal preacher by God."

"Really. Some Baptists lived up the street from us," I recalled. "Their boys used to beat up my little brother. You know, 'cause the Jews killed Christ."

He grunted, clearly not amused. "That was Christian of 'em."

"So where's your family now?"

"Let me see." His lips pursed under the wide mustache. "Daddy's in a nursing home in Dallas. Mother's real fat; she just got a new husband. My younger sister's a Jesus freak and a Quaalude addict. Brother sells insurance in Oklahoma, and my older sister's a dyke."

I stared. "For a living?"

He affected an upper-crust accent. "No, for a living she teaches ballroom dancing."

I giggled.

"I love your laugh," he went on. "It's carbonated."

"And how do you know your sister's a dyke?"

He winked. "I seen the wingtips in her closet."

Ben and Wanda were all but forgotten. I could have sat there till daybreak listening to him talk. Seemed like hours before we heard stirring in the theater. Reluctantly we left our little haven, both knowing we'd agreed to something still unspoken.

Several nights later we drove out to the old WPA fire tower, a square wooden box atop a spiraling metal staircase. The three-story derrick stood on a buckled ridge of pine and oak, the only man-made structure for miles.

We climbed the steep steps, a six-pack in Depty's hand. At the top he stretched out on the floor, up on one elbow while I sat cross-legged in front of him. The night was perfumed with honeysuckle, the sky pricked with a thousand stars. We smiled at each other and looked away.

I sipped on a beer, sloshed some on my shirt. "I'm a mess," I declared. "Maybe you better kiss me now."

Depty sat up. "I been wanting to do that for weeks."

We bumped heads. "I don't know why I'm so shy around you," I confessed.

He stroked my hair. "All wild things are shy."

His mouth brushed mine. Then he was holding me and me him, and it was a long time before we let go.

A half-moon was rising as I drove us away from the fire tower in Ethyl. A few miles down the road, blinking blue lights came up behind us. The cop insisted I go down to the Carrollton police station for a breath test. Alone, I might have gotten off with a warning, but seeing me with longhaired Depty Dawg swayed the officer's decision. I passed the test and took it for a sign. I'd always suspected I was a wild child in a good girl's body; wishful thinking no doubt. My brief stint as a thief had gone badly but now, taking up with Depty

Dawg, my theory was confirmed: I'd kissed him and become an outlaw, all in a few hours' time.

We drove to the ramshackle cottage where he sometimes crashed. No one was there that night but us. I helped him off with his boots. We undressed, our bodies gleaming whitely in the dark. I reached up for him as he came down to me, and we melded away together.

5

Exodus

S o began our love affair, which was to span two years and ten states. The next morning was the first of many spent touching and whispering, playing and laughing so hard we cried. It was also the morning my education began.

Depty jumped up naked and put on a record. "Listen to this," he commanded, sliding back into my arms.

"*Hey, Mr. Tambourine Man*," he sang in harmony with the singer. "*Play a song for me.*" He'd begun my musical tutelage with Bob Dylan.

What I knew of folk music was admittedly sketchy. Weaned in the '60s on Elvis, *My Fair Lady,* and *A Hard Day's Night,* in college I was introduced to Crosby, Stills, Nash and Young; Elton John; Joni Mitchell. Depty Dawg brought with him a tremendous knowledge of music of all kinds; his only criterion was that it be heartfelt. Over time he would introduce me to an eclectic mix of Doc Watson, George Jones, Jackson Browne, Jerry Jeff Walker, Bruce Hampton, Frank Zappa, Emmylou Harris, and Kinky Friedman, to name a few.

But mostly there was John Prine. We would spend hours listening to his albums, marveling at the lyrics, passing the words between us like bubble gum shared in the mouths of ecstatic teenagers. We pulled apart the stories his songs told, the layers of meaning within the simple phrases, the way common occurrences could shimmer with poetry.

"First time I heard his song 'Billy the Bum,'" Depty told me. "That's when I knew I got stories to tell too." He cocked his head clownishly. "Hey, that rhymed."

I kissed him. "You're a poet."

He lifted his left foot, the toes crimped from polio. "Longfellow."

I wasn't kidding. In our time together we would share many things, Depty Dawg and I. But it was this love of words and poetry, music and feeling, that bound our deepest selves. The bond was inexpressible, yet somehow we had recognized it.

That first morning though, all we knew was that we were dazzled. Depty promptly named our privates Elmo and Lucy. Elmo was too modest, in my opinion, and not very literary. The latter was for Lucy in the Sky with Diamonds.

The one-acts were having a good run at the Mill, but the living situation was beginning to sour. A rivalry had sprung up between Depty and my co-star Leo, playful for the most part, or so it seemed to me. Only once Depty Dawg and I were officially an item, his grievances with Leo became official too.

Leo and I portrayed suitors in a physical, farcical play.

"The feelings are manufactured," I insisted to Dep. "An illusion in a made-up world. I'm not responding to Leo but to his character. And the character isn't real."

"At that moment he is." Depty could look hawkish when he frowned. "You seem like you're feeling something."

"I wouldn't be doing my job if I wasn't." I thought he would understand artifice, being an artist himself. "Do you feel everything you sing?"

He was surprised. "Why else do it?"

I'd not reckoned on his formal code of romance. He brooked no rivals, in life or in art. He picked at Leo relentlessly: Leo was effete and full of himself. Leo gave it back in kind: Depty was a drifter, a ne'er-do-well. Their bickering erupted in drunken pawing at a party with me providing the background hysterics. I needn't have bothered. Their standoff was the stumbling dance of idiot bears wearing strapped-on antlers they had no idea how to use.

Jo fretted that my affair with Depty Dawg would break up the ensemble. But there were other forces at play that would affect the troupe more. There was grumbling among the artists. McGukin had not been able to come up with our stipends; neither Zonko nor the band had been paid. He reminded us that we'd all come on board knowing the Mill was a new venture requiring costly renovations. He was sure things would pick up over the summer and he'd make it up to us then. Meantime we had a roof over our heads and food to eat, didn't we?

We mutinied anyway. Already in disarray, the theater ensemble disbanded. The batikist took her goddesses off the walls. Zonko Joe and Depty Dawg went down to the kitchen and fed all of McGukin's filet mignon to the dogs. The only artist who would remain at the Mill was Ben. Wanda had moved in with him after that memorable afternoon, shed her baby fat, let her hair grow back a soft cinnamon brown. Ben started wearing a shirt. Emerging occasionally from his studio, they'd sit by themselves in the bar, billing and cooing like tame pigeons who'd been mating successfully for years.

To bankroll our exit, the Banning artists held a yard sale at Bunk Duke's Package Store on Main Street in Whitesburg. I painted a sign: *Flee Market* (pun intended) *Each Item 25 Cents*. We peddled off the theater's props and costumes. I don't recall how much we made; it couldn't have been a lot.

The next day Depty Dawg and I packed Ethyl with what little I had left. During our stay at the Mill, Meander had given birth to a litter of four kittens, hiding them away in some out-of-reach cranny. After a fruitless search, we had no choice but to gather her up and leave the kittens behind. She sat in the backseat hyperventilating, whether from heat or maternal panic we couldn't be sure.

Thus it was that Depty Dawg and I drove away from Banning Mill to start life on our own. We had no money, no place to live, and no concern about it. We had each other and, for the time being, that was all that mattered.

6

Legendary Loves

It was way too soon to tell my folks about Depty Dawg. And it would be months before I got up the nerve to put him and my mother in the same room. At twenty-five, I was tethered to her by invisible and opposing ties: I adored her and she terrified me; she was so easily wounded. Early on, I had learned to keep secrets from her.

In the summer of 1975, Momma was fifty-two, the same age I am today, riding a bus back to Georgia to retrace my gypsy past. Her hopes for me then were probably no different from any middle-class, middle-aged Jewish mother of her generation. She was born to Polish immigrants in Brooklyn in 1922 and raised in insular poverty, speaking only Yiddish until she was five. As a teenager during the Great Depression, Jeannette dreamed of being an actress; that desire would be absorbed by the quest for safety which she found, to some degree, in my devoted father. If ever they fretted over my decision to pursue theater, they never tried to dissuade me. Momma understood the spell of the stage. She'd given me my first dose of theatrical magic when I was four, taking me to a rehearsal in a red-curtained community theater downtown. The worn plush seats scratched my legs, but nothing could mar the thrill of seeing my mother onstage, a radiant glamorous ingénue in a Peter Pan bob. Years later, I would return the favor, inviting her to all my college performances—a crackerjack assortment of psychotics, tomboys, and corpses—all of which she claimed to have thoroughly enjoyed.

Sex was another matter. By the time I graduated college, the myth of my virginity had been perforated.

"I'll never see you walk down the aisle in a white dress," Momma had sobbed, after I'd confessed to sleeping with a boyfriend.

That wrenching conversation had closed with an admission of her own: she and my father had been happy in bed, but he was her only partner to date, and she'd always been curious what other men were like. Far as I know, she never found out.

I have so many questions to ask her; you rarely think of them until it's too late. She died of cancer six years ago, and my broken-hearted father followed, gone in an instant five months later.

Though I've lived in New York State for almost three decades now, coming south is always coming home. The bus drops me in Roanoke at dawn. By afternoon I'm standing in the graveyard where my parents are buried under a crabapple tree. Being at the cemetery always recalls their funerals, coming so close together they felt like one event.

"It's me, *Tsibila*," I whisper to their headstone, using my childhood nickname, Yiddish for "little onion."

Engraved on the tall, gray stone is a quote from *Genesis: They became one flesh.*

At their separate burials, the rabbi had spoken of their legendary love; their domino deaths had solidified that perception. I'd always thought of them as two unhappy people in a happy marriage, if such a thing was possible.

They had met on a blind date. "And we're still blind," Momma would quip for the next fifty-five years. The matchmaker had been a mutual friend, Eugenie, an incurable romantic who arranged for Sam and Jeannette to meet at her house. Sam was a mild and handsome young man, whose nickname in high school had been "Hot Lips." He got to Eugenie's house first, had answered the door when Jeannette rang the bell. She was wearing a turban, fashionably askew above lively dark eyes. It was raining, her cheeks were flushed. Daddy always maintained it was love at first sight.

He wanted to get married right away. Jeannette was hesitant; she was nineteen and insecure. She refused to go out with Sam during the day because—another secret she would later admit—she had facial hair. Then Pearl Harbor was attacked and, mustache or no, she called him and told him she loved him. Sam enlisted in the army; they became engaged. Jeannette had an ID bracelet engraved with her fiancé's name and serial number. On the back she inscribed, *I Love You Always, Jeannette.* Thirty years later, my dad would give that bracelet to me.

My parents were married in Brooklyn in 1943, on a warm July morning. The groom wore his staff sergeant's uniform. The bride had rented a long satin dress that had to be returned by afternoon. She'd earned her white lace; both she and Hot Lips were virgins. Before the ceremony they had purchased a sex manual and gone to Prospect Park to read it together. To hear them tell it, it was very helpful.

Then Sam went off to war, and the newlyweds sent hundreds of V-mails across the Atlantic, letters aching with longing, bravery, and dread. After Momma died, my father dug out their wartime correspondence. Following Daddy's death, my brother, Josh, and I went through the letters. We were shocked to discover our parents had lives before us, nicknames for each other—Bambi and Pussface—that we'd never heard. The seeds of their sorrows were in those pages too: Momma's fears and fragilities, Daddy's futile efforts to make her alright.

When the war ended, the young couple transplanted to Virginia to help run the family pajama factory. Thus their three kids were born to the hybrid life of being southern and Jewish. I entered kindergarten with a name no Johnny Reb could pronounce. "Is that like the *Civil* War?" classmates would ask.

As a girl I badgered my parents, "Why are we Jewish?" Their replies had to do with the passing on of culture and beliefs. That was the answer to a different question. What I really wanted to know was this: how is it I entered life female and Jewish, born to these two people in this particular time and place? Though I couldn't quite form my question, I was already curious about identity, the riddle of existence, and my own aliveness.

Today in my fifties, I stand mute before their grave, inquiry stilled in the presence of mystery. I flash on Larue's ashes, still in a plastic box in my bedroom in New York. Alive, the dog weighed sixty-five pounds; now she fits in a container no bigger than a shoebox.

Weeks ago, I had pried the box open with the help of a longtime close friend Yukon, an ordained monk at a nearby Zen Buddhist monastery where I, too, am a student. At fifty-two, Yukon has a burly merriment suffusing his muscular frame, and impish blue eyes.

We ran our fingers through Larue's dry ashes and shards of bone. "Is this it?" I murmured, touching a fingertip of her ashes to my tongue.

I could see her bounding into the road, blonde head thrown back, answering the noon siren with an aria of ear-piercing yips. Fifi Larue we had called her then, the canine diva.

"Where did her spirit go, her energy?" I queried Yukon. "Does it return to the whole?"

He thunked my forehead like a boy shooting a marble. "It can't return," he exclaimed, eyes dancing. "It never left!"

"Please." I held up a hand. "Don't confuse me with reality."

Death used to seem final; now I don't know any more. At the cemetery I leave a stone at my parents' grave, a Jewish custom that marks visits to the deceased. My mind can't wrap itself around the fact that they've been dead for six years, another instance where death has erased time. The measurement is useful, but all it really conveys is the lapse of moments necessary for them to be utterly present and utterly gone.

. The next morning I leave Virginia for Georgia. In the Knoxville bus station, turkey vultures circle a dumpster, long wings lined with silver, rosy in the first light. The dumpster logo reads BFI—Browning-Ferris Industries—the first I've seen since coming south. Blaze used to joke that BFI stood for "Blaze Foley Inside," a reference to his mythic homeless state. I've turned the corner into his country.

On the crowded bus an empty seat places me beside a woman in her seventies, skin the color of almonds, with heavy-lidded blue eyes and a great many gold rings. Leona is traveling with her sister to a wedding in Atlanta. A terminally ill daughter lies in a hospital in Detroit, the fourth of her fourteen children to die, but she's come on this trip anyway.

"You get familiar with death," she tells me. "You just got to let go and let God."

Her story segues into mine. When I tell her of hearing Depty sing for the first time after so many years and the groundswell of feeling it brought on, she finishes my sentence: "You loved him."

She ought to know. Leona once had a boyfriend she was crazy about. But they were teenagers and had to part; she couldn't even recall why any more. Eventually, she married someone else, lived with him for thirty-four years, had his fourteen kids. On the day of her husband's funeral, she received a call from this boy from her past, ringing to say how sorry he was. They chatted a while, then she thanked him for calling.

"You're welcome," he replied. "Will you marry me?"

She was dumbstruck. "You haven't seen me in forty years, fool."

"Leona, you're the only woman I ever wanted to marry."

Weeks passed before she would see him. Leona had been a coltish teenager; fourteen pregnancies later she weighed over two hundred pounds. When her old flame saw her again, he pronounced her unchanged. They married a year later.

Leona pats my arm. "Love returns any way it can."

The bus pulls into the Atlanta station. I take her hand. "Leona," I say. "I think you must be an angel."

Leona calls across the aisle. "Hear that, Sister? This girl thinks I'm an angel."

Her sister snorts. "Love is blind," she says back.

7

Waller

Leona's sister could have been describing Depty Dawg and me, fleeing Banning Mill in those first heady weeks, living on kisses and blissed-out faith. Though I was more or less a newcomer to the county, Depty had already put down some kind of roots. Soon after leaving the Mill, he introduced me to Waller.

The abandoned fish camp squatted on a granite outcropping overlooking a muddy river crumpled with lazy eddies. The indigenous Creeks had named it Chattahoochee: *treacherous waters*. From a distance it appeared to bend languidly through the countryside; closer inspection revealed strong currents coursing over rocks and snags hidden below. Nobody swam in that water, except turtles basking on rotted logs, and the bank beavers coming through in summer to thin the woods for their riverside lodges.

A mile upstream on the opposite bank, Georgia Power had plunked down Plant Yates, a mammoth coal-powered electric plant. The ladder of lights on its two tall chimneys blinked night-and-day through the trees. Occasionally, the plant would belch noisily, spewing God-knows-what into the water. But the power company had provided a five-hundred-acre green belt around the old shack, and there was not another house visible on this side of the river or the other.

Sas and Glyn had purchased the ramshackle cabin in 1970. Sas was a civil-rights activist from Alabama, small, dark and full of fire, part-Apache, part-Morgan le Fey. Her third husband, Glyn, hailed from Kentucky. An assistant to the Dean of Arts and Sciences at nearby West Georgia College, Glyn had the distinction of being the only longhaired, bellbottomed faculty member. The snaggletooth prof sported embroidered shirts and a peace symbol around his neck; he drove trucks with names like Dirty Luv. At the college, he worked beside an ambitious young man named Newt, who served as director of environmental studies, a novel social science. Glyn taught another oddball social science himself. His Alternative Lifestyles class was a laid-back exploration of "off-the-wall" housing, a phenomenon of the '70s Carroll County seemed to excel in, as evidenced by the teepees, shanties, and geodesic domes that had sprouted along the Chattahoochee and its winding tributaries Snake and Whooping Creeks.

Depty Dawg and Zonko Joe would sit in on Glyn's class if they were in the neighborhood, working on campus for Professor Gingrich for instance. (The professor purportedly dubbed Depty Dawg his "own Bob Dylan.") Once, in Glyn's class, Glyn introduced the two saw-dusted carpenters as consultants.

"What do you consult on?" a student had asked them.

"Carpentry, homesteading, and LSD," Joe had replied.

Those were the basics for alternative lifestyles then. The rundown fish camp on the Chattahoochee had barely been habitable when Glyn began to remodel it, but the recurrent theme of its existence on the river had always been hospitality. At one time, the ferry had a stop close by, and over the years the shack served as restaurant, bar, gambling house, and brothel. Now Sas and Glyn's home became the natural gathering place for hippie neighbors, itinerant artists, and ex-student anarchists like Zonko Joe. Waller was where you came to talk politics, do drugs, and watch the water go by.

The name had come about when a friend remarked that life on the river was so laid back, all you wanted to do was "hang out and waller like a hog." Sas' kids had picked that up right away, calling the place Hog Waller for a time. Then the Hog was dropped—from inertia as much as anything—and it was just Waller or, formally, *the* Waller. In its heyday there was rarely a time when the cabin was not full of people in varying degrees of inebriation and exhilaration, when there was not music on the porch, chili in the kitchen, sex in the loft, and high jinx in the yard.

To get to Waller, you had to bump over rutted back roads winding down to the river and the shack perched at its edge. A garrulous pack of dogs greeted your arrival. If you were new to the place, Glyn would come out to welcome you and give you the official "first-time" tour.

Dusty sunbeams spilled through skylights the afternoon I first entered the two-story cabin. Rays shimmered over a maze of gold laced along the rafters.

Glyn looked up with proprietary pride. "We grow cobwebs here," he explained. Spiders were useful and their webs art, a new concept for a girl who grew up in a house where we never used the fireplace for fear of dirtying the curtains.

Sas' paintings hung on the walls: colorful canvases of mothers and children in vine-like embraces; a newsprint collage of a pregnant, brown-skinned woman wearing a button that read "Nixon's the one." The cover of the fuse box in the front hall was painted in black letters: *Power to the People*. A working phone booth sat nearby; inside, the sign over the phone read, "Mom is timing you."

For all its slapdash hilarity, Waller was home to a family raising children. Glyn and Sas got up every morning and went to work, he to the college, she to the loft to put in long hours as a computer programmer. They had few rules for their frequent guests, the cardinal one being that no drugs were taken in front of the kids. Sas' three children all had bedtimes, and every morning took the bus to local public schools.

"Welcome to Waller." Sas greeted me with a bowl of chili and a cold beer, putting them both in my hands before charging back into the kitchen roaring, "Menfolk on the porch!"

Glyn grinned and shrugged, leaving me to my own devices. Depty had already disappeared. I followed Sas into the kitchen where female conversation simmered in a stew of tie-dye, cigarette smoke, and patchouli oil.

A wand-thin woman in an orange bikini sat at the counter, rolling a cigarette from a bag of dried herbs.

"Mullein leaves," she explained. "I dry them myself. Good for the lungs." She lit the smoke and inhaled, rasping, "Hi. I'm Roxanne. I'm a witch. Right now I'm into coffee enemas. Wow. Clean you right out."

She exhaled professionally. Her triangular halter barely concealed small, conical breasts. By contrast, I was more modestly dressed, too self-conscious for free love, much less free glimpses.

Roxanne and her elfish daughter, Spring, lived in a plastic house built by her boyfriend, Buddy. Its translucent walls were made of sheets of heavy plastic stretched from post to post, and patched here and there with scraps of rusted tin. The opaque shanty resembled a wilted fungus but was warm inside in winter, the light diffuse as a greenhouse. Its inhabitants were hothouse flowers too, with a blonde fragility direct sun might shrivel. Buddy was a local boy, a recovering Vietnam vet. He'd been a helicopter pilot in-country, till he convinced his commanders to stop sending him out on missions, since the only way he could get himself to fly was by taking LSD.

Roxanne gazed out the kitchen window at her bearded boyfriend. "I always wanted a guy like Buddy," she breathed. "You know. A Sagittarius with nice muscles."

At the moment Buddy was standing with his back discreetly turned, indulging in the Waller male tradition of peeing off the porch. To preserve the antiquated septic system, Glyn had obligingly lowered the railings to accommodate the equipment of any man over twelve. Buddy had christened the bees drawn to the urine-soaked ground as "piss-drinking Waller swallers."

As a gesture of new friendship, Roxanne now offered to lend me her enema bag. Refusing politely, I drifted outside to look for Depty Dawg. On the porch Glyn was expounding from his rocker to a circle of rapt young men.

"West Georgia College had the first humanistic psychology department in the country," he declared. "Where else can you get a master's degree in shamanism?"

"Far out." Buddy was perched cross-legged on the railing.

Glyn grinned crookedly. "That's directionally correct."

From the porch the Chattahoochee was barely visible behind the cottonwoods and sycamores leaning over its banks. House-sized boulders perched above the floodplain; like icebergs, only their tops were visible from the cabin. The tenants of the teepees lolled on the rocks, the women in long dresses, the men in feathers and ragtag cut-offs. From their postures and expressions, I guessed they were doing mushrooms. In the floodplain, Sas' young daughters and neighbor friends were swinging on a rope hung above a shallow inlet. Faint calls and laughter floated through the woods.

"You're that actress, aren't you?" a voice at my shoulder said. I turned to find a blonde teenage girl peering seriously into my eyes.

"Uh, I guess." I took a swig of beer. "I'm not sure who I am these days."

"Have you seen Greg?" She was asking after Sas' teenage son.

"You know what? I believe I saw him vanish into his room with Depty Dawg."

The girl grinned and headed into the cabin. I knew that smile: Greg charmed everyone who crossed his path. His mother's native genes had given him a finish like polished gold; skin, eyes, even his smile had a tawny glow. Glyn had christened longhaired, happy-go-lucky Greg "The Punk," and he and his adolescent pals made up the cabin's infamous "Punk Patrol." The Patrol was unabashedly in awe of Depty Dawg. They all aspired to be musicians, and to them Dep was the real deal, a traveling blues man. It was Greg's winning grin that had pulled Depty away the moment we arrived—that, and the promise of a guitar to play.

I followed the blonde into the back room. Every inch was crammed with teenagers, scrunched together to make room for a wheelchair. Tony had broken his neck in the Snake Creek rapids the summer before, but that had not cancelled his membership in the Punk Patrol. At the moment all eyes were on Depty Dawg, sitting on the edge of a bunk, finger-picking a borrowed guitar.

Seeing me in the doorway, Dep grinned. "Intermission," he announced, putting down the guitar and pulling me onto his lap for a kiss. The Patrol snickered and dispersed, pushing Tony out with them.

"Missed you, little onion," Dep whispered, arms around me.

I leaned against him, breathing in his warm beer-and-cigarettes smell. His hand encircled my arm.

"Sleepy?" he inquired.

"Amorous."

He buried his face in my hair, laughing. I played with the ID bracelet on his wrist. Before I came down to Georgia, my father had given me my mother's wartime gift, and just the other day I'd given it to Dep as a token of my love.

"Where should we stay tonight?" I wondered aloud.

"Here, if you want." He waggled his eyebrows. "We can get us a blanket and go down by the river."

Waller offered us haven. It wasn't unusual for Sas to feed twenty people at a time, or at night's end, to find fifteen bodies flopped on the porch and the living room floor, much less the couples courting in the woods.

Tonight we would be one of them.

8

The Tree House

H omeless and penniless, Depty and I crashed where we could, though we yearned for privacy, for some place of our own. Zonko Joe's property lay five miles east of the Alabama border, on the outskirts of Roopville, population 300 or so. There, in the thick pinewoods, sat a hand-hewn wooden shelter. Dep thought the little tree house, as Zonko Joe called it, might do for us, at least temporarily.

The turn off Highway 5 was marked by Opal Shirrey's all-purpose store. Ethyl scrambled over red dirt roads, crisscrossing a creek several times before reaching Joe's property. At the end of the driveway, a rusted trailer slumped beside the skeletal frame of an unfinished house.

Depty had told me its sad history. Joe and a former girlfriend had started work on the house the summer before, hoping to move in by winter. One morning she went out for a tuna fish sandwich and never came back. She would surface months later, herding goats in Mexico, but by then construction on the house had stopped long before. Joe was inconsolable.

"Too bad you're not a songwriter," Glyn had said to him. "You could turn all this sorrow into a song and profit from it."

"Yeah," Joe had replied. "But you can't build a melancholy house." And so it had stood there, a two-by-four Miss Havisham, abandoned and forlorn.

Alongside the unfinished house was a footpath down through the woods to the creek. One of the tree house's many charms was that you couldn't drive to it. You had to park your vehicle by the trailer and walk a quarter of a mile through a wide firebreak. The swath of open field sat in the shadow of tall metal derricks that carried power away from another nearby electric plant, this one on Yellow Dirt Creek.

Head wrapped in a red bandana, Zonko Joe led us through the mowed field. Thick power lines buzzed above us. It was June now, and the meadow was buzzing too. Bumblebees and butterflies were in their cups, drunk on nectar sipped from the nodding umbels of Queen Anne's lace and mauve-colored milkweed flowers. The path dipped down toward the diaphanous border of the creek.

"See?" Joe remarked. "It's not so primitive." He indicated the stream. "You have running water—" Pointing up to the power lines, he added slyly, "And electricity."

Before reaching the brook, the footpath turned at a heavy-limbed black oak, widening to become an overgrown carriage road. Thirty feet into the woods, there stood the tree house, almost invisible beneath the tall pines and tangled understory. It wasn't exactly a house, not yet; nor was it actually in a tree. Three simple platforms of varying heights, each with its own sloping roof, made a single shelter within the circle of pines. One pine grew up through the middle platform, and maybe that was why Joe called it the tree house. There were no walls, no inside or out, only the grove of white pines all around and a ramble of rhododendron sliding down to a shallow creek whose name we never knew.

The open structure had been built on a hill. To one side, the woods rolled away in a swale that filled with runoff when it rained. The stream meandered on the other side, where the slope flattened into small sandy beaches, thin as new moons.

We hoisted ourselves onto the middle platform, the one the pine grew through. The platform's front edge was four feet high and closest to the ground; the back edge was the shelter's highest point, looking out over the creek from ten feet up in the air.

At the front, the topmost platform served as a loft bed, built to accommodate a double mattress. Depty sat to test the bare foam cushion. Gazing into the woods, he murmured, "Be kind of nice to have our own boudoir awhile." He pronounced it *boo-door*.

The soles of his sneakers rested on the middle platform. A short set of stairs led down to the lowest platform, where Zonko Joe had installed a propane cook stove.

"The place is ready for you," Joe announced, a characteristic twinkle in his eye. "If you are ready for it."

We could have it rent-free. In exchange, all we had to do was keep an eye on the property and his dog when he went to New Orleans to work in the fall.

We didn't hesitate. Not that we were experienced campers by any stretch of the imagination; it simply didn't take any to imagine ourselves living here.

I looked at Depty, he looked at me, and we said, "Okay."

The next day Joe and Dep nailed a plank from the ground to the middle platform, so we could walk into the house instead of having to climb aboard. We brought in a rocking chair, a wooden spool for a table, two crates for seats, and covered the foam mattress with borrowed sheets and pillows. Against the rough tapestry of trunks and blossom-hung vines, our boudoir resembled a rustic bower from an ancient druid's tale.

Without walls, objets d'art were hung on the ceiling. Above the bed we taped a round paper swirl of watercolors, a leftover prop from the Mill. Brushstrokes of green, blue, and red flowed round and round, reminiscent of rolling down a hill with your eyes open—the perfect metaphor for our current mindset. We refrigerated food and beer in the creek, hung washcloths on limbs by the water and pronounced it the WC.

That night we fell asleep in each other's arms under an apricot moon. In the morning we woke to the birds and the butterflies and the babble of the creek.

I sat up, holding the sheet against me. Depty put a warm hand on my back. Yellow sunlight poured into the woods, spangling the dew on leaves and needles, each drop a glimmering star in a tiny galaxy of woodland suns.

"Honey," I breathed, looking down at Dep. "I think we just landed in paradise."

9

Udo

Depty named our paradise "Udo." When asked what that meant, his face would crumple in a wry smile, and he'd reply with a stuffed-nose twang, "You know."

Udo encompassed the universe of the tree house. It began at Joe's trailer and included the unfinished house. It was the pines and the path through the field where, after a rain, the grasses shook their rust-colored heads, releasing clouds of seed. Udo contained the red clay and the black oak marking the turn to the tree house. It was the song of the creek, the spiders weaving webs above our bed, and the moon shining like a stage light down the firebreak, or casting shadows along the pewter stream. And it was Depty, carrying me piggyback through the starry darkness and us lying down together, navigating love and sleep, while deer passed silently nearby and the whippoorwills called through our dreams.

Before we blew out the light at night, candle flies gathered on our pillows—huge moths with translucent wings fine as parchment, fluttering by the flame of our lamp. As we slept, spiders wriggled over our heads, working at their silken looms. Spiders had always made me shriek, but now that they shared this home with us, I wanted to let go of my old dislikes and terrors.

Depty quoted *Proverbs*: "The spider taketh hold of life and lives in kings' palaces."

Through the night they labored blindly in the rafters of our paupers' palace. In the morning we woke and the place would be all decorated, corners hung with silver and pearl.

Each day I tried to be up before Depty. I wanted to be awake when his eyes opened, to catch that first sleep-washed flare of blue. Then we'd smile and reach for each other.

Our love was like the tree house: it had no walls. I could be completely myself with Depty Dawg. I could be stupid; I could be reckless; I could fling myself at him and he never turned aside, never asked for less. I thought him beautiful, not for his talent nor his dreams, but for the weight of him, how small and sure I felt in his large embrace. He would come completely to rest in my arms, a rough leg thrown over mine, my fingers playing on his back. I didn't know a man could have such delicate skin.

Dawn dappled the trunks of the trees. Then Joe's Irish setter, Sandra Jean, would be by our bed, grinning in the early slanting light. The birds were awake before the sun too: saucy little woodpeckers tapping up the pines, the plain brown thrushes with their liquid calls. In a house without walls, you have no neighbors; every living thing lives with you, knows your songs, your scents and secrets.

The chickadees followed me as I walked naked down to the creek, dipping the pail in the cold clear water to bring back for coffee. They chattered back and forth amongst themselves: what manner of beast was the big nude man in cowboy boots, making peanut butter and chocolate syrup sandwiches for breakfast? One morning the woods reverberated with popcorn-making as Depty glued popcorn balls together with peanut butter and coated them in chocolate.

After breakfast, he would pick up whatever guitar he had with him, to play for the birds and me. By now the woods were fully awake. Butterflies floated through on painted wings as if drawn to Dep's softly sung gospel.

He had no walls either; no veneer. Like an exquisite live wire with no insulation, he was easily shocked, sensitive to slights, real or perceived. He didn't talk much about his past, except through stories about other people or in tales at his own expense. But I knew he had wounds that had not healed, and they were felt most keenly in the old childhood hymns. He cried when he sang the refrain to "Where the Roses Never Fade," and I did too, on hearing him. *I am going to a city/Where the roses never fade/Here they bloom but for a season/Soon their beauty is decayed/I am going to a city/Where the roses never fade.*

"Do you believe in God?" I asked him one morning.

He waved a pick at the trees and brook. "I believe in the God that made all this. And the One that made you," he added.

I smiled. "Were you baptized?"

He gave me the peace sign. "Twice."

"Didn't take the first time?" I teased.

He chuckled. "I'm double-dipped."

"So that means you're saved? Jesus saves you?"

He put up a testifying hand. "I don't wanna talk about Jesus. I just wanna see His face."

"But what does it mean to be saved?" I persisted.

"According to my mama, means I'm going to Heaven." He shrugged. "Don't know about Heaven, but I know for certain there's a Hell."

His fingers moved on the strings. "Come on, little onion, sing one with me."

I shook my head. "Momma always said I can't carry a tune."

"No such thing as can't." Frowning, he crooned: "*Farther along we'll know all about it/Farther along we'll understand why/Cheer up, my brothers, live in the sunshine/We'll understand it all by and by.*

It was irresistible. In the privacy of Udo, I could join my voice to his and know that he would make it come out all right. As the last notes faded on the guitar, he leaned me back on the bed.

"We ought to hit the road as a duo," he mused. "Depty Dawg and sweet Vidalia Onion. Guaranteed to make you cry."

I wrapped my arms around him. "Hmm. Dawg with Onion. Sounds like the lunch special. But thanks for the vote of confidence." I bolted up. "Oh my God, look at that!"

A tiny dinosaur with a pulsing throat and bright blue tail sat on the bedclothes, peering at us curiously.

Dep grinned. "Move along there, Spike." He shooed the lizard off the bed, then stood. "Gotta go drain my dragon."

I snickered. "First time in my life I ever suffered from penis envy."

My efforts to pee off the side of the tree house amused him greatly, especially at night. He'd watch from the bed as I squatted over the edge of the middle platform, my butt in the air, one arm clinging to a post to keep from falling off. I'd never felt so clumsy, or so free.

Which is not to say my own sorrows were absent. I still hadn't told my mother about Depty Dawg, much less the tree house. I didn't know how to describe this bright, odd hillbilly who had stolen me away to Udo. Or our carefree poverty, willingly entered into. We'd already lost my father's bracelet in our first transient days. I was losing all my ambition too, as if this forest universe inhabited by Depty Dawg absorbed all need for expression or the craving for fame.

"I have this longing to be ordinary," I explained to him.

His eyes sparkled. "And that's why you live in a house with no walls?"

I giggled. "Touché. Because I also have this terrible fear that I am."

Good at playing the actress, the buoyant face I showed to the world masked an abyss of self-doubt. The sickening hollowness my insecurities summoned could surface unexpectedly, even in paradise.

I had given my mother the telephone number in Zonko Joe's trailer. One afternoon she caught up with me there. Evading her questions about my life, I could smell her fear through the line. After we hung up, I walked out to the unfinished house and sank beside Depty waiting for me there.

He put an arm around my shoulders. "What's the matter, little onion? You unhappy here?"

"You kidding?" I climbed onto his lap, big as an armchair. "Don't ever think that."

"Well, what then? You miss acting?"

"No. Forget it. It's stupid."

He lifted my chin. "Let me be the judge of that."

I sighed. "It's just that—sometimes? I feel like I'm invisible. Like I have to look in a mirror to make sure I exist." I'd never dared tell anyone this before. "There's this feeling—I don't know—like I don't have a face."

He touched my cheek. "You got a face."

"I'm serious, Dep."

"So am I." His brow dipped. "I know what you mean. It's like a wind blowing through you and nothing to stop it."

I pressed my cheek to his. "I don't want to end up in an unfinished house."

He held me close. "I see you, Sybil."

In a love without walls, nothing is left out.

10

Alternative Lifestyles

O ur poverty was carefree, I was discovering, so long as I didn't care. Money was not a problem for Depty and me. We never had any.

"I hate to have it rattling 'round my pocket," he would declare. And the whole time I was with him, I never heard that sound.

Our life in the tree house was governed by simplicity, not lack. Who needed television, a dishwasher, or curtains, when we had spiders for company, no dishes, and a delicious amount of privacy? Groceries, beer, and Depty's Kools were all we needed money for; that, and enough gas to drive to Opal's to get them. The way we figured it, the less we had, the less we were responsible for, and we had nothing, except Ethyl.

If we were broke, it wasn't because we didn't work. Soon after taking up residence in the tree house, I got hired to cane chair seats at Mule Muzzle Antiques on Main Street in Whitesburg. For fifteen bucks a chair, it was not exactly lucrative work; one seat could take two days or more to weave. Still, I came to love how the pattern slowly emerged in a symmetry of bamboo hexagons.

Now that he was a Zonko-trained carpenter, Depty Dawg sometimes hired out on his own. A new friend in the county was putting him to work. Billy was a computer whiz of Greek ancestry whom we'd met at the Mill. At forty, he was pear-shaped and swarthy, with eyes the color of Kalamata olives, and hair long enough to sit on. His well-told tales of growing up over the Second Avenue Deli in Manhattan enthralled two homegrown southerners like ourselves. I knew a little about Brooklyn from visiting my grandparents; Manhattan was always that shining island across the water, sharper, less friendly, and therefore more glamorous.

Besides being a deft weaver of urban myth, Billy could also play a mean set of spoons. He and his wife, Margery, were another pair of aspiring homesteaders in the county. They had just purchased a house outside Whitesburg, commuting daily to their jobs as statistician and researcher, respectively, at the Yerkes Primate Center in Atlanta. Recently, they'd acquired four pregnant ewes in the hopes of selling spring lamb chops to local chefs, and Billy had hired Dep to help him put up a new sheep shed behind their house. I'd been meeting Depty there once I was finished at the Mule Muzzle.

At five o'clock, the unused canes were hung on the wall to dry. Georgia sweltered in late June; I was looking forward to a beer and a cold soak in the creek with Depty Dawg. Pocketing my pay, I inched Ethyl down Main Street, aware she still bore her Virginia license plates. Sooner or later, Police Chief Hightower would figure out we were here to stay, and we'd have to come up with enough money to make her state legal. Slipping by the cops' *greed* trap, as Depty called it, I turned onto Old Black Dirt Road.

Billy and Margery's modest, one-story bungalow was perched on the edge of an oak-shaded pasture. At its far rim sat a patch of one-hundred, newly-planted blueberry bushes. The dogs barked my arrival; Margery was nowhere in sight.

Heading toward the sheep shed—which just that day had gained a roof—I overheard Billy say, "Yeah, sure, everybody talks about the poor, but who really cares?"

"Artists maybe," Depty replied. "I'd like to think so."

The two grimy carpenters sat in the shed's shade, airing their armpits and drinking frosty beers. I was surprised; for once Depty wasn't wearing a shirt. He could be so modest, I often wondered if he still thought of himself as fat.

I fell into his arms. His blue eyes glittered. "Hey, little Sybil."

"Hey, big Dep," I said back. Pressing my face to his shoulder, I turned to sit between his knees.

"Careful," he cautioned, handing me his beer. "I stink."

"She don't care." Billy wagged a finger at us. "I know this dance you two are doing. It's soul-nabbing."

I tilted the bottle to my lips as Depty whispered in my ear, "They gonna have a baby."

Out sputtered the beer. "Really?"

Billy swiped playfully at Depty. "I said we're *thinking* about it." He shot me a peevish look. "What's the matter, *little* Sybil? We too old?"

Depty minced like a proper church-lady. "Thou shalt not fornicate after thirty."

I poked him with my elbow. "Yeah. I'll remind you of that."

Billy put up a droll hand. "We won't do it again. Promise." Then he toppled over in comic mirth.

"What is so funny?" Margery strode into the shed wearing oversized jeans and a shapeless green sweatshirt. Born and raised in Macon, Georgia, Margery had a no-frills approach to life. Her long brown hair was pulled back off angular features, enlivened by turquoise eyes and a flashing smile.

"Get up, Sybil," she commanded. "You got to see these damn sheep."

She led me out to a makeshift pen where four fat ewes stood chewing placidly, thick shaggy coats seriously out of season. One wore a blue ear tag, another a green.

Margery pointed left to right. "We named them First, Blue, Green, and Dummy."

I giggled. "I'm trying to picture them as shish kabob."

"They don't look smart enough to eat." Margery's raucous cackle belied her contained demeanor.

"What you going to do with all that wool?" I asked her.

She gave me a sideways glance. "Start knitting baby blankets, I reckon."

Margery was an inspiration to me: womanly without adornment, intelligent without apology. At thirty-eight, she was about to become a mother for the first time; whoever heard of such a thing? The world was opening up in ways I couldn't have imagined. The women around me were pioneers in a brave new female frontier, out of the realm of those like my mother who were frozen with fear. I wasn't made of ice, but I didn't feel quite ready to join up with the likes of Margery or Sas.

When the first lambs were born, Depty and I drove over to see them. They were silky white, already gamboling about on sturdy stick legs.

Dep scratched his brow. "Think I understand innocence now."

And Billy showed us how to hold the lambs in our arms, how to nurse them with bottles of warm milk.

Our life in the county was—to misquote the old song—a mix of two Williams: Hank and Tennessee. We were surrounded by a number of true characters: the tenants of the teepees, the witch in the plastic house, the two ageless spinsters who lived in a shack down the road and longed for real "lye-noleum" for their plywood floors. We retold their stories to each other, puzzling how to reshape them for fiction and song. We couldn't wait to quote the hilarious things people said, the way quirks of speech reflected human foibles.

"That gal was so dumb," a man in Opal's was overheard to say. "Her eyes was ringing up 'No Sale.'"

That summer I also worked at a little hospital in Franklin, one county over. The job basically consisted of opening huge cans of green beans and carrots for the patients' lunches, collecting garbage, and washing dishes. The employees still called the place "the asylum," and used to be, if you committed someone there, you got $25 and a sack of white potatoes. Unless, of course, you were African-American—then all you got were the potatoes.

Depty cringed when I repeated this to him. "Who told you that?" he asked, indignant. Seemed like he took all injustice personally.

The young toffee-colored woman who ran the kitchen had informed me of the policy. Selma was tall and bony, her pitted face fringed with tight braids. My first day on the job, she'd inquired after my *nationality*, curious if my dark features, curly hair, and full lips meant I had African blood. Momma always said I was olive-colored, unless she was depressed, in which case I was sallow. We were of Polish and Russian descent, with a little Kublai Khan thrown in, courtesy of centuries of the bronze Mongols' encounters with peasant *shtetl* girls.

When I explained this to Selma, she declared, "Well, that must be it then. 'Cause you are the most peculiar hue I ever seen."

After that, Depty Dawg began introducing me, with pride, as his half-black Jewish girlfriend. And he always stopped by the kitchen to shoot the breeze with Selma whenever he picked me up at work.

One afternoon in the car going home, I tried to have a conversation with Elmo. I hit my head on the steering wheel and we started giggling so hard, Depty had to pull over. We were still laughing when we got back to Udo and put ourselves in park.

It didn't matter so much that we weren't actively pursuing our art; we were living it. We sat for hours reading the dictionary, reveling in words: *ethereal, conundrum, plethora*. We punned through the days, called each other by our names spelled backwards. Our minds collected idioms the way magnets draw nails—a simile I earned that summer when I became a carpenter's assistant, helping Depty and Bubba, another new friend in the county, build a tool shed for Mama Kate.

At eighty-one, Mama Kate still ran a home-style restaurant out of her kitchen, serving up a scrumptious plate of ham, biscuits, collards, and yams for only two bucks. Her laurels rested on the fact that in 1954 she'd been

Georgia's Mother of the Year. Now, bent over like a seven, she sewed a new quilt every three weeks, managed her small farm by herself, and remained eminently quotable.

"You won't believe what Mama Kate just said," I exclaimed to Dep and Bubba the day we framed in her shed. I was in her kitchen getting us lemonade, when she blithely informed me she was going to a livestock auction to buy a blind calf.

I asked her, "Why do you buy a blind one?"

"Well," she had answered. "I can't eat the eyes."

Bubba's laugh went off like a string of firecrackers *rat-tat-tat-tat*. He was an Atlanta aristocrat masquerading as a redneck Robin Hood, a mischievous hipster with thick black locks down to his waist.

Depty was already searching his carpenter's apron for a pencil. "We got to write that one down, darlin'."

I pointed to the stub tucked behind his ear. "If you was a snake, you'd have bit it," I told him, borrowing one of his own sayings.

Laughing, he swiped the pencil into his hand. "My mama used to say that."

"So listen, y'all," I went on. "I'm off to the store for Mama Kate. We need anything?"

Bubba counted out bills for a six-pack, a gold-link bracelet clattering on his wrist.

Depty kissed me. "Bye, Syllable. Don't forget to move your vowels."

Rat-tat-tat-tat. Bubba snorted. "Ya'll kill me. Godless heathens living in a tree."

Dep put a fist in the air. "Hillbilly is beautiful."

"Hey!" Bubba shouted. "When ya'll gonna trade lives with Helen and me?"

Bubba's wife was his perfect counterpart, being blonde and voluptuous, with peach-down on cheekbones that rivaled her Trojan namesake. Like Roxanne the witch, Helen knew about herbal remedies, though she preferred her coffee in a cup. She had showed me how to use alum and comfrey to heal a cut, and what teas to drink for cramps. Helen had made us turtle soup from a resident of their lake, yelling for Bubba every time the huge snapper tried to climb out of the pot.

Our friends were the same age as us, but to my mind they were the grownups, married and settled on land of their own, with Woolly Booger, a silky black bull they intended to eat. By contrast, Dep and I were weightless odd-ducks, still at loose ends. It was a case of the grass being greener. Bubba and Helen admired our Woodstock Nation housing, and were curious to try it out a night or two. In return, we could play house at theirs. Their life came with a stereo, toilet, refrigerator, and baby.

Seth was a toddler with stick-straight blonde hair and an ever-present pillow. He spoke a vivid gibberish, long explanations he assumed we understood.

"Be ga do bi do ga bi da be bo na."

Depty sat him on his knee. "De bi do ga see."

Seth nodded solemnly. "See ga no be de."

"Oh." Depty's eyes widened, and they both laughed.

For two days we tried our hand at diapering, feeding, and rocking. It was scary but sweet, and the novelty of it buoyed us along. On the second night we held Seth's hands and waded into the lake.

Afterwards, removing his large wet sneakers, Depty showed Seth his crimped toes. "Me Big Foot," he growled.

Seth giggled and hit him with his pillow.

We cooked hot dogs over a campfire and lay out on blankets under the starry sky. I cuddled the little boy until he fell asleep. Then we laid him between us.

"This is practice," Dep whispered. "For our turn when it comes."

July was hot and muggy, the air in Udo thick as a bath. Glistening with sweat, Depty stood on the path to the tree house, yelling up to me in the trailer.

"Okay, little onion, you hold it in again, I'm going to stretch it out!"

"Be careful!" I called back.

Every musty corner of Zonko Joe's trailer was crammed with albums, more than eight hundred by his count. Gingerly, I pushed the plug of an orange extension cord into a socket. I could swear I heard a car pulling into the driveway, but where was Sandra Jean's customary bark? Before I could investigate, the cord whipped out of the wall, uncoiling like a snake.

I ducked. "Dep, hang on! It pulled out—"

"What are ya'll doing in here?" came a man's voice, making me jump again.

A rumpled, bearded hippie had stuck his head in the door. Grody Mike often dropped by unexpectedly, spending hours in the trailer with us listening to music. His shirt hung crookedly, buttoned wrong; his jeans were ripped;

and he'd lost his shoes sometime last week, he informed me now. Rumored to be a genius, in any other setting Grody Mike would have been labeled a nerd. Here in the county, his oddness was embraced.

A native of New Orleans, on his first visit to Waller, Mike had passed out in the back of Glyn's pick-up where, for convenience, the empty beer cans were thrown. The next morning he was discovered snoring under a pile of cans and immediately pronounced *grody*. He returned to New Orleans a changed man, quit his job as manager of a string of Timesaver Stores, and came back to Waller to live, possibly forever. Grody Mike had aspirations of being a painter, and one wandering eye.

"Dep's running an extension cord to the tree house," I explained to him now.

"He what?" Grody turned his head to stare at me through coke-bottle lenses.

"Yeah. He thought it'd be nice if we could play records down there. We been talking about having a housewarming, you know."

Grody's laugh was the caw of a pixilated crow. "Far out. Maybe somebody will give you walls."

Depty came in now, dejectedly dragging a length of orange cord. "Ought to be some way to use all this juice we got here," he fumed.

Grody Mike collapsed on the couch in silent laughter, slapping his leg three times. "Yeah, let's blow up the trailer. I love doing science projects with hippies."

He wiped his glasses on his sleeve. "Forget it, Dep. They don't make cords that long." Grody had an uncanny way of pointing out the obvious.

"Wait," I shushed them. "Ya'll hear something?"

Little squeals and peeps were coming up from under the floorboards. We tromped out to inspect. There, under the trailer lay Sandra Jean, exhausted beside a pile of mewling puppies. I counted them: twelve in all.

"When did that happen?" I exclaimed. "The whole world is procreating."

Depty grinned. "While we're just recreating." He pointed to a red-and-white puppy. "We'll take that one for our own."

"You sure, honey?" I fretted. "We can barely afford to feed ourselves."

"By the way," Grody threw in. "Your application for food stamps was approved."

I stared at him. "What are you, our social worker?"

He crouched on his haunches. "I was at Waller when Glyn got the call. Guess ya'll put him down as a reference. The woman wanted to know if your name really was De-pu-ty Dog? And did you really live in a tree house?" He cawed. "What a country."

Depty rubbed the puppy's nose, so black it was blue. "You'll be Betsey Ross, our bicentennial dog," he declared, referring to the year to come.

Then, putting an arm around me, he drawled in his best road hog growl, "We got food stamps and a dog, baby. Nobody can say we ain't American."

11

Interdependence Day

If Udo was our private lovers' universe, Waller was the way station where we refueled friendships and caught up on new trends in alternative living. At Waller, we first encountered the über miracle of duct tape when Glyn showed us how he had repaired his sweat pants with the shiny stuff. Glyn was our altered fashion guru: frugal, quirky, and redneck chic.

Quirky and redneck were the norm at Waller. You never arrived there without an ecstatic greeting from Ape-shit, a nondescript mutt so named because whenever she saw you, she just went, well—ape-shit. Said to have mated with every dog in three counties, her offspring had the gene pool to prove it. Her son, Crooked Tail, an assortment of snap-on parts with brain waves like a dial tone, was thought to be the father of at least two of Ape-shit's litters.

Dep shuddered. "And Lord knows what their puppies look like."

Then there was the pride of Waller cats. Early on, Meander had happily joined General Ledger, Critter, and a male named Ugly Daughter.

"How are the kittens today?" I asked Sas, coming into the cabin on the Fourth of July.

Smiling mysteriously, she crooked a thin finger. "Come and see."

Shortly after we'd fled the Mill, Meander's lost litter had showed up at the cabin in a cardboard box. The four scrawny kittens had somehow survived without their young mother, but now, unfortunately, Meander wanted nothing to do with them.

Setting the box on the porch, Sas and I had sat in the kitchen pondering their future. After a while I went out to check on them and found one missing. We couldn't imagine how so puny a creature could have climbed over the edge of the box. Searching in vain, we looked in again on the remaining three—another one gone.

We went back to the kitchen and staked out the box. Pretty soon, along came Ape-shit, lifting a third kitten between her jaws. We followed her and the kitten down to the stone cellar under the house, where the two lost kittens lay in the bower the dog had dug in the dusty clay. When we brought the last one down to her, Ape-shit drew them all in, nuzzling and offering the warmth of her body.

We were awed. The urge to mother had transcended species. Sas showed us how to make a sugar tit—a twisted rag soaked with warm milk and sugar for the kittens to suckle. That was two weeks ago, and we'd come by almost every afternoon since to feed them.

Sas' eyes gleamed as she led us into the cool dark cellar. "I'm closing down the sugar-tit operation," she announced, pointing to the four kittens vigorously attached to Ape-shit's nipples. "That damn dog has started making milk!"

"Good Lord," I breathed. "We ought to nominate Ape-shit for Mother of the Year."

Depty laughed. "Better watch it. Them kittens'll grow up to be sons-of-bitches."

Sas winked. "Yeah, they'll probably lift their leg to pee."

We watched them a while in respectful silence, till Sas' son, Greg, leaned across the cellar doorway.

"There you are," he called out merrily to Dep. The tawny fan of the Punk's long hair was backlit by the sun. "Come on, sports fans—let's play ball."

Depty ran off after him, tilting across the yard. The annual Waller whiffle ball game was a Fourth of July tradition, played in the floodplain beside the inlet creek. Dep was excited. This year, the lopsided kid who couldn't run fast was about to play shortstop for Zonko Joe's team. I would be on his team too, as would a spindly young man visiting Waller for the first time today.

"Have y'all met Steve?" Joe asked us.

Steve stuck a hand into the air and left it there for us to find. Blind from birth, he was said to be a brilliant piano player and guitarist, though West Georgia College had refused him as a music major because he couldn't sight read. But that mere detail was not going to keep Steve from playing whiffle ball this afternoon, or from pitching for our team.

Zonko Joe stood behind home plate being Steve's eyes, helping him adjust his pitch from ball to ball.

"A little wide and to the right," Joe coached Steve after a pitch, as both teams stood taut with amazement.

Greg came up to bat. Steve threw two strikes, then *crack!* Bat and ball connected; up flew the plastic orb. The shortstop leapt into the air and came down in a heap, ball in his glove. We cheered, Depty bowed, and Greg ran the bases anyway, hands in the air, sharing Dep's applause.

Waller was the world as we'd always pictured it, where dogs could nurse kittens and pitchers could be blind.

12

ħomecoming

I t would take coming back to Georgia for many of these memories to re-surface. Now here I am, falling like Alice down a rabbit hole in pursuit of a forgotten wonderland. Am I seeing the past through rose-colored glasses, or was it truly that way? And how did I come to be in our friend Billy's car twenty-six years later, driving away from the Atlanta bus station onto once-familiar roads? Route 166. Highway 5.

Oh my God, I'm back in the county.

The weather is overcast and damp, typical for November. The countryside looks much the same: lots of withered kudzu. More houses along the highway, more Confederate flags than American; a county yet divided. Red clay hills still roll to low horizons where clouds lather over dark groves of loblolly pine. I didn't know how it would feel to be back, but my return is having the desired effect: the landscape is drawing out shreds of lost conversation—something Depty once said about the rain, the way it deepens the hues of winter fields, bringing out the rust and sere, making brown a primary color.

Billy sits quietly behind the wheel. At sixty-seven, he wears his hair short and his beard long, both white as salt, with the same insistent curiosity in his eyes. As if on cue, we start chattering away like the old friends we are.

He catches me up on the Waller crowd. First, his son, Basil: twenty-six years old and living in New York City, a drummer and carpenter no less.

Billy beams. "Good man. Really good man."

"I bet."

"Let's see." He thinks a moment. "Glyn and Sas divorced—'79—'80? Who can remember?"

I throw up my hands. "Not me."

"Glyn remarried," Billy continues. "Divorced again. Sas is back in the county. Her daughters are married with kids. Greg was killed in '87. You knew that, right?"

I nod. "Sas told me. Years ago. On the phone."

Inspired by Depty Dawg, Greg had gone on to play guitar with Jump Street, a band in Atlanta. At twenty-eight, he was struck in his car by a drunk driver and died instantly.

Billy grips the steering wheel. "That was the end of an era. Since then Waller's never been the same. Bubba's still kicking," he goes on. "I wrote you he has Hepatitis-C."

"Yeah, how's he doing?"

Billy shrugs. "Good days and bad. Beautiful Helen, gone for decades. Seth is all grown up, a fine young man. Who else? Joe's in New Orleans. Married with greyhounds. They rescue abused racers."

"That sounds like ole Joe. And Grody Mike?"

"Get this," Billy chortles. "Hotshot water engineer for the city of Austin, Texas. Two kids. Absolutely devoted family man. He's coming in a few days. He wants to see you."

Then all at once we're on Old Black Dirt Road, which is now neither old nor dirt, covered with a recent layer of shiny black asphalt. We pull into Billy's driveway. I've been warned to avoid Koko the rooster. Margery shoos him into his coop.

At the back edge of the yard is the site of the sheep shed Depty helped to build, torn down years ago, replaced by something sturdier. In a fenced-in field, their last two ewes, fat with wool, still chew without expression. Probably they should not have named their sheep; over the years the flock expanded, but not their pocketbooks.

Billy points to the fence. "Dep and Grody put that in for us, remember?"

"I do now."

The house has had a lot of work done on it: a new second story, bedroom and bath. Across the lawn at the rim of a forested ridge, the swath of high bush blueberries is ten feet tall and crimson in autumn.

"Was that hill always there?" I had pictured the yard as flat pasture.

Billy laughs. "Your eyes were on other things then."

Margery comes over now, smaller than I recall, resilient despite a recent battle with breast cancer. I'd forgotten how blue her eyes are, how deep her accent.

"Oh, Sybil." She puts her arms around me and suddenly I'm home again.

Glyn, Bubba, and his second wife, Pam, are coming over for dinner. Glyn arrives first. Almost seventy and far less shaggy, there's not a scrap of duct tape anywhere on his attire, but he's still got that crooked-tooth smile and warm Kentucky hug.

"Glyn," I say into his shoulder. "I never told you how sorry I am about Greg."

"That was a long time ago." He grins. "Great funeral. Best I ever went to."

It was held at Waller of course, down in the whiffle ball field. A fierce wind had blown up, bringing in a brief squall of thunder and rain. Everyone had taken a handful of Greg's ashes to fling in the air or pour in the river. Some of the girls fed the trees he'd wooed them under. Punk Patrol Emeritus Jumpin' Jimmy ate his.

Glyn has remained a master of rough-lumber engineering. Lately, he's been finishing a new studio planked together from the fifteen sheds that sprang up along the driveway at Waller over the last three decades. The quarters, as he calls the new building, is where the film crew will stay when they arrive on Sunday, and where the week's filming will take place. I'd almost forgotten that's why I'm here.

The door swings open again, and in comes Bubba followed by Pam, whom I've never met. Gaunt from his illness, Bubba has morphed from Robin Hood to Don Quixote, jousting with his mortality, still unabashedly warm. Pam is curvaceous and gravel-voiced, with huge dark eyes. Versed firsthand in the legacy of legends, she was once married to the English rock star Steve Marriott, who died in a fire caused by his smoking in bed.

Pam knew Depty only as Blaze. As she hugs me, she says, "I've heard a lot about you."

"I'm almost afraid to ask," I reply, and we laugh.

We sit down to dinner. Billy holds his wine glass aloft. "If there's a heartache Whitesburg can't heal, I don't want to have it."

Glasses clink around the table. It feels so natural being here. These old friends are like a constellation of faraway stars: when I look at them, I see the past. Our faces reflect time and distance—we've become middle-aged, some of us bordering on elderly—yet the constancy of affection is unchanged. I know almost nothing of their lives, nor they of mine, and that gives this reunion a gentle warping, as if no time had passed at all and these aging faces around the table are mere premonitions of where our lives are headed.

Bubba breaks my reverie. "Can't believe it's actually you sitting there."

"Tell me about it."

His laugh still *rat-tat-tats*, but it's lost a lot of breath. He snaps his fingers. "Hey! You remember the night in the tree house when you peed in the Frito bag?"

"No way! You're making that up."

I glance around the table. Billy and Glyn are laughing. Margery has her face in her hands.

Bubba is incredulous. "We were working for Mama Kate. I came to get y'all in the morning. Damn, it could get chilly by that crick! You had to pee in the night, but it was too cold to get up, so Blaze went, 'Here, darlin',' and handed you an empty Frito bag. You were so mortified—you don't remember that?"

I don't, but I'm so desperate for memories I'm willing to steal them. I notice he calls Depty Blaze now; they all do. Their history with him is so much longer than mine. They were witnesses to his decline, and their memories of the younger man are obscured by the man he became.

In the past few weeks, Blaze's story has become a picture I find I can enter, like a hologram I know intimately, or a dream of my own life. I read somewhere that if you cut a hologram into minute pieces and shine a laser through one shard, the entire image will be projected; every part contains the whole.

I know there is more of him yet to encounter, and still so much to absorb. For these friends, he's the past; they've had years to process his fate. For me, the unfolding of his life is happening in the present, too real at times to take in all at once. So when Glyn mentions in passing that Blaze got fat again, and I start to bawl, Bubba puts an arm around me, grinning.

"Some things never change."

"Quit teasing her," Margery admonishes him. "She'll pack up and go away for another twenty-six years."

"Yeah." Bubba arches an eyebrow. "Where you been all this time?"

"That's what I'm trying to find out." I wipe my eyes on a napkin. "Tell me the truth, y'all. Do you think things would've turned out differently if I'd stayed with him?"

"It's called self-preservation," Pam states. "I can tell you about that." She shivers up her spine. "Big time."

Billy taps my knee once, hard. "I think you gave it your best shot."

I blow my nose. "Then why do I feel like I hurt him more than helped him?"

Billy waves his arms. "Stop! You'll disappoint me. I thought you were smarter than this."

"Shut up, Billy," Margery tells him blandly, then turns to me. "You're wrong, Sybil," she says. "You slowed him down."

13

Ghosts

On Sunday Margery drives me over to Waller for the first time since I've been back. The film crew is coming in from Austin this afternoon, and I want to be there to greet them when they arrive.

The main intersection in Whitesburg has been turned into a roundabout where logging trucks and SUVs do a traffic dosey-doe. Bunk Duke's Package Store is boarded up, replaced by the inevitable Stop N Shop. The other concession to the twenty-first century is down the road: Lamp Music South, a Christian music recording studio-slash-tanning salon.

Turning off the blacktop, we wind down gravel roads Depty and I traveled almost every day. I can't say I remember them exactly, yet they resonate anyway, as if the molecules of air we breathed still cling to the dust raised by Margery's car. In Jewish mythology there's an Angel of Forgetfulness who visits you in the womb to lead you through the life you're about to live. Then you're born, and you forget what you've been shown, until those moments of déjà vu when you live for the first time something you've always known.

We pass through an open gate. The driveway to Waller tilts toward the river, and time is bending back. I'm in Ethyl with Depty Dawg, on our way to see our friends, bumping down the drive as rutted then as it is now. Dep is at the wheel; I'm sitting against him, his hand on my thigh. In a minute the cabin will appear at the bottom of the road and Ape-shit will be wagging her unrestrained hello.

There are no dogs to greet us now. Ape-shit died years ago. She never did get to be Georgia's Mother of the Year. But in the spring of '76, the hippies on the river finally had enough of local police harassment and pulled off a boycott of Whitesburg stores and gas stations. Not only did they remove the offending cops, they also managed to put a Punk Patroller in office. Campaigning on Main Street in his wheelchair, nineteen-year-old Tony Boatwright became the youngest mayor in Whitesburg's—and the nation's—history. As mayor, he dedicated the fire plug at the corner of Main and College to Apeshit. The official proclamation read: *She has provided her services unselfishly to the members of the canine community.*

I gaze around the yard at Waller. The lights on the electric plant towers still blink through the woods; a measure of time, a heartbeat. Leaning against the tree trunk is a weatherworn sign: *Flee Market Each Item 25 Cents.* Along the top are the worn words *Banning Mill Ensemble.* Glyn has kept it all these years, his lone purchase at our impromptu bazaar.

Arms open wide, he comes out to greet us. "Welcome back to Waller."

The place has changed so little, really. The house still smells of wood smoke and mildew, the incense of old country cabins. In the foyer the phone booth is no longer used, though the *Power to the People* on the fuse box has not faded. The back bunkrooms have been gutted to make one large bedroom overlooking the river. We step out onto a porch that now wraps around the entire shack. Sunlight glitters on the surface of the river.

"Blaze helped me build these decks," Glyn tells us. "When he'd come back from Texas to spend his summers here."

Tromping over boards Blaze nailed in place, Glyn leads us back inside. Above the living room, cobwebs still grace the rafters, an enduring tradition.

Glyn grins. "I give starter sets for wedding presents now."

My laughter is cut short. On the wall is a large grainy photo taken at the Mill during a rehearsal of *The Bear.* Leo is knelt before me, I'm about to swoon, and Jo is watching intently like a maestro conducting a duet. We look very ardent and very young.

"When did you put that up?" I sputter.

Glyn strokes his beard. "Let me see, which wife was that?" He shrugs. "Twenty years, thirty maybe. Great picture, don't you think?"

I don't know what to think. My brain can't quite grasp that I've been here all along. I can't bring myself to ask if Blaze ever saw the picture, but surely he must have. How brave of him to return to the county time after time. But then Waller was always home. I wonder if he ever imagined our paths crossing here again. They never did. Until today.

Sitting down to breakfast in the kitchen at Waller, I'm aware of ghosts in the room. So many people from that long-ago time damaged or dead from alcoholism, disease, overdoses, accidents, and violence. What once seemed like innocent play has ended in imploded lives and graveyards.

It never occurred to me then that Depty might be alcoholic: everybody drank and smoked and dropped; me too. No doubt those indulgences have contributed to my dearth of memories. So naïve, I hadn't yet learned that all actions have consequences.

Bubba was right, though: some things don't change. Waller still offers up the county's best breakfast—a feast of crisp bacon, cheesy eggs, biscuits, and homemade French fries.

I bite into a biscuit smeared with Margery's blueberry preserves. "So where is Helen these days?" I ask innocently.

"Poor Helen." Margery's glance at Glyn conveys a shorthand of history between longtime friends.

Helen disappeared in the late '70s, another victim of drugs and alcohol. She lives in Atlanta now, but I wouldn't recognize her.

Glyn reaches for a French fry. "Did you know Blaze wrote 'Picture Cards Can't Picture You' for Helen?"

"Blaze had an affair with Helen?" Margery replies, almost as stunned as me. "When was that?"

Glyn considers. "'78? '79?" He says to me, "You weren't around then."

He scrapes eggs onto his fork. "I'm not telling tales out of school. Blaze confessed to Bubba. You know his song 'Officer Norris'? That was about the time Blaze and Helen got arrested in Newnan. I ought to know. I bailed him out, took Seth, and left Helen there to sleep it off."

I can't swallow. Helen of Troy. So she was the married woman Blaze had mentioned on his CD, and Seth was the child.

My heart feels like it's been through a garlic press. From his songs I knew that Blaze had other loves in Georgia; I never figured I'd know any of them. Helen had been a friend; I can't say I knew her well. I never suspected the addict in her.

And I don't mention that I think "Picture Cards" one of Blaze's most beautiful songs, or that I saw the words before the song appeared. They no longer belong to me and it seems greedy, much less petty, to say anything about it now.

14

Livin' in the Woods in a Tree

For the record, I was a Depty Dawg fan before he ever wrote a song about us. His name (albeit misspelled) and then his voice beguiled me, though I was not alone in that. Wherever he sang, the music flowed out from him, and that grace extended to me, reflected in his star shine.

Then, in those first smitten weeks in the tree house, Depty Dawg began to write. He composed two songs, one after the other on the same day, in an explosive burst of creation.

The refrain of the first tune went *Your brown eyes/your brown eyes/oh what they do to me.* Zonko Joe pronounced it possibly the most annoying love song he'd ever heard. Personally, I was thrilled—but then no one expected me to be objective.

The second was a John Prinesque portrait of our life in Udo:

Met a kinky little woman with crazy hair
Big brown eyes and a faraway stare
Mamas wouldn't think we'd have made a pair
Now we're livin' in the woods in a tree
Some folks think we're a little deranged
That's the way it is, probably never will change
We don't care 'cause you got to be strange
When you're livin' in the woods in a tree
Cook our breakfast whenever we rise
Play a little music for the butterflies
Say pretty things lookin' into our eyes
Laughin' in the woods in a tree
Got a lot of friends we can go and see
Some got kids that'll sit on your knee
I love her and she loves me

Sleepin' in the woods in a tree
Gonna have a party when our boat gets here
Try to have some food and a thing of beer
Dance with the people that we live near
Laughin' in the woods in a tree
We're both a little shaky with the other sometime
Maybe 'cause of things that we left behind
But we watch our steps as we start to climb
To the house in the woods in a tree

Depty sang the song for the first time on the porch at Waller, shyly producing the lyrics on crumpled legal pad paper. Across the top he'd printed the title: "Livin' in the Woods in a Tree."

Billy leaned back in his rocker and gave me a knowing smile. "You're his muse."

"I think the tree house is the muse," I blushed.

Whatever was inspiring him, more songs followed. And for those of us who knew him then, one of the unforgettable joys of that summer was waiting to hear what Depty Dawg would come up with next. He was writing directly from his life, and so was writing all of ours:

Big Chief Hightower
Hold you up about an hour
Every time you drive through Whitesburg
Big Chief Hightower
Hold you up about an hour
Every time you drive through town

Melodies were pouring out of him like an underground spring that had made its way to the surface at a fertile place and time. Lyrics mining long-silent feelings were finding expression now in song. He'd begun the first of these excerpts from "I Won't Be Your Fat Boy Any More" as a teenager in Irving, Texas:

Well, I used to go drinkin' and look for my bride
Walk in the parties and the girls would hide
They didn't want no fat boys in their rooms
Always used to tell me we can be good friends
And you can sleep on the pallet when the party ends
I won't be your fat boy any more

Ten years later, in Georgia, he would finish the song with a happier ending:

Now I got a little woman that I kiss each day

She likes my lovin' and some of my ways
Glad I'm not a fat boy any more
Her hair's real curly and her eyes real brown
She rubs my belly when I'm layin' down
I won't be your fat boy any more

Sometimes Depty wrote in the tree house. Then I'd circle him the way you do a hot brilliant fire—carefully, and all the while loving the heat. Perched on the edge of the loft, arms akimbo over a guitar, he'd finger-pick through melodies, one note at a time.

His flame set my own muse bubbling. As a kid, I'd dabbled in poetry and short stories, even a play or two. Now while he worked, I sat at the table scribbling down ideas for a screenplay or novel. But none of my efforts could match Depty Dawg's in those first early days.

Mostly he wrote alone, while I was away working or visiting friends. He hesitated to tell me he needed privacy to write.

"I don't want to hurt your feelings."

"Honey, you'll hurt my feelings if you *don't* write."

So I'd come home and he'd have a new song, or a piece of one, to play for me. He scrawled down the words for us to read together. Now it was *his* lyrics we were tasting and savoring. I was awed, and so proud. His poetry was a magnetic force binding us ever more closely.

More than anything, I loved the artist in Depty Dawg, and being a kind of midwife to his art was its own fulfilling rapture.

15

JAB Blues

We had come from different worlds. My grandfather was a *shmata*-peddling Orthodox Jew on the streets of Brooklyn. Dep's was a fire-breathing Evangelical fiddler from the Ozarks. As a kid, Mike Fuller had listened in his bedroom to Chet Atkins and Red Foley, while I swayed in the living room to Eddie Fisher and Harry Belafonte. He was raised as a Christian Fundamentalist; I was a Jewish-American belle.

Unlike her first cousin the Jewish-American princess, a JAB by definition is not necessarily spoiled. Instead, her birthright comes with a sheltered upbringing, a pair of rainbow-tinted glasses, and a sense of propriety that hides a helpless passivity. No one ever mistook me for Scarlett O'Hara until I started having hot flashes.

In essential ways though, we were more alike than different—both Aeolian harps, extremely sensitive, easily played by whatever was in the air. Mavericks in a new age of non-conformity, we were hungry for identity, yet we both fervently believed in what Depty called *old-fashioned love*. That each was affecting the other powerfully was not lost on us; that we'd landed together in the tree house was a joyful reminder of how unpredictable, how lucky life could be.

In many ways, Depty Dawg was worldlier than me. He'd been on his own longer, hitchhiking around, earning a road-honed cynicism I admired. As a rule, Jewish-American belles do not hitchhike. Still, it was reassuring to know that if the need arose, it'd be no problem since I'd be with a pro. I never expected to test that theory out so soon.

My younger brother, Josh, graduated from high school the same spring I moved into a tree. Born seven years apart, we'd always been close, allied by necessity in a topsy-turvy household. At eighteen, Josh was tall and lanky, topped by a bushy hairdo he called his *Isro*. Now, he and three friends were coming to Georgia to check out Udo and meet my new love. It was the first time Depty was introduced to any of my family and I could understand his anxiety.

Josh held out his hand to shake Dep's. "Nice to meet you, Deputy."

"It's Depty," Dep corrected him. "Depty Dawg."

"Should I call you Mr. Dawg?" my brother replied.

Later that evening when Josh smoked a little too much hash oil and fell out of the tree house, Depty began to feel more at home with him.

That night our guests camped on a slope by the creek. In the early morning hours, an unexpected downpour gushed run-off into their tent. After breakfast, we loaned them Ethyl so they could drive to Myrtle Beach and dry out. The plan was for Depty and me to hitchhike there in a few days' time and ferry them back to Virginia. I figured, what the heck, it was time; I'd be safe with Depty Dawg. What I didn't figure was that we'd be hitching across South Carolina—an iffy proposition for a longhaired hippie cowboy with a half-black belle in those *Easy Rider* days.

Our first ride took us from Atlanta to the South Carolina border.

"See?" Depty opined. "Piece o' pie."

He spoke too soon. We stood by the highway for a very long time in a very hot sun, car after car bypassing our outstretched thumbs. Suddenly a vehicle swerved sharply toward the shoulder. Dep yanked us out of harm's way and the car sped off, honking.

A battered pick-up truck slowed and pulled over. The elderly farmer behind the wheel gestured for us to get in back with the hay bales.

"Much obliged," Dep told him through the window. "I saw that car coming at us, I thought I have met my Maker and He is a Buick."

The man did not smile. "Only reason I'm picking y'all up," he drawled, passing a rough hand over thinning hair. "Is 'cause they found two dead just like you on the side of the road last week."

My legs shook. "Just let us off at a pay phone, please."

We climbed into the flatbed, leaning against the bales. The truck turned back onto the highway. I lifted my face to the wind, trying not to cry.

"Is it always this much fun?"

Dep squeezed my hand. "We'll be all right."

Straw stuck through my T-shirt. "Ever hitchhike with a girl before?"

"Never had a girl before." He pulled out a Kool and cupped the match flame.

"Yeah, there's always women hanging around musicians," he went on. "Only them kind want something from you you can only give yourself."

"What's that?"

He exhaled. "Your dreams."

I sighed. "I'm afraid I'm no different, sweetheart."

"What you talking, Vidalia? You got your own dreams."

"They seem awfully distant right now."

"Naw." He ripped open an imaginary envelope. "The Oscar for Best Actress goes to—Jean Carlot."

"Who's that?"

"You, darlin.' In cellulite."

I snickered in answer. Depty kissed my fingers. "It won't always be like this."

"I know," I replied. "I got faith in you. You're bound for the stars, Depty Dawg. I'd bet money on it, if I had any."

"Don't wanna be no star." His hat shaded his hawk profile. "I wanna be a legend."

"What's the dif?"

"Stars burn out. Legends last forever."

I peered at him. "You think that's possible?"

"To be a legend?"

"To live forever."

He winked. "It's just a matter of time."

"Well." I put my head in his lap. "The sky's the limit. But when Mr. Green Jeans lets us off, I'm calling Josh."

At nightfall, the farmer dropped us at a truck-stop forty miles from the shore. Miraculously, I got my brother on the phone at his motel. Depty waited for me by the gas pumps, head down, his hair a dark frame around his face. I waved to him through the glass. He looked so vulnerable sitting there, broke and stranded in an unfriendly world.

The next day we drove Josh and his friends back to Virginia. It hardly seemed the moment to introduce the folks to Depty Dawg. We let our passengers off at a strip mall below their apartment and hurried back to our safe harbor.

Depty and I rarely fought. Which is not to say we didn't get mad at each other. I myself was not very practiced at conflict. Raised to be an obedient belle, anger was not on the list of emotions I was expected to express. Still, there were moments—like those nights when he had too much to drink at Waller—that frustrated me.

"Dep, come on, it's late, let's go," I'd whine for the umpteenth time.

His appetite and stamina for carousing were far greater than mine, and he was so damn big that just organizing him physically into the car could be a production, especially at night. Fortunately, there was always Grody Mike or Glyn to steer him in the right direction. It didn't happen often. Most of the time he stayed sober enough so that, as the evening wound down, we were both more than happy to go home to the tree house and each other.

I, on the other hand, could piss him off. One time in particular he really let me see the anger jealousy could fuel. The year before, while still living in Atlanta, I'd modeled occasionally for a nude-drawing class. The instructor was very protective of her models, so I might lie hidden in a blanket or sitting in a chair, turned away with only an ankle showing.

It was the kind of paradox only youth allows. I was ambivalent about my body. A late bloomer in sex, I'd learned that men were attracted to me, but I lacked the confidence needed to believe it. That was the trouble with being smart and a good girl; I used my intelligence perfecting my neuroses. The mirror proved my existence and revealed my flaws: my mouth was too big and my butt too small. I didn't have Helen's curves, or Roxanne's gossamer hair. More than that, I had a sensitive boyfriend and no interest or intention of making him insecure. The modeling job was just that, a job; at least that's what I told myself then.

Dep's slippery handling of our finances was all right with me most of the time. But every month I had to come up with thirty bucks to pay off the loan my father had co-signed for Ethyl. The modeling job was available, so once, out of desperation, I took it, omitting a few essential details when describing it to Dep.

By the time he came to pick me up at the school, he'd figured it out—and he was fuming. Snatching my bag, he flung it into the backseat. "You lied to me!"

I didn't deny it. "Look," I replied, tearing up. "I don't care that we're poor. But you think it's easy getting you to hang on to thirty bucks?"

He hit the steering wheel. "I can't stand the thought of it." His eyes glistened like he might cry.

"Oh, Dep, I'm sorry." I put my arms around him. "Some pair of hippies we make."

"Take that money," he told me. "Don't let me even see it. But don't do this again, promise?"

I kissed him. "I promise."

"All right." Brightening, he started the car. "Now let's go home and take off our clothes."

16

Romantic Codes

Depty's vulnerablity could be startling, especially when it ran so at odds with his freewheeling views. By the time we met, he'd had his share of one-night stands, but where true love was concerned, he adhered to a strict code, a conservative blueprint for how lovers should be. One of its guiding principles was that they not mention previous loves to each other. I was not fully aware of this when I blundered onto the subject of Kay.

Kay was a charismatic actress with black Mediterranean eyes and honey-gold hair, another theater student from college. For several months after graduation, she and I had acted together in an avant-garde North Carolina stage company called The Poor Theater. Based on the work of Polish minimalist Jerzy Grotowski, it would have, among other things, a fatal name for a theater.

One afternoon, during the company's doomed run, Kay came to my apartment and announced with trepidation that she was attracted to me. Secretly, I was thrilled. I'd fallen in love with her four years before, the moment I laid eyes on her in fact. She was the most expressive person I'd ever seen, passionate about theater, determined to make it professionally. All through college Kay had been the golden girl of the stage; now, suddenly, she was drawn to me. Even as a kid, I'd sensed that women could be attracted to other women, especially if they were nice. Though I'd never actively pursued a woman, I had practiced kissing on all my girl-friends in high school. It was probably just a question of time till one pursued me and I responded.

When the final curtain fell on The Poor Theater, Kay and I got hired to act at The Olde West Dinner Theater in Johnson City, Tennessee. Local patrons of the arts referred to The Olde West as the *diner the-ayter*. The acting ensemble lived in paper-thin cubicles tacked onto the back of the restaurant's kitchen, a detail of provincial stage life that always irked Kay.

"People who work at Woolworth's don't have to live at Woolworth's," she'd point out regularly.

In the spring of '73, The Olde West season required more actors than the theater building could accommodate, so Kay and I were sent to live in a trailer by a lake some miles away. The move gave us the privacy and freedom to carry on our hidden affair. The fact that Kay was married seemed a distant obstacle. Her husband was off acting in a dinner theater in North Carolina. It was a first for us both.

Tennessee springs are cloaked in magenta redbuds. That spring we mirrored the landscape, blossoming with sensation. Before Kay, I'd had only two lovers, both young men from college. Sex was terrifying but irresistible, pleasure locked away behind a fear of losing myself. Kay coaxed me out of hiding. Through a looking glass, I discovered my body on hers, learned its rhythms and responses by reflection.

She and I taught each other many things that spring. I grew a little stronger, absorbing her resilience as if by intimate osmosis. When she went back to her husband at the beginning of the summer, it was painful, but I told myself it was a natural ending. I was skittish about commitment, it didn't matter with whom. I'd tortured my college boyfriends with my ambivalence. With Kay it was easier to make excuses: what I wanted was to be as alive with a man as I'd been with her.

Two years later, when I fell for Depty Dawg, the fullness of that Tennessee springtime came to bear. I wanted to be with him, it was that simple, and his tenderness and loyalty overrode my fears. So it seemed obvious—to me anyway—that these two people should meet and know each other. In taking up with Depty Dawg, I had entered his world, though it was seamlessly becoming mine. Still, I had come from somewhere, and I wanted him to know it for himself.

Dep was fragile when I told him about Kay, hurt and confused. Awkwardly I tried to reassure him: it was because I loved him so that I wanted them to meet, wanted her to know him too. I convinced him to go to North Carolina where Kay and her husband were working at a dinner theater, certain that once they heard him sing, every barrier would fall away.

We started out in high spirits on a clear summer's day. Margery had recently lent Depty her Empire State guitar, a beautiful antique instrument with a bell-like sound. Strummed by many hands over many years, the body was worn away in places.

"There's magic in here," Dep declared, fingers moving up and down the frets.

He had just begun to write his own songs, and so we were filled with that excitement too. It felt like a benediction, the guitar coming into his hands at this moment. To celebrate, we split a hit of mescaline before getting out on the highway. We figured we'd be past the little jog of South Carolina and well into North Carolina before the drug took hold.

We figured wrong.

By the time we got to the South Carolina border, I was babbling, and Dep was barely able to drive. With a little money in our pockets for a change, we decided to get a motel room until we calmed down.

Dep pulled off the interstate in front of a Holiday Inn. "Okay, little onion. You go get us a room."

"Me? Are you kidding? I'll just giggle like a madwoman. They'll lock me up."

He grinned. "They see me coming, they'll lock me out."

"Well," I wondered aloud. "Do you think they'll get suspicious if we just sit here for four hours?"

He saw my point. Back Ethyl went onto the highway till another motel loomed, another ramp was traversed, and the same inability to cope presented itself. At last we came to a park-like rest stop, thick with shade trees around a shimmering lake. It looked deserted; what's more, it felt safe.

We parked the car, glad to rest our bodies, if not our brains. No sooner had we taken our first relieved breath than a South Carolina state trooper car pulled up beside us and four bullish cops with no visible necks slammed out of its doors.

In those halcyon days of hallucinogenics, I could go from hysterical laughter to visceral crying in ten seconds flat. Fear shrunk the time lapse that day, bringing on sobbing in under two seconds and drawing an officer over to my window.

"Everything okay in here?"

Depty drew me to him, an arm around my shoulders. "Her granddaddy died today." His voice cracked. "We loved him so much."

I pushed my face into his shoulder to stifle a sudden outbreak of the giggles. The cop recoiled. "Oop, sorry," he murmured, and walked away.

After a while we dried our eyes, stretched our legs, and ambled around the lake. The police didn't bother us again. It was almost noon by the time we got back into Ethyl and drove straight out of South Carolina into the Smoky Mountains.

Still tripping, but in a softer, euphoric phase, we tumbled from the car onto a grassy slope. Depty put his arms around me and I rested against him, his heart beating through my ribs, the haze of clouded ridges expanding endlessly before us.

The visit with Kay was a disaster. We were strung out, exhausted, and she wasn't exactly thrilled about meeting my new boyfriend. Her rehearsal schedule kept her busy and distracted. There was little opportunity for Dep to play. He was restless; he didn't want to stay. As we got ready to leave, Kay pulled me aside.

"I don't understand how you can give up acting to live in the boonies," she chided me, not mentioning Depty by name.

"If you could see where we live," I began. "Our whole life is art." But there was not time enough to tell her all about it.

My attempt to make Kay and Dep accept each other had misfired. On the way back down to Georgia, he was determined to drive through Deep Gap, North Carolina, where the blind bluegrass legend Doc Watson lived. He had this idea to show Doc the old Empire State guitar. The possibility seemed to console him, as if he wanted to remind me what his life had to offer mine. I didn't need reminding. Udo had lulled me into believing a perfect world could exist, and I refused to acknowledge that it couldn't extend everywhere. I didn't want to be limited; I wanted us to live in a boundless world. My insistence that they meet had been selfish, but my life seemed to exist in dislocated fragments I could never seem to stitch into one durable design.

I didn't mention Kay to Dep for a long time after that. And I wouldn't hear from her again until she and her husband moved to New York City to pursue their acting careers.

In her letter Kay wrote, "Say hello to the moon for me. We can't see it from here."

17

Number the Days

~~~~~~~~~~

And then I got pregnant. It wasn't surprising, not really, since we weren't using any birth control. But as I hadn't had a period in over a year, I didn't think it possible.

The summer before, while still in Atlanta, I'd discovered a lump in my left breast. The benign tumor was removed, and I was taken off the pill. It was typical, the surgeon said, to go without a period for months. I thought that meant we were safe.

My breasts grew sore, my belly bloated. Depty's response, like mine, was mixed. We couldn't picture having a child now when we were still children ourselves. Nor were we sure it was fair to bring another into a world where we had no money, a house without walls, and no clear vision of where our lives were going. The women I admired had worked this all out. Sas was a mother, wage earner, and artist; Margery an educated scientist with a swelling belly of her own. But they were older than me, and far sturdier.

At the same time, we couldn't help be astonished, excited even. We had procreated, in tune with the world. We'd put our bodies together and something new had come out of our passion. Foolishly, we fell in love with this small seed unfurling inside me.

We took to spending long hours alone in Udo. One afternoon, a thunderstorm polished the leaves of the leathery rhododendron to a shine. We were stretched out in the boudoir listening to the rain subside, water dripping from the tree house eaves.

"Sounds like a clock ticking," Depty murmured sleepily.

I turned to him. "Dep? You ever wondered how many days you been alive?"

Eyes closed, he gathered me in his arms. "Vidalia. The things you come up with."

"No, but think about it. How many days have you lived through?"

He smiled. "I've lived through all of them so far."

"But have you ever counted them?" Lying on my stomach, I did the math on the pillow. "Depty Dawg, you have been alive nine thousand, three hundred and forty-two days. So far."

"Whoo-ee! Don't seem like so many when you string 'em out like that, does it? How many is it for you?"

I figured again. "Nine thousand, one hundred and ninety-three." I rolled onto my back. "Where do we come from, that's what I'd like to know."

"And where do we go?" he countered. "'Least with Heaven you got an address." He put a hand on my belly. "Come from nothing seems like."

"I know," I agreed. "Seems like there ought to be a bell or a light, or something goes off when a person gets made."

He called down the bed. "She didn't mean that, Elmo."

I laughed. He lay back, looking up for a time. "Always thought I'd just come and go on this earth," he began softly. "Know what I mean? Just kind of blow across it and be gone. But now I got something holding me, keeping me here—"

"You mean the baby?"

"I mean you."

I put my cheek to his. "Oh, Dep. What should we do?"

Our confusion was growing; the indecision was painful. We knew we had to act, one way or the other. Finally, we went to a local women's clinic to see what they would say to us. They offered us the chance to have an abortion that day, for free if necessary, since we had no money of our own. We went outside to mull it over once again.

I sank to the curb. "What if I'm like Meander? You know? Just too clueless."

"You'd make a good mother, little onion, I know that."

"Well, what about all the other reasons: overpopulation, nuclear war, life sucks?"

The lame response attempted to conceal my terror of repeating my mother's tormented domesticity. I was determined not to end up, as I'd often pictured her, shackled to the kitchen sink.

"Are you ready?" I implored him. "Tell me the truth, are you ready for this?"

He plunked down beside me. "Ain't had much of a role model in the daddy department."

Frowning, he pulled off his hat. "Didn't you ever want something that you didn't want? You got to decide, Sybil. I can't make you do something you don't want to do."

I burst into tears. "And will you love me, no matter what?"

He held my hand to his heart. "No matter what."

Dep sat in the waiting room while I went in to talk to the nurse. Everyone there was very gentle with me. Perhaps they suspected I had no idea what was about to happen. Once I made up my mind, I was grateful to be able to take care of it safely. Still, I was completely unprepared to be hooked up to a machine and have this imagined little life sucked out of me. The experience undid me with its coldness, and the sudden sense of loss was shocking and deep.

Afterwards I lay on a cot in the dark recovery room, staring up at the ceiling. *Maybe there wasn't any such thing as a perfect world after all.*

Depty came in on tiptoe. "You okay, little onion? You look awful."

"It's gone," I whispered.

"Come on," he blinked. "Let's go home."

He lifted me up, took me by the arm, and walked me out to the parking lot. We sat in the car and cried. We promised ourselves this would never happen again; we would work hard and make our dreams come true. I didn't care any more if they were Depty's or mine, so long as they were strong enough to make us whole.

18

Revelations

Years would have to pass before I let myself feel that pain again. Being here in Georgia has brought on a springtide of bittersweet memories, crashing on rocky shores. I need some private hours to sort through the scattered details, washed up like broken shells after a storm at sea. Yet neither solitude nor time is mine for now.

The film crew from Austin arrives at Waller late Sunday afternoon. For weeks, I've been hurling impatiently toward my interview with them. Now that it's upon me, I want to run screaming in the opposite direction. Just hearing their car come down the drive, I'm wracked with self-consciousness. I have a sneaking suspicion that at this point they know more about me than I do. Who knows who I'll be tomorrow when they turn the cameras on?

Meeting them assuages some of my anxiety. Kevin, the director, is a forty-something bookish professor, not at all the brash filmmaker I pictured him to be. I feel an instant kinship with him, a wondering gratitude. His desire to tell Blaze's story on film has set in motion this belated reunion with Depty Dawg.

"Why do you want to make a movie about Blaze?" I ask him first thing.

Kevin runs a hand over close-cropped gray hair and mumbles, "I don't know."

That works for me.

His soundman, Kai, is an exuberant clown with a brown braid bobbling on top of a buzzed head. First cameraman Mike has a winning smile, quicksilver intelligence, and the gift of gab. Andy on second camera is elegant and sweet, already missing his wife. Young and earnest, they are straight arrows, every one. The fact that they never actually knew Blaze has not diluted their affectionate obsession with him now. This past summer's filming at Waller was the culmination of six years of hard investigative work. And Waller had enthralled them. Not one of them had ever peed off a porch before.

Filming begins early the next day in the quarters. The rough, spare cabin has mismatched windows facing the fiery autumn woods, and long shimmering views of the Chattahoochee. This morning, its rooms are abuzz with the set-up of cameras and sound equipment, cords and wires underfoot, umbrella lights arranged to accommodate the shifting morning sun. A small-scale film set, but real nonetheless, complete with clappers to start the cameras.

Jean Carlot's first starring role, courtesy of Blaze Foley.

Today Ms. Carlot will be playing a grief-stricken, fifty-two-year-old girl, trying to come to terms with a discarded past. When I tell the funny tree house stories, the crew stuffs their fists in their mouths to keep from laughing out loud. Other times, I look up and they are crying.

Kevin has questions for me. "Did Depty ever talk about his childhood?"

I shake my head. "I only know his heart was broken long before he met me."

Kevin persists. "Did he ever mention his high school girlfriend, Nell?"

"Nell? Who's Nell?"

Blindly jealous of the women who came after me, I hadn't even considered the ones who might have come before. Depty had said there weren't any, but now I see that his romantic code reached all the way back to Mike Fuller's teens. Kevin hasn't been able to locate Nell, but in their interviews the Fuller family recalled her as a church-going girl with soulful brown eyes who had loved chubby Mike very much. Only she couldn't tolerate his drinking and rambling, playing music in bars. He was riding a motorcycle then—

"Excuse me?" I interrupt Kevin. "Did you say motorcycle?"

"Yes. And he was calling himself Tex."

Tex? Why didn't I know this? Did he not tell me, or had I forgotten it, packed it away with other D. Dawg data in some misplaced mnemonic file?

From earlier interviews, Kevin gleaned that friends from Tex's bar life persuaded him to drop innocent Nell and get a real woman. But real women, Tex soon discovered, were not very satisfying. He wanted to return to Nell, but she had refused to take him back.

So, like it or not, here was a precedent to our story. I can't decide if I should be glad or sad that I wasn't the first woman to break his heart. And it doesn't help any that my conundrum is being captured on film.

Yet now I can see what I wasn't able to then: Udo was a respite. For eight months Depty Dawg had stayed still and never wandered, and in that time he had begun to write. "Livin' in the Woods in a Tree," a few verses of "I Won't Be Your Fat Boy Any More," and "Big Chief Hightower" are the only ones of his earliest tunes I could recall. There had to be others from that enchanted time, but Blaze stopped singing many of them in public, and they'd been buried in my mind's archives for so long, I'd lost the key to that file.

At noon, we break for lunch. Over cold-cut sandwiches and potato chips, Kevin turns to me blithely and asks, "Did you know that in 1980 Blaze was engaged to a woman in Houston?"

I blanch inwardly. "Really?"

In the short time since my return to Georgia, I like to think I've perfected a bland smile of indifference whenever someone inadvertently drops a new Blaze Foley fact on me. I assume it's working now because Kevin is smiling back, his bluntness mollified by his obvious kindness.

"Yeah," he offers. "We heard they were the perfect couple, always laughing and joking."

Mike is concentrating on his chips. "We also heard she called off the wedding at least twice."

And now Kai chimes in. "Wasn't she the one made him change 'Big Cheeseburgers' from brown eyes to blue?"

"Oh." I clear my throat. "So that was her. What was her name?" To hide my upset, I take a sip of water.

"Fifi Larue," answers Kevin.

Out spews the water. Having gotten the crew's complete attention, I laugh wildly. "You're kidding me, right?"

"No," Kevin replies slowly. "Why?"

"Fifi Larue was my dear dog's name, may she rest in peace."

Four sets of stares respond to my announcement, uncertain if this is good news or bad. Finally, Kevin breaks the silence.

"You're kidding us now, right?"

"Nope, sorry," I sigh. "Couldn't make that up. Was Fifi a blonde? The dog was is why I ask."

"We don't know," Kevin admits. "We haven't interviewed her yet."

"Ah," I say. "Well, let's hope she still has her sense of humor."

A small miracle has occurred. Margery has found what she thinks is an old recording of Depty Dawg, made sometime in the mid-'70s. It's on a reel-to-reel tape, and she's also located two reel-to-reel players, though both are broken. We wrap up filming for the day and rush over to her house to see what can be done. In no time, Margery's dining table is littered with parts as Kevin and Kai dismantle the ancient machines to create a working one.

Similarly, Margery, Billy, and I piece together the past. Margery remembers being pregnant at the time the recording was made. A newfangled procedure called a sonogram had revealed the baby's gender, and Dep had written an instrumental in honor of his pending arrival in the spring. On the night we went over to record "Basil's Song," Margery had insisted on taping every tune Depty Dawg had finished so far.

Two-and-a-half decades later, we watch as Kevin and Kai perform some arcane wizardry only they understand—and all of a sudden Depty's voice is filling the room once more. We are transfixed. Here he is, asking shyly, "What should I do?" and then follows the whole collection of those first songs, sung in his clear, young voice.

Billy and Margery are wide-eyed, wet-eyed, much the way I was on hearing him again for the first time in New York. Each new tune is greeted with a shout of recognition and then a breathless silence, as song after song brings back the man we knew—reviving the days when he was birthing himself as an artist, and we were all there to witness it.

Here were love songs I'd forgotten—how was that possible? Lullabies he'd sung me to sleep with in the tree house. Though the yearning for home has become more poignant with time, the first verse of his serenade echoes the restlessness that had already claimed him.

When I woke up this mornin'
I was wonderin' where I'd be
When the sun comes up tomorrow
But nobody answered me
Don't know the days that haven't been
So I'll wait around and see
And I hope that she'll be with me
Anyplace that I might be

Here, too, was an ode to moonlight, with the revealing last lines:

Layin' with the one I love
Lookin' at the moon above
Bein' where we really want to be

> The autumn winds for now are still
> The moon shines on
> It always will

That was Depty—the autumn winds stilled for a season. When the ballad ends, Billy turns to me. "So how does it feel to be a muse?"

My eyes brim. "The job description's not all it's cracked up to be. It can be heartbreaking actually."

The next song surprises us all, its portrait of inner city life so vivid we can't imagine how it could have faded from our collective memory. Recalling their conversations in the new sheep shed, Billy is certain the song sprang from those philosophical afternoons. What we can't understand is why Blaze dropped it from his repertoire. The final lines contain an uncanny prophecy for the twenty-first century:

> Social change is still just talk
> The things you see in urban walks
> Should make you sick and lose your lunch
> Inside your high-rise diners
> You make the laws you own the land
> You hold them down where you can stand
> One of these days you'll get yours aplenty
> One of these days you'll get yours aplenty

It turns out that Margery's tape is a composite, recorded at three different intervals from 1976 to 1978, capturing the artist's transformation from Depty Dawg to Blaze Foley. At the final session, much to my delight, he sang "Big Cheeseburgers and Good French Fries" with the original lyric intact:

> Got an angel of a woman with big brown eyes
> Friends in the country and old neckties
> I love big cheeseburgers and good French fries
> Could go fishin' but the fish draw flies
> Could go swimmin' if it ain't too deep
> Rather just sit here and cool my feet
> Know I ain't lazy 'cause I don't like to sleep
> I might just be lazy to you

A wry celebration of his emerging new identity, the song isn't only about him—it's about all of us who knew him then, Zonko Joe for one.

> Story's been told, it's been said before
> All there is to it and here's some more

Friend comin' over from the liquor store
Joe he dance till his feet get sore
Love my woman and my woman loves me
Don't go skiin' 'cause I can't ski
That kind of thing don't bother me
So it shouldn't be botherin' you

It's late by the time we say good night, each of us exhausted and exhilarated. For Kevin, the recording is an affirmation of years of effort, a chronicle of Blaze's creative evolution, and a jackpot discovery of his earliest songs. For Margery and Billy, it's not only a triumph of documentation but even more, a link to the memory of an innocent past before time took its destined toll. The tape was packed away in a box in their house all these years, waiting for the moment to reappear. What a gift to Depty and me; we were luckier than we even knew. We had been made welcome in these generous households where we were given a warm audience and a tolerant mirror. Our contribution would be his music, and our persistent happiness.

That is the treasure I carry away from this night; that, and the sense of *we* in those first songs, how clearly and deeply Depty Dawg saw us then as one.

19

Inner Prizes

Depty Dawg had said he wanted to be a legend, not a star. For him, celebrity meant compromise and trappings; being a legend was the opposite of that. His myth would be his own creation, and he would love it, since it meant breaking the rules, laughing at the demands of success. He told me he had role models for this growing up: Hank Williams, Johnny Cash, Merle Haggard.

"It's about who you are, how you live." He plucked the guitar strings like a spider on a web. "What you stand for."

I wasn't sure I understood. "You mean, like what you have to say?"

"Oh, I definitely got things to say." He drew on his cigarette and stowed it, ember-up, in the tuning keys. "It's got all to do with your style," he riffed.

Style began with the right handle. "If I'm gonna make a name for myself," he mused, "first I got to have one."

He couldn't be Depty Dawg forever—no one would take him seriously—and the name Mike Fuller had fallen away with his weight. So now with his knack for naming, he set out to invent a new one for himself. He tried out possibilities on me.

"Vidalia," he declared one night, tucked under the sheets. "I been thinking of calling myself 'Red Butler.' What you make of it?"

"Not very much," I admitted.

He smirked. "Well, frankly, my dear, I don't give a damn."

He got everybody with that.

The Foley came first, in honor of Red Foley. Clyde Julian "Red" Foley had come out of Kentucky during the Depression, a true gentleman of country music with a warm, fluid baritone and a soft spot for new talent coming up. Mike Fuller had heard him on the radio when Foley emceed for the *Grand Ole Opry* out of Nashville. Later, he watched him on TV as master of ceremonies for the short-lived *Ozark Jubilee*. Now, Depty Dawg wanted to anchor himself in Red Foley's authentic tradition.

He played with the first name Blue—even Blues—Foley. Too gimmicky, he decided. Ultimately, he would settle on Blaze, a moniker with a dash of self-irony and a smattering of romance. Glyn suggested he could bill himself as the illegitimate son of Blaze Starr and Red Foley. It was a fit, though it would be some time before he stopped thinking of himself as Depty Dawg.

He also envisioned having his own music company. "That way I can help other musicians. That's what fame's for, Udo?"

The name of his company would be a take on the word *Enterprises*. He scribbled down the words for me to see how they looked on paper. And when I read *Blaze Foley Inner Prizes* written in his jagged print, I fell in love with the poet in him all over again.

Sometime in late September of '75, Depty and I turned to each other in the wall-less tree house and asked, "Is it getting cold in here to you?"

With the forest just beginning to reveal its coat of many colors, the lack of walls was becoming an issue. Though we needed protection from the season's winds and rains, we were in no way ready to leave Udo. So one shining October morning, a troupe of our friends tromped down the footpath with lumber, hammers, and saws over their shoulders—coming, as in the barn raisings of old, to help us plank up the tree house. In a day's time, it became a finished house with walls and windows, a new set of stairs leading out a back door, and a homemade Dutch door for the front.

We had cherished the old airy bower and the limitless feeling it gave us. The enclosed shack was sturdy and odd, full of cracks and crannies the wind could slip through. The first night we marveled at every unknown inch.

I ran a hand along the seam where the sides now met. "Is there anything you take more for granted than a corner?" I queried.

Depty peered out a window, all that remained of the spaciousness the walls had grown up around. A sliver of new moon floated through a netting of bare branches.

"Like it's caught in the trees," he mused. "Strange how a frame changes the way you see something. You get less but you see more. Know what I mean, jellybean?"

"And look here." I pointed out a parallelogram of crisscrossed moonbeams splayed on the woolen blanket. "The window has captured the light."

Having walls around us deepened our sense of home. I was possessed with a new creative impulse: decorating. Sas helped me choose thick-weave white cotton for curtains. Hand-stitching a top hem, I shredded the bottoms for fringe. Then we threaded gnarled branches as rods through the top hems, and Dep nailed the whole contraption over the windows. The ragtag curtains gave the house a neat, hobbit-like look. We secured a wooden box as a shelf for our few books and knickknacks, closed in the space under the loft for a closet. Our artwork now hung vertically as opposed to horizontally.

The new, improved tree house framed our dreams. At night, we curled around each other, imagining what we would do when our fortunes were made.

"We'll get us a wooden sign that says 'Udo,'" Depty opined. "Hang it on the big oak. And plant fig trees in the front yard—that's Bible food, little onion."

An owl hooted on the other side of the creek. I pointed to the ceiling. "We could put in a skylight. Imagine lying here, looking up at the stars?

"And I guess we'll need a sleeping loft for the kids," I ventured, treading lightly on a still-delicate subject.

He kissed me. "Who wouldn't want to grow up here? We'll dig us a well too, and hey—we'll have us an outdoor shower. With hot water by God."

The list went on and on. Our house had a definite shape now. It was the future that knew no bounds.

Autumn came, bringing with it the first cold weather. During the summer we had built a shed-sized greenhouse—loosely modeled on Roxanne's plastic house—in the meadow under the power lines. The first killing frost shriveled all our pots of marigolds and maryjane. But inside our little house was snug.

We'd been given a tiny metal stove. The night of the first freeze we filled it with wood and paper and lit a fire, excited and proud of ourselves.

"Vy-ola!" Depty exclaimed.

The little stove burned wonderfully hot. We fell asleep on top of the covers. Next morning I woke to find us under the blankets and the tree house cold. Looking over at Dep, I busted out giggling.

"What you snickering at?" he asked, yawning awake.

"Your—your face—"

It was covered with a layer of soot. The blackened skin made his eyes shine like agates.

"Mine?" he answered. He was laughing now too, since my skin was stained same as his.

"Guess we're both half-black now," I cracked.

And not only our faces, we soon realized. Our hair, our hands, anything that stuck out from the blankets, was smeared a greasy onyx. Turned out the little stove was for kerosene, not wood. The flames had heated the toxic residue inside the canister, creating an oily smoke. We were lucky to be alive.

Blankets, furniture, curtains, planking—everything was covered with the tarry gook. It would require long hours of scrubbing to remove the soot from the walls, not to mention a long hot shower to get it off our skin. Unfortunately, the sudden cold snap had cut off all the electricity in the county, and no one we knew had hot water for days. Several would pass before we were able to wash ourselves properly. After a while, we even forgot our faces were still streaked—until we encountered a friend or neighbor and wondered why they were doubled over laughing.

A hurricane roared through the county that fall. Dep and I stayed with Betsey Ross and Sandra Jean in the trailer, listening to the wind howling through the trees, the rain hammering on the tin roof. The next morning we walked down to the tree house with the dogs, to see how it had survived. Pines had fallen all around it, though the shack itself was unscathed.

Setting out for Bubba and Helen's to borrow a chain saw, we were stopped by the trunk of a huge sweet gum fallen across the road. We turned back, going the long way out through flooded roads, arriving at their house hours later. There, we elected to stay a few days in their spare room until the rain had stopped.

The electricity was out again, so Helen was making hamburgers on the woodstove. "Recognize this booger?" she whispered, sliding a patty onto a bun.

My eyes grew large. "No, really? He finally did it?"

Bubba had been talking about butchering their bull, Woolly Booger, to make steaks for their winter table.

"Poor Bubba," Helen drawled. "He couldn't bring himself to do it. Had to get Buddy to come down and shoot him. Then he got the butcher to mix the meat with bought hamburger, so he wouldn't know which bite was Booger."

Alternative lifestyles had their moral dilemmas.

When the sun finally came out, the four of us went back to the tree house with a saw, to cut the fallen pines into logs small enough for a new stove, one that burned wood this time. Bubba drove the heavy stove down the firebreak in his truck, and together we heaved it into the house.

Vy-ola! Depty and I soon mastered the new woodstove, banking the embers to keep a fire going through the night. Glyn gave us bricks to make a wall behind the stove that absorbed the heat and prevented the wooden planks from getting scorched. Some nights we laid two bricks on top and once they were hot, wrapped them in towels to put at the end of the bed to keep our feet warm. Other nights we'd bake potatoes in the stove and put them at the foot of the bed. Then in the morning we'd get up and make hash browns.

We were learning how to use what we had, what was given; we could make do with so little. And we were delighted to become another stop on Glyn's Alternative Lifestyles tour. Each semester he took his class on a field trip to view the county's geodesic domes, teepees, and plastic house.

"Gems on the necklace," he called them, a strand now strung with the house in the woods in a tree.

20

When in Roanoke

"**O**h, honey," my mother sighed over the phone after I'd told her, at last, that I was living in a tree house. "Don't you dream of something better?"

What could be better? It was time to introduce Depty Dawg to my mom.

"Did you prepare her for me?" he asked anxiously as we drove north to Virginia once again.

"How do you suggest I do that?" I teased him.

My father had already been prepared, when a business trip three weeks earlier allowed him a brief layover in the Atlanta airport. We'd ridden over to meet him and spend a few hours. There he had taken our picture, and now I could only imagine how Momma had reacted to Dep's battered cowboy hat and my worn-out bellbottoms.

"Let me prepare you," I told Depty in the car. "One word of Yiddish: *f'mished.*"

"Famished," Dep repeated dutifully.

"It's *f'mished,*" I corrected him, laughing. "Rhymes with pished. And it's what my mother's going to be when she meets you."

I was hoping I was wrong. I was hoping Momma might see in Depty Dawg the genius that I saw. After all, she and my father were both thwarted artists. Her meteoric career in community theater had been shattered by heightened sensitivities and a lack of nerve. And Daddy had long before surrendered all his creative ambitions. As a teenager, Sam had sat in his bedroom in Brooklyn, designing airplanes and dreaming of a future at the aeronautics school in Dayton, Ohio. But he was an only child, and Grandma wouldn't let him go so far away. Besides, my peddler-grandfather had a different vision of the American dream: business, not flying, was the path to success. His son would play the pajama game just as he had done. Daddy rebelled briefly, becoming a wedding photographer for a time, but when that endeavor failed, he, too, wound up in nightwear.

Still, my parents' marriage had fulfilled all the longings of their wartime letters: they had sent their three children to college, an unavailable option for them, the offspring of immigrants coming of age in the Great Depression. No doubt they were praying I'd regain my senses and give up this unsettled life for marriage to a Jewish, preferably professional, husband with scads of well-behaved grandchildren for them to spoil. Instead, here I was: their college grad-turned-actress-turned-hippie daughter, bringing home this big galoot with hair below his shoulders, a thick handlebar mustache, and my IUD dangling from his ear.

I'd gone back to the women's clinic to be fitted for the copper intrauterine device, so we would have birth control at last. My insides had wanted nothing to do with it. Cramping painfully, I lay moaning on the cool tiles of the exam room floor. The gynecologist had removed the IUD, already mangled from the pressure of my womb. He gave it to me and I gave it to Dep. Always the snappy dresser, Depty put it in his ear.

As it was, Momma took one look at him, turned around, went into her bedroom and started crying. My prediction had come true, except it wasn't funny. Her response shamed me; I couldn't bear for Dep to see her behaving this way. Following her down the hall, I was walking in footsteps imprinted in childhood, as full of dread today as I had been then. She was given to unpredictable moods, long bouts of crying and recrimination.

I stopped in the doorway. Momma was sobbing on the bed. So many times I'd stood in this same spot pretending to be sorry for things I hadn't done; it was easier than trying to plead my innocence. This time I knew what I'd done, and I wasn't pretending anything.

She lifted her wet face, grimacing, "What's that smell? Like something burning."

I guessed what she meant. My hand-me-down coat of black lambs' wool reeked of wood smoke.

"I love that smell," I countered, sending her head back to the pillow. "Momma, you don't have to do this. We can just leave."

"We never see you." She sat up, petulant as a child, and blew her nose. "I don't know what to say, Sybil. I guess I expected more."

"You haven't even said hello to him." I was surprising myself. I had rarely dared to talk back to her.

From the living room Dep's voice floated down the hall into the bedroom. He'd resorted to the only thing he knew to do: *"Farther along we'll know all about it/Farther along we'll understand why,"* he sang to my father.

"You ought to hear him, Momma, before you write him off." I turned on my heel and rejoined the men in the living room.

Depty winked at me as I entered. *"Cheer up, my sister,"* he crooned. *"Live in the sunshine/We'll understand it all by and by."*

It would be the music—its undeniable spell—that finally coaxed Momma out of her bedroom. That, and the opportunity to wash our clothes.

Deputy, as she and my father insisted on calling him, might not be the man they envisioned for me but they were unable to resist that voice, or those songs. In time, Momma responded to his vulnerability as well. In many ways, they were similar: charismatic and warm, hugely compassionate and easily hurt.

She got around the fact that I was living out of wedlock—with a Gentile no less—by putting us in separate bedrooms.

"Talk about hypocrisy," I grumbled to Dep.

"I can't even spell it." He shrugged. "When in Roanoke, do as the Jewish people do." He took me in his arms. "We'll go to sleep and dream of each other."

"We do that anyway." I bit his ear. "Meet me in the bathroom at 3 a.m."

He never did. Deputy was on his best behavior, bumping around the kitchen, drying dishes, making polite conversation. I got a good glimpse of Mike Fuller then, the well-brought up, gentlemanly boy. My mother fed him macaroons, matzo balls, and blintzes, as if the way to a man's beliefs might be through his stomach too.

Clearly he'd won her over when she asked, "Deputy, don't you think Sybil has a nice nose?" One of those profound questions Jewish mothers like to ask.

"I'm sorry, Mrs. Rosen," Deputy replied. "We Pentecostals don't care about noses."

To her credit, Momma laughed. He got her and my father chuckling too, with carefully edited stories of Udo. I reminded them of the tree house Daddy had built in our backyard, a simple platform high in the crotch of an oak, though I may have failed to mention that I used to go up there to smoke cigarettes and read dirty books.

For all their nervous concerns, my parents were romantics at heart. They'd been in love for thirty years, had survived my mother's depression, my father's lack of success. I knew they wanted to believe in the feelings between Dep and me, in the sincerity of his intentions, and the promise of his talent.

Three days passed, mercifully swift. As we were saying goodbye, Daddy took out his wallet to show Deputy the snapshot of us that he'd put there.

Dep's eyes glistened. "I doubt my own daddy ever kept me in his pocket."

Nevertheless, we were relieved to go home to Georgia and our boudoir. The visit, we decided, had been a qualified success.

21

Three Dawg Nights

Our food stamp supply was terminated at Thanksgiving when Depty Dawg tried to use all of November's allotment to buy a turkey big enough to feed everyone at Waller.

"There's a song in there somewhere," he declared, snuggling with me under blankets in the tree house.

The forest was bare of leaves, the winter light pale and crystalline. It could get really cold at night, even with the woodstove cranking, even with Betsey Ross and Sandra Jean sleeping on the bed with us—an arrangement Depty considered my own personal version of a three-dog night.

Some mornings we woke to find the glass of water by the bed frozen solid. So during a cold snap we would often stay at Bubba and Helen's, partying and playing music till all hours of the night. Or on Old Black Dirt Road, regaled by Billy's storytelling. There we could take a bath which, for conservation purposes, we did together; it didn't take much water to fill a claw-foot tub with Depty Dawg and me both in it.

Margery's belly was growing. The nesting instinct had arrived overnight.

"It's true," Billy informed us. "For days she's been going around with twigs and little pieces of string in her mouth."

Late one night Depty and I trundled off to bed in their back room. Drifting toward sleep, I murmured, "Dep? I got to pee."

The indoor bathroom was being renovated in readiness for Basil, so the only working toilet was the old outhouse in the yard. I pushed off the covers and tried to stand. Woozy, I fell back in bed.

"Can't have you wetting the bed, darlin'," Dep said, and throwing on his pants and boots, took me in his arms and carried me to the outhouse shed. Leaving the door open a crack, I lowered myself onto the cold seat. I could see him in his shirtsleeves, sitting against a fence post, smoking a cigarette under a ramble of icy stars. He looked so happy, so content.

I put my head down on my knees. Next thing I knew, I was on a big white bed in an all-white jumpsuit, save for my butt which was covered in blue cloth. And after that, I was being taken back to bed.

In the morning I told Depty about the dream. He interpreted it as a warning from my subconscious, letting me know a part of myself was about to freeze.

Because apparently I'd called out to him from the toilet, "Dep, take me in—my ass is blue."

It was a time of great possibility. We were cozy in the tree house, staying afloat odd-job by odd-job. Depty was buoyant, full of good humor, cranking out words and melodies at a breathtaking rate. He'd even begun to talk about going out to Texas to peddle Blaze Foley's songs. Nothing we could dream up seemed beyond our reach.

The air was raw and damp by the creek. We'd come home late one night after an exasperating evening at Waller where Dep had too much to drink. I knelt down in front of the woodstove, hurrying to make a fire.

"Let me just get this going," I called, balling up newspaper.

"Shut up, you cunt," he spat out. Shocked, I turned to look at him. He was standing on the platform above me, a hand raised in anger, his face a fiendish mask.

My breath was white. "Who you talking to?"

The question deflated him. He sank onto the loft, pulling off his boots and getting under the covers. The outburst had been so unlike him I could almost convince myself it had nothing to do with me.

"It don't," he insisted the next morning.

"That's a little hard to believe," I quavered.

"I would never hurt you that way, Sybil. You gotta trust me."

"Then what was it?"

He shook his head. "You don't wanna know."

"Dep—you can tell me anything."

He put his hands to his eyes and began to cry. "Sometimes I think I ain't glued together right."

I didn't know what to say to that. A tear slid down his cheek toward his ear. I leaned my face into his and licked the tear.

He drew back, startled. "What are you doing?"

"Gluing you right."

I gathered him in my arms, wishing I felt as confident as I sounded. Who was I to heal him, the girl who had no face? Last night I'd glimpsed his poisoned face, and I wasn't certain my love alone could be the antidote.

Fortunately, Christmas came early that year. John Prine was giving a concert at the Southeastern Music Hall in Atlanta, and we had tickets for it. Our tree house landlord, Zonko Joe, was back in the county and going too, as were a couple of musician friends, Dave and Gail. We had sometimes crashed in a shack at their place outside Carrollton in our first itinerant days.

Dave was a gentle guitarist with brown shafts of hair to his waist, and Gail another Virginia mountain girl with a gift for drawing and macramé. Dave had backed Depty at the Mill; they'd even talked of forming a trio with Gail. Only when Dep disappeared into the woods with me, Dave and Gail became a duo instead, called Head Over Heels, which they were.

On the way to the concert we chattered excitedly in the car. Bubba had a friend working backstage, so there was the unimaginable possibility that we might even get to meet the man himself.

"What would you say to him?" Joe asked Dep.

Dep scratched his head. "I'd say, 'When I grow up, I want to be just like you.' If I could write one song that moves me like his do—"

"Your songs move me," Dave insisted. He never failed to credit Depty with teaching him how to fingerpick or encouraging him to sing out.

Dep let the compliment slip by. "I'm talking about a tune like 'Sam Stone.'" The Prine dirge described the homecoming of a heroin-addicted Vietnam veteran.

"That just captured the whole end of the war for them guys," Depty mused. "Makes me cry every time I hear it."

I knew that at nineteen Mike Fuller had gone to a recruiting office in Memphis to volunteer for the war. He was overweight, but they'd turned him down because of that short left leg. Depty Dawg no longer understood what had possessed him to do that.

"Used to be stupid," was all he could figure. "It's hard to be human, Udo?"

We hoped Prine would sing "Sam Stone" that night, and we were not disappointed. The concert was held on a bare platform in a small black-box hall. We sat cross-legged on the floor three rows back from the stage, close enough to see the sweat on Prine's fingers. The stage lights flickered above him, turning blue, red, and green. Finally, he squinted up at the light booth through a rainbow of haloes.

"Don't worry with them lights," he cajoled the techies in his West Virginia drawl. "I can change colors all by myself."

Depty beamed; his eyes never left the stage. Between songs he talked to Prine from the audience. At intermission, he crept up and stole the empty Heineken bottle his hero had left there, which I would keep through all our travels, together and alone.

After the concert we did get to go backstage, Dep and I. Up close, Prine was a shy, smiling man with thick eyebrows and a shock of black hair. Depty towered over him saying nothing, thrilled beyond words I think. It was a little awkward actually, our tongue-tied attempts to convey without fawning what his music meant to us. I'd hoped Depty might mention his own songwriting, but he didn't; sometimes his self-doubt could override his zeal. Prine let us stumble around a minute more, shook our hands graciously, and we were out of there.

By the time we left the concert hall, it was sleeting; the highway back to the county was sheeted in ice. We stopped at Waller to let out Zonko Joe and decided to stay the night ourselves. Dep parked Ethyl, and in we went to catch some shut-eye on the living room floor.

In the morning I looked out the window and saw nothing where the car had been. Turned out she'd rolled down the hill and might have careened into the floodplain, save for the oak that stopped her. We winched her to Glyn's truck, but gravity and the weather were against us. Soon his truck was down the hill, bumper-to-bumper with Ethyl. When we tried to pull it up, we succeeded only in adding a third vehicle to the line-up. A fourth soon followed, like a string of taffy-eating kids who'd gotten stuck to each other.

We figured they might have to stay that way till the January thaw when, over the top of the driveway, appeared a tractor driven by a man who lived down the road. Word had gotten out about the pile-up at Waller and now—like a good neighbor in a John Prine song—the farmer was coming to set the hippies' cars free.

22

Departure

The nation's bicentennial year arrived. By January of '76, Depty Dawg had a full bag of brand-new songs; he was writing and practicing constantly. His confidence was growing and with it, his ambition. He was eager to get out in the world and become Blaze Foley. He said we couldn't stay in the tree house forever; we had to make lives, not to mention money, if we were to realize our goals of family and careers.

It would be hard to leave paradise. We debated it constantly: should we stay? Should we go? In the end we resorted to flipping a coin.

Dep held a nickel on his palm. "Heads we stay, tails we're gone."

The coin somersaulted through the air and landed on his open hand for me to read.

"Tails." I smiled up at him. "Guess it's meant to be, honey."

He lifted me off my feet. "Austin, Texas, here we come!"

To his mind, Austin was the true home of country music, not Nashville, not any more, with its rhinestone cowboys churning out watered-down, prettified tunes. The gritty, authentic sound was coming from Texas now, where a red-haired renegade named Willie Nelson had single-handedly turned redneck rock—a fusion of country-western and rhythm-and-blues—into a national pastime.

It sounded good to me. In Austin I might be able to act again, and maybe even write. Dep thought I could do whatever I put my mind to. It made sense that we would have to leave Udo to take on grown-up lives. We were ready to move on; I believed our love could survive anything. The prospect of adventure, and the fulfillment of our dreams, was intoxicating, irresistible. So what if they were Depty's dreams? I'd hitched myself to his star, and I was willing to go anywhere to see it rise. His gift was so real, and so rare, success felt inevitable.

Our friends were not convinced. Margery, especially, was disconcerted. She was still two months away from giving birth.

"Why do you have to go now?" she argued, pulling a sweatshirt over her rounded belly.

"Depty feels ready," I explained.

Frowning, she put a hand on her stomach. "I'm ready too, but I have to wait."

I smiled. "He can't do here what he wants to do musically."

"What about Atlanta?"

"He says Austin's the place. Besides," I went on, "the door fell off the tree house this morning."

Margery's blue eyes widened. "Oh," she said. "You didn't tell me that."

And so it was decided. The dogs would stay with Grody Mike who'd be moving into the tree house after us. Having finally paid off Ethyl, we sold her for fifty bucks; we didn't have the money to keep her on the road anyway. In a few weeks, Grody would drive us to New Orleans for Mardi Gras. Afterwards, Dep and I would hitchhike to Dallas to see his younger sister. From there we'd thumb to Waco, where we could make a little money working for friends before going on to Austin.

Our final days in the county ticked away. Roxanne the witch came down to say good-bye, and to ask if I had borrowed her enema bag? I had not. We said tearful farewells to Bubba, Helen, and Seth, to Margery and Billy, to Glyn and Sas and the family at Waller. We would miss our friends immeasurably.

The last morning in Whitesburg I went to a local nursery. The old man in charge tried to put his rabbity little tongue in my mouth, but he had just the thing I was looking for: jasmine.

Udo had given us so much. It had sheltered and nurtured us and we, in turn, had loved it as best we could. Now we wanted to leave something of ourselves there, the lingering scent of our life together. That afternoon we planted the fragrant vine at the foot of the tree house. Kneeling, we pressed our hands into the wet earth and gave our blessing to the star-shaped flowers whose common name was poet's jasmine.

"We'll be back," Depty whispered.

23

Our Little Town

I t's the final night of filming the Blaze Foley documentary at Waller. Kevin and his crew had hoped to get out to the tree house with me, only I'm not sure how to find it, and now there isn't time. The crew has to start back to Texas early tomorrow morning. Over the past five days I've given them our story, and they, in turn, have taken tender care of me. We won't say goodbye, just *see you later*. I'll be coming to Austin in two months' time to visit Blaze's grave; it's long overdue. Turns out Georgia is only the beginning of my journey back to him.

As the crew packs up their equipment, a spiffy white car comes down the driveway with Grody Mike at the wheel. A quarter of a century has passed since he and I last saw each other, and I can say with certainty that Mike is no longer grody, though the name persists. Nattily dressed in a button-down collar and white-cabled sweater, he wears his salt-and-pepper beard neatly trimmed. Like all of us, he's wider and rounder, though his pixilated caw is the same. We play twenty-five-year catch-up. He's a working man in Austin now, with a wife and two teenagers he adores.

The next morning he and I drive out to look for Udo. Zonko Joe's property was in a suburb of Roopville called Star Point, a fact I never knew before. Grody Mike hasn't been back for decades either, not since Joe sold the land in the late '70s. It takes a while to get our bearings; roads have been widened and familiar landmarks like Opal Shirrey's general store no longer exist.

At last we find the dirt road and what we think is the property. The power lines have been removed; only skeletal remnants mark their former row across the field. The unfinished house and trailer are gone. In their place is a locked gate across the driveway and a white frame house beyond.

I buzz the intercom. When a man's voice answers, I say we used to live on this land and were wondering, could we look around? The man comes out to open the gate. Red-haired and blue-veined, he has pale indoor skin and no recollection of any house in the woods. He bought the land from the guy who bought it from Zonko Joe; lots of things have changed in twenty-five years. Still, we are welcome to take a look.

Grody and I follow the extinct power lines through the still-visible fire-break. Lack of use has erased the footpath. When Depty and I used to come home at night, we could have been on another planet, so hidden away did we feel. Thick woods on every side sheltered us from the road, which now seems closer, and new pre-fab houses encroach on the withered meadow.

The indelible imprint of a carriage road connects field to woods; this may be the way to the tree house. The black oak is no longer there, but we turn into the woods anyway. The creek runs alongside, singing the same moonlit song. The pines are skinny here, save for a few older ones, with the same dense understory of rhododendron and grapevine. We're gripped by a feeling of familiarity. Our pace quickens; we must be close. We wonder what could remain after so many years. If the tree house was torn down, which is likely, any planks left to rot would have long returned to the soil. We reconstruct the lay of the land, the hill the shelter was built on, the swale that dipped away. I remember how the rain gushed into my brother's tent. When the forest was logged and the incline laid bare, erosion may have altered the grade, making it steeper, unrecognizable.

But what if the jasmine is still here? Secretly, that's what I'm hoping to find. Jasmine can grow to be thirty feet tall, and its presence in these pinewoods would mark the site indubitably. That, more than anything, would tell me something of Udo has endured.

We don't find the tree house, or the jasmine, much as we want to, hard as we try. After a while we stop looking and settle on a narrow sandbar beside the stream. Grody Mike has just told me its name, Milligan Creek, another new fact.

Bronze-colored leaves rustle in the breeze, scattering glints of light like thrown diamonds across the brook. How delicate these woods are in the last throes of autumn. The refrain from Blaze's ballad "Our Little Town" drifts through my head:

Tonight I'll be alone and blue

With empty arms that long for you
I only hear the lonesome sound
Since you left our little town

"Why did we ever leave here?" I wonder aloud.

"The man had work to do." Grody Mike has retained his way of speaking in declarative sentences. "It's a full-time job, being a legend."

He sits back on his haunches. An eye was lost to glaucoma years ago but he can still slide the other, conveying a mixture of shyness and slyness. Dipping a hand in the creek, he braids the water with his fingertips.

"It was the love," he begins, out of the blue. "The not holding back. Hearts wide-open. That's what made you and Dep so attractive. I'd never seen a couple so dedicated to each other. I wanted to feel that with someone."

We watch a leaf fall slowly into the stream to be carried along by the current. "I found my love with Dee," Grody goes on dreamily. "There's nothing I wouldn't do to make my wife smile."

He cuts his eye at me again. "See, I have this idea why you and Depty split. I think he saw the difficult road ahead and couldn't bear to see you suffer. At some level, he pushed you away."

I frown. "Grody, what are you talking about? I broke up with him, remember?"

He caws. "Yeah, well, that was convenient."

I am dumbfounded. "How do you know this?"

"He talked about it," Grody admits. "He let you go. He wanted to do it."

"Well, if that's true, then why do some of his songs sound so angry?"

"It hurt!" Grody shakes his head. I can hear him thinking: *Women.*

He goes on. "He intended to become Blaze Foley, win the fame and fortune due him, and come back for you."

"That's not how I remember it," I say lamely.

Grody caws again. "You're not listening."

I am. I'm just too *f'mished* to admit what I'm feeling. As in, *what do you mean, he left me?* So what, I was just another "baby" in a song? Someone—some*thing*—to be written about?

Only wait a minute, isn't that what I did to him? Used his memory as muse, as grist for the literary mill? Blaze himself had addressed this dilemma in "Faded Loves and Memories":

Faded loves and memories
Where I go, they follow me

> And I just can't seem to lose 'em
> So I might as well just use 'em
> One more time, one more sad old country song

I shake my head, trying to clear it of past assumptions. I'd come back to Georgia to recover the truth, but everyone, I was discovering, had their own account of it.

Had Blaze Foley's ambition cost Depty Dawg his heart?

24

ℜowhere to ℜide

Returning to New York by bus in early December, I'm raw as the weather, still buffetted by doubt. The trip to Georgia has replenished my memory of our beginnings—and called into question all my presumptions about our end.

At times, I suspect I've glommed onto Depty's ghost out of my own unrequited longings and hunger. Other times, I feel like Larue, like a bitch intent on marking my territory, claiming this song or that as my turf. I don't know if it's regret, or just pride, that compels me to retrace an identity I threw away years ago: that of being Blaze Foley's true love.

Alighting at the Kingston bus station, it's hard to believe it's been only three weeks since I left home. A honk directs me to Marnie, who's come to pick me up.

Another old friend from college, Marnie played Sister George in that long-ago production at the Mill. Today, she is still acting, and her pale Mayflower beauty, hickory smoked on a Carolina childhood, has gotten her many gigs on TV and in print commercials.

Lately I've begun to wonder why the Sister George days stayed with me so vividly, while so much of the tree house era had grown dim. Waving to Marnie now, it occurs to me that it's the longevity of our friendship that keeps those remembrances fresh. Each time we reminisce, they're reprinted, colors revived, details engraved anew. When I left Georgia all those years ago, I lost touch with the friends who would have refurbished Depty's memory time and again. Maybe that's why I had to write about him in the years after we parted, revisiting him through my imagination in solitary pursuit.

Memory is so fragile, so elemental to our sense of identity, perhaps language and poetry, music and song evolved as its helpmates. We tell our stories in the belief, mistaken or not, that words are less ephemeral than the flesh that stores them. We try to trap our experiences by recording them. That stem word *cord* comes from *coeur,* French for *heart.* Stories and songs attempt to recapture the heart, the essence, of our lives. It's hard to trust what you cannot hold on to.

Marnie welcomes me back to the Catskills with a mischievous grin. Several months ago she and her husband bought the house two doors down from the one I've been renting on the Little Beaverkill. Even before I went down to Georgia, they were already in the throes of renovations with a local contractor named Frank.

"Did you know Frank used to live in Austin?" Marnie asks slyly, driving us back into the mountains.

Her question puts me on immediate alert. Frank and I had met only a few times, yet I can easily picture his blonde ponytail and tranquil pale eyes. Turns out, not only did he live in Austin, he's a musician, a bass player.

Marnie can barely contain her glee. "So I asked him if he ever heard of the songwriter Blaze Foley?"

"'Blaze Foley!'" She mimics Frank's wide-eyed response. "'Sure, I know Blaze. Never met the man, but I was the engineer for his live CD.'"

"No, c'mon." I put up my hands to fend off the impact. "Don't tell me that."

Fumbling in my backpack for the CD—yep, there's Frank's name, with his credit for mixing and mastering at Phoenix Mastering and Recording in Austin.

"Gee," Marnie concludes, punching my arm. "Looks like ole Blaze has moved into the neighborhood."

Such is the stuff of legends.

Part 2

Autumn Winds

25

Miles to Go

Two months after my return from Georgia, I'm on my way to Texas and Blaze Foley's grave. It's the end of January now, and the thermometers in New York have plunged to zero. The Catskills are white and unmoving, the air so cold it glitters with crystals.

The night before I leave, Yukon the monk helps me try to bury Larue's ashes in the grove of pines behind the house. The ground is frozen, impossible to dig; no resting place there. It will be summer by the time we finally scatter her ashes in the percolating stream beside the cottage where she last lived.

For now, Yukon sends me off with his blessing. In our long friendship, good-byes have been frequent.

"My gypsy queen," he breathes, passing a hand over the top of my head. He wears a woolen cap pulled down to just above his eyelids. "It's a love story through space and time."

"There's no such thing as time," I grouse. "I'm convinced of that now." I don't know whether to laugh or cry. "Do you think I'm going crazy?" I ask him.

He peers at me and shrugs. "If something can heal you, let it."

And then I'm sitting in Marnie's car at the corner bus stop, waiting for the westbound bus. Huddled by the heater, bundled like Heidi in every warm layer I own, I have two hundred dollars in cash to my name.

Marnie envies me the trip out of the cold, though she fears I might get lost in the past, or caught up in some new future, and not come back to the Catskills. The bus pulls up to the corner. I tell her I'm coming home, but I don't really know where home is any more.

This is my second foray in search of Depty Dawg, and if I've learned anything, it's this: buses are for crying. Folding into the rough seat, I stash the backpack under my knees, look out the window and let 'er rip. Don't get me wrong: I like it. Bus time is dream time; I've come to appreciate its surreal invisibility. The communal experience has a built-in privacy, especially at night when all the other passengers are either sleeping, under earphones, or crying too. I'm not done grieving for Depty Dawg. My tears have become a mirror of his, as has this restlessness. It's my own zigzagging footsteps I'm also refilling.

In the dark hours the bus rolls across northern Indiana, girding an expanse of steel mills along the glacial Great Lakes. The tangle of metal and flame shimmers against the inky sky, like tethered dragons breathing fires so brilliant they can be seen from outer space.

The bus races neck-and-neck with eighteen-wheelers bound for Chicago. When the trucks outrun the bus, which they inevitably do, their blinkers cast red pulses over the uneasy dreams of the riders inside. But tonight I'm awake when they pass, and the height of the bus makes it possible for me to see into the cabs.

The number of young women driving trucks these days is nothing less than awe-inspiring. Bare arms gleam in the dashboard's muted glow; in the privacy of the cabs they bop to the latest Merle Haggard or Emmylou Harris CD. The nights are long and they have miles to go. Eyes on the road, they talk through the blackness on their cell phones, red-tipped fingers holding up thin cigarettes. Dice, feathers, beads, and crucifixes adorn rearview mirrors. One lady has a big pink stuffed dog in the seat beside her; maybe it's company, or maybe she's bringing it home to someone, a lover or a kid. When did a room of one's own become a truck of one's own?

Passing through Chicago in the middle of the night, I dream of changing buses and wake at sunrise to bleak Illinois cornfields. I'd forgotten how much I love the flatlands of the Midwest. Depty Dawg introduced me to them, and for a mountain girl the prairie is exotic. All that big sky gives me a kind of galactic vertigo. You can almost feel the planet tilting into the sun, the curved horizon balanced like a gyroscope around its metallic core.

By afternoon the bus has crossed into Missouri. Turkey vultures circle above the highway, riding warmed updrafts of air. Buzzards migrate south in winter, navigating the interstates and snacking on road kill all the way down.

I transfer buses in St. Louis where it's suddenly spring beside the wide Mississippi. Peeling off layers of fleece outside the bus station, I suddenly realize my suitcase is missing.

And I can hear Depty laugh: *How much are you willing to lose to find me?*

26

Fat Tuesday

I n February of 1976, Depty Dawg and I had nothing to lose, except Margery's Empire State guitar and a battered attaché case filled with Blaze Foley songs. The nickel we flipped to decide our fate had long been spent. Udo was behind us; the wide world beckoned. Embarking on an adventure to jumpstart a legend, our first stop would be New Orleans—and Mardi Gras.

We set out from Waller with Grody Mike and Dottie, another former Banning Mill escapee. Depty Dawg and I curled up in the back seat, his guitar within reach. He didn't like the idea of putting an instrument in a trunk, so we were used to sharing small spaces with it.

Along the highway, yellow daffodils trumpeted the return of sun-driven breezes. Grody's dented car headed into spring through landscapes new to me: swamplands stalked by long-legged shorebirds, cotton fields snowy with the season's first crop. The countryside opened up in lower Alabama, flattening and spreading to become water. Stark gray bayous gave way to broad shining Lake Pontchartrain, the blue wash of the Gulf of Mexico along its farthest shore.

Here, where the Mississippi ends its impressive journey from frigid Minnesota lakes to a tropical gulf coast, the river's meeting with the southern sea gave New Orleans a hot, unbridled quality, unlike any other place I'd ever known. The Cajun *patois,* rattling streetcars, and live oaks bearded with Spanish moss—all this was mysterious and familiar, seen only through Tennessee Williams' sensual, jaded eyes.

In New Orleans I went from being half-black to half-Cajun, or half-Creole. Everyone was half-Something. If America is a melting pot, New Orleans is where it comes to a boil. The history of the South is penned in DNA, inscribed on dark erotic faces of African, French, Spanish, Italian, Irish, Indian, and Caribbean design. Historians can prattle on about borders and treaties; in the end it all comes down to sex.

The mixing of gene pools was so commonplace here, language tried and mostly failed to keep up. Take the regrettable term *mulatto*, which I was asked if I was on several occasions. Originally it was meant for children of African and European descent, usually the result of slave women coerced by their owners. Likewise, *quadroon* smacks of Spanish currency, but the word was coined for the offspring of a white father and mulatto mother. Many kids of ex-slaves were one-fourth African, hence the *quad*, and their progeny were *octoroons*, for their one-eighth portion of African genes. In New Orleans, there are no peculiar hues.

Depty and I were fascinated by these distinctions, and the stories they told. Our hostess, Cynthia, was a caramel beauty of African, Caucasian, and American Indian lineage, animated by a saucy wit. When I wondered aloud what I'd be—being half-black, southern, and Jewish and all—Depty suggested *macaroon*. That sounded Scottish to me.

"How about *crackeroon*?" Cynthia quipped.

She and her husband, Jim, had been friends of Waller since the '60s, when Jim served as a VISTA volunteer in Atlanta's inner city. Now he worked for the mayor of New Orleans. The four of us from Georgia would camp out on Jim and Cynthia's living room floor, though sleep was the last item on our list of things to do.

Before Fat Tuesday we careened from party to party on mambo feet, drinking beer and gobbling oysters galore. Seemed like everywhere we went there were big burlap bags of oysters waiting to be shucked and slurped. Mardi Gras, I learned, was a smorgasbord of French-Catholic traditions, seasoned with pagan spring rites, and served up in different dishes along the Gulf Coast. In some locales it was called Carnival, meaning *fleshly excess*. Infused one night with the carnival spirit, the Whitesburg Four took a shower together in Cynthia's bathroom, all fully dressed.

For his Mardi Gras costume, Grody Mike shaved the entire left half of his head, beard and hair both. In profile he looked completely different: bald on one side, hairy on the other. Viewed straight on, he just looked weird. Fortunately, New Orleans welcomed the weird, and the poor. Pay phones were only a nickel, and you could get a big bowl of beans and rice for only fifty cents.

On Fat Tuesday we were up before the sun. Jim had gotten us seats on the one parade allowed in the French Quarter that day. The Krewe of Kraw was an assembly of ragtag pick-up trucks that hauled huge vats of crawfish and kegs of beer to give out to the revelers for free. The weekend before, a traditional "crawdad" race had decided who would reign over the Krewe. Live crawfish were placed in the center of a circle, and if yours reached the edge of the circle first, you were crowned. Our ruler that year christened himself Succulence the King and showed up Fat Tuesday in a bright red cape.

Depty and I didn't wear costumes. We were odd enough, we decided, and just being in the company of Grody's half-head lent us a certain bizarreness by proxy. Besides, we were busy in the back of the truck. From it we could see the whole expanse of crowded streets—the garish playful costumes, infinitely imaginative. A family of five dressed like tomatoes, round as pincushions and descending in size from beefsteak to cherry. A man clad in a leopard loincloth with a feathered headdress so broad the crowd had to part to let him by. On-duty cops wore pig masks; homegrown jazz bands played on every corner. From the high narrow balconies lining the French Quarter, residents rained down squalls of confetti on the noisy crowd, opening to let the parade of pick-ups pass.

We rode waves of uplifted hands, filling them with splashing cups of beer and handfuls of crawfish dripping with spices.

"How do you eat these?" people asked.

"Eat the tail, suck the head," was the customary reply. And in one section of the French Quarter largely populated by gay men and women, that mantra rose in a hue and cry that lasted a full five minutes.

From our perch above the crowd, I was thrilled to deliver refreshments to the merrymakers in the street, to be part of the celebration in this generous way. The Krewe started drinking early. By afternoon, I was sleepy, and Depty was soused. When King Succulence's preening got on his nerves, he tried to pick a fight with him.

"Hey!" Dep taunted, leaning precariously from the truck. "You suck!"

I'd rarely seen him drunk in daylight, and never in so large a crowd. His flailing carelessness unnerved me; I was scared he'd hurt himself or, God forbid, someone else. When the parade was over, I pleaded exhaustion, and with Grody Mike's help, got him back without incident to Cynthia's floor.

"Sweet dreams, Big Foot," I murmured, covering him with a jacket.

He rolled over and threw an arm around his guitar case. Soon he was breathing deeply.

"Ah." Grody Mike's grin darted out from his half-beard. "The bad sleep well." He turned to me. "Hey—want to go listen to some jazz, just you, me and Dottie?"

"No, thanks." I took his hand. "What am I going to do without you?"

"Y'all can always come home." Leave it to Grody to point out the obvious.

The front door closed behind him. I scooted in beside Depty and lay my head against his damp shoulder, listening to him scuffle in his sleep. Going back to Georgia was out of the question. Yet, for all the mad magic of Mardi Gras, I was already missing the quiet spell of the tree house, and the safety of our little town.

27

Tumbleweed

A day later, we were on the road again. Grody drove us through the French Quarter to the western outskirts of New Orleans to catch a ride on Interstate 10. Like Depty Dawg, the French Quarter was still recovering. Mountain-high mounds of wine bottles towered above workers with push-brooms, bulldozing knee-high piles of confetti into the gutters. We pictured tons of the rainbow-colored slivers washing into the Gulf and settling to the bottom, the faintest wash of polka-dot sediment attesting, millions of years from now, to the city's brief, phantasmal reign.

The prospect of hitchhiking across Louisiana was daunting—to me anyway—but all we had were our thumbs, and Depty thought we'd have more luck if mine was the one out. Standing once more beside a highway, I polished my digit, a ritual inspired by Sissy Hankshaw, hitchhiker extraordinaire of Tom Robbins' *Even Cowgirls Get the Blues*. That cracked Dep up; better still, it worked. We got short rides consistently, always from men. Also consistent was some form of the question, do ya'll like to go skinny-dippin'? Depty took it all in stride, and he could quote Scripture, which helped.

By late afternoon we were still hours from the Texas border, and our present ride was only going as far as Lafayette. Depty had hoped to be farther along by dark.

"Let us off at the next truck stop," he directed the driver. "That be fine."

"Honey?" I fretted at his side. "Is this a good idea?"

"Trucks go long distance," he explained, after we'd been dropped off at a desolate café in an empty field. The ramshackle building was circled by a herd of resting freight-haulers.

"Think of them as motels on wheels," he instructed me. "Don't worry, I can handle truckers. My daddy was one."

In the café he spied a pair of chatty, rough-hewn truckers sitting at the counter. Bonnie and Roy were on their way to Kansas City. They were willing to tuck a small suitcase, one guitar, and two wayfarers behind their front seat, so long as Depty was willing to sing for them sometime before we hit Shreveport. It was only a hundred miles to Dallas from there.

The sun was gashing red and purple as we settled in the back of their cab. Outside of town, Roy pulled off onto deserted back roads, the colors of houses and barns indistinguishable in the graying light.

"We been livin' in the truck all the time," he informed us, *Born to Be Free* tattooed in cursive on his sizeable forearm. "Ever since I come back from 'Nam."

Bonnie had a tomboy figure and dirty blonde hair; a loose bottom plate clicked like castanets when she talked. "Suits me fine. Ain't never been able to sit still, not in all my life."

Roy smiled at her. "You're tumbleweed, babe, same as me."

"That's right," Bonnie clicked. "And tumbleweed don't stick to nothin' but itself."

The radio kept them company on long hauls. Like Depty Dawg, they knew what music got played where, and they loved it all: gospel, country, Cajun, soul, rhythm-and-blues, and the plain ol' blues. The landscape was as much composed of airwaves as it was asphalt.

Roy patted the dashboard above the radio. "Yep. She's our constant solace."

After an hour or so of easy conversation, Dep opened his guitar case. That was my cue to plaster myself against the window to make room for his knees. In the black sky above, constellations were winking on one-by-one in patterns more familiar than the white lines dashing below me. The truck rumbled past tattered billboards, closed gas stations, and slumbering trailers, as Depty sang and the dark countryside opened to receive us.

At midnight we came out on the highway and Bonnie took the wheel. Roy passed out, snoring, in the passenger seat. Dep put the guitar away and drew me to him.

"Get some sleep," he whispered. Obligingly, I closed my eyes. "We appreciate y'all giving up your boo-door for a night," he told Bonnie.

I opened one eye. She looked like a little kid hunkered over the wheel.

"You sure can sing," she allowed over her shoulder. "That could be you on the radio I swear."

I leaned forward. "Ever heard of Blaze Foley, the country music sensation?"

Bonnie lit a cigarette. "That you?"

Dep shrugged modestly. "Here's hoping".

"You his agent?" Bonnie asked, looking at me in the rear-view mirror.

"No, his mother," I giggled.

"Country music sensation, huh?" she went on. "Ya'll on vacation?" Her laugh ended in a hoarse cough. She spit out the window. "Want some speed?"

I sat up; I wasn't going to get any sleep anyway. We swallowed the pills with the last of our Dr. Pepper. Depty bummed a smoke from Bonnie and rolled down the window. The cool night air washed over us.

"They got it all worked out," he mused. "Livin' like turtles with home on their backs."

He pictured us on a Blaze Foley road tour, a truck's empty trailer transformed into a moveable, windowless house. Outside it'd look weatherworn, with "Foley Trucking" painted on the rough tin.

"Inside it could be like the Taj Mahal," he improvised. "Nobody'd have to know but us."

"We could take the tree house with us," I said, caught up in the fantasy. "With grapevines hanging, a trickling waterfall, and the moon full every night."

He shook his head. "Can't believe I doubted how I'd feel once we left there. About us and everything. Udo. The way your mind can talk stupid."

He tossed the cigarette out the window. Orange sparks sprayed in the wind before disappearing into the blackness. "Anywhere you are is home," he whispered.

28

Big D

At daybreak, Bonnie and Roy let us off outside Shreveport, promising to keep the radio tuned for Blaze Foley. By noon, we were in a black sedan driven by a middle-aged salesman going straight into Dallas. He'd picked us up out of parental concern, he told us—a reminder of how young we must look standing by the side of the road.

Dep sprawled in the back seat with the guitar and immediately fell asleep. I sat in front, keeping our benefactor company. This was my first glimpse of big sky. In the distance, a black anvil-shaped cloud moved over the flatlands, the only thing seeming to hold the barren earth down. The horizon was so low I could see the storm in its entirety. Blue lightning flicked within the tall thunderhead, fringed at the bottom with gray streaks of rain that evaporated before reaching the hot, dry plain.

In Dallas, the salesman dropped us off at the house of a friend from high school, a bona fide third-generation Jewish-American belle. Sarajane had come through Waller the summer before, spending a night on the tree house floor. She was tall and bosomy with waist-length chestnut hair; as a teenager, she was Legolas to my Gimli, and I was more than happy to trail in her magnetic shadow.

Then one day, when Sarajane was fifteen, her mother Betty unexpectedly left town, changed her name to Samantha, and became a Christian Scientist.

"America, America, where all your dreams can come true," Depty rhapsodized when I told him her story.

At twenty-three, Sarajane had survived her parents' divorce with elegance and grit. These days she freelanced as a jeweler and magazine stylist in the Dallas-Fort Worth area. As it happened, her mother was visiting her when Depty and I popped in unannounced. I couldn't believe Samantha's transformation: the curvy, bouffant JAB had become a demure church-lady. Everyone was in the business of reinvention, it seemed.

"We're bonded with Crazy Glue," Sarajane informed me. She didn't bother to hide her opinion of Depty Dawg either. Far as she was concerned, he was a wrong turn down a dead-end street. That stung; it was too easy to see the bum and miss the poet. We didn't stay with her long.

Dep got in touch with his younger sister. Marsha was living in Irving, a suburb of Dallas. He hadn't seen her, or her seven-year-old daughter Stephanie, in years. At twenty-one and already on a second marriage, Marsha was large-boned and striking with glossy, russet hair. She had her brother's bright intensity and the same undertow of sorrow.

"Just can't seem to get myself together," she declared, ricocheting around her apartment looking for a match. "The Lord's going to help me with that." Pulling a pack from under her Bible, she held it up. "See what I mean?"

She lit a cigarette and veered onto the subject of the family's traveling gospel days. Her brother had made up songs for them in the car. Marsha still called him Mike.

"What was that one about the dirty nickel?" She snapped her fingers. "You know, Mike? That one you found between the seats? That one Mother told you not to touch."

Mike jumped up, jamming like Elvis on an imaginary guitar. "It's so dirty," he crooned, grinding his hips. "So doggone dirty."

His sister held up an invisible microphone. "Don't you touch it, you better not touch it." Then they doubled over, laughing.

From the late '50s on, the Fuller Family trio was composed of their mother Louise and the two eldest children at home at the time. At first, that meant their older brother, Douglas, and their sister, Patricia. But when Doug left home at nineteen to get married, eleven-year-old Mike took his place. After Patricia moved away, it became Marsha's turn. At six, she sang lead.

"I do love to sing," Marsha exclaimed now, a hand in the air. "Before—and to—the Lord."

She and Mike had harmonized with Louise from Texas to Georgia, bartering hymns for their bread and board. Depty had described their performances: "Mother'd tap her foot and play the ukulele and Daddy'd sit out in the station wagon and drink Ripple." Sometimes the kids came out of church to find Daddy passed out in the front seat.

I could feel the presence of secrets in the restraint they used when speaking of their father. Edwin had *nerve problems* was all they would allow. I could guess what that meant; my family had secrets too. We excused Momma's erratic behavior with the embarrassed euphemism: *She's sensitive.*

Marsha showed me a snapshot of Edwin. She and Mike had inherited his dark, sharp features, only he was bantam-small with a '40s movie-star kind of suave. His kids were still little when he drove a truck for Braswell Freight; he'd be gone weeks at a stretch. For a time, his growing family carved a path across the South, attempting to keep up with him. But when Edwin quit trucking and resolved to stay at home, his family kept moving—this time to lose him. Daddy was tenacious; he could always find them.

Recently, however, he'd come to a screeching halt in a nursing home, and now we were on our way to visit him. Depty hadn't seen his father in five years, not since he was fat and still Mike. By '71, the family had broken up, was scattered all over. Mike was living alone in a trailer in Memphis when Edwin caught up with his youngest son and insisted on moving in with him. Mike had fled, leaving no forwarding address.

The nursing home was a long, shabby building squatting on a barren lot. A smell of disinfectant pervaded the visiting room where we sat, waiting for Edwin to join us. The drab furnishings were softened by a buttery light seeping through opaque curtains.

Edwin was fifty-five and looked eighty. His addictions to pills and alcohol had shriveled him so he could hardly stand, let alone walk, without crutches. He sat chain-smoking unfiltered cigarettes, quaking yellow fingers holding up a growing line of ash. His lap caught the fallen ashes—and his tears— when his children sang "Where the Roses Never Fade," their voices gliding together in the old remembered harmonies.

Afterwards, we walked him, tottering on crutches, to the outdoor bathroom. Mike closed the door behind their daddy, to turn and smile at Marsha, an unreadable smile conveying knowledge only they could have.

"What was it like, seeing him again?" I asked that night as we fell asleep in a tangle on his sister's couch.

"Can't believe I used to be scared of that." Depty sighed into the dark. "Think I'd rather die young than be that way when I get old."

I put my head on his chest. "Don't say that."

But I understood. Growing up, people used to say to me, "You're just like your mother, so sensitive." That was shorthand for *crazy*, a life sentence I was hoping to outpace by running as fast and as far as I could into a life vastly different from hers.

In Dallas I thought I got a glimmer of what Depty Dawg was running from—or maybe toward. Either way, it was unavoidable. If his father, or my mother, were any indication, we were already broken, beyond repair.

29

Wacko

ven I was anxious to get back on the road. The following day we said
goodbye to Marsha, and set out for Waco. By early March the Texas
highways were ablaze with wildflowers: bluebonnet, larkspur, Indian
paintbrush, black-eyed Susan, bull thistle.

"Names alone tell a story," Dep mused, sitting on a suitcase in the warm
sun, watching me polish my thumb yet again. It was only a short jog to Waco,
where the promise of money and safe haven awaited us.

LaNelle was a college friend of Margery's whom we'd met on Old Black
Dirt Road. At one time a psychological researcher, lately she'd acquired a law
degree to practice alongside her attorney husband. Johnny was easygoing
and preppy in crisp white shirts. He and LaNelle were in the midst of restor-
ing their ornate Victorian mansion. As luck would have it, they needed a
carpenter.

LaNelle put us up in a back bedroom and bath on the second floor. The
single twin bed sat high off the ground in an antique wooden frame. The
ancient wallpaper was adorned with faded rows of red-coated soldiers that
marched with fife-and-drum when we turned out the light. Down the hall
was another bedroom with dizzying paisley walls reminiscent of the Mill. But
without a doubt the mansion's most memorable feature was a curving cherry
staircase with a flat banister, perfect for sliding down.

Soon after we arrived, Dep began to build a flight of new stairs in the old
barn behind the house, while I worked outside in the shade, caning four dining chairs that had belonged to Johnny's grandmother. LaNelle brought us
lunchtime sacks of cheeseburgers and French fries. She wore her brilliance
like a jaunty sun hat, another quotable character we wanted to follow around,
recording her quirks and fabulous tales. Our favorite was the one we were
living firsthand.

In a tumbledown shed in the corner of the yard lived two aging turkeys, Bach and Gobble. Former research subjects of LaNelle's, the birds were a domestic breed, the kind that usually ends up young and fat on somebody's Thanksgiving platter. Having escaped the fate of their peers, they were still laying eggs in old age—even more remarkable since Bach had begun life as Gobble's *son*. Bred to produce desirable white meat, domestic turkeys are genetically engineered to develop well-formed breasts, and the females tend to lay prodigious amounts of eggs. Bach's breasts grew so large, he decided he was female and started laying eggs at the rate of his/her mother. Now their old bodies were running out of calcium, and the eggs were coming out already cracked, so to speak—shell-less blobs of yoke and mucous lying in the nest. We accompanied LaNelle to the local Purina factory where she had more calcium added to their feed. Soon Bach and Gobble were laying eggs in shells. They were delicious, by the way—the eggs, not the birds.

Waco was a respite from our new sense of dislocation. We'd been lucky so far: every time we free-fell, a net had appeared to catch us. Depty felt at home in Texas; his cowboy hat and boots were the norm here. Marsha came down to visit several times during our two-month stay. She and Dep knew some of the local musicians; at night they would gather in a back sitting-room. Dep got a lot of composing done in those weeks, trying out melodies and lyrics on whoever assembled in LaNelle's high-ceilinged parlor.

Texas was already casting its rough-and-tumble spell. He'd begun a song about a woman who dealt cards in a saloon:

> It was June or September
> Don't rightly remember
> The first time I laid eyes on you
> It was June or September
> Seattle or Denver
> First time I laid eyes on you

Like us, LaNelle and Johnny were fans of Kinky Friedman, a ribald, Jewish, Texas songwriter. Dep and I especially loved his tune, "They Ain't Making Jews Like Jesus Any More." Kinky seemed to epitomize Austin's irreverent energy, a spirit so like Depty Dawg's we were certain he'd be a hit. We grew eager and impatient, time to make the future present.

Just before setting out for Austin at the end of April, we got the news: Basil had been born at last to Margery and Billy in Whitesburg.

"Let's go!" LaNelle yelled, and within minutes, the three of us were on the highway headed east to Georgia.

There wasn't a second to get over to Waller, or to even get homesick. We held the newborn infant in our arms, turned around, and sped back to Texas in thirty-six hours' time.

Back in Waco, we resumed our plans to take on Austin. The thought of our thumbing there horrified LaNelle. As a deterrent, she took us to the Waco courthouse to show us mug shots of roadside murderers. And a few days after our return from Georgia, she ferried us down to Austin herself.

An old friend of Dep's had invited us to stay with him when we arrived in town. In the late '60s, the two teenagers had worked side-by-side at the Sears in Irving—Lindsey in automotive and Mike Fuller in paint. Lindsey had the distinction of being Mike's first friend to grow his hair long. Now he and his wife were offering us sanctuary till we found work and a place of our own.

Soon as we were settled in at Lindsey's, I started looking for a job, and Depty Dawg went to check out Austin's country music scene, to see how Blaze Foley might make it his own.

30

Lovers and Music

Austin is where Blaze Foley's legend would ultimately take root, and where it is still unfurling. I can feel its gravitational pull on me as I touch down at the Austin bus station, twenty-seven springs after Depty Dawg and I first landed here. I don't know what I expect to learn by coming back to Texas, but I'm committed to being educated. Consumed by the desire to heal the past, I'm letting the grief lead me where it wants to go, geographically and emotionally.

Kevin picks me up at the Austin station. "Welcome back," he says, jumping out of his van.

It's heartening to see a familiar face. After so long an absence, Austin is as much a stranger to me as I was to it in May of '76. Crisscrossing loops of freeways and Gotham-like glass skyscrapers have pressed Austin's small-town boundaries outward and upward. Timeless landmarks remain: the gold-domed State Capitol building, and the infamous Texas Tower, looming twenty-seven stories above the university campus on Guadalupe, the funky strip of shops and restaurants still referred to as *the drag*.

Heading south, the van crosses the slow-moving river that cinches the city like a green leather belt. Several blocks below the water, Kevin pulls off the busy boulevard and parks behind the tidy purple bungalow that houses Abraxas Productions.

The modest offices contain editing consoles and video screens that vie for space with Kevin's books and belongings. I follow him around as he gathers up dirty clothes and throws them in a closet. Lately he's been sleeping on the editing-room couch. In the past year, he's lost a job, a lover, and a home.

"Oh, no!" he cries, holding his head in clownish despair. "I'm becoming Blaze!"

On the wall above the couch he has constructed a timeline of Blaze's life, dates and bare facts only. So much of Blaze's chronology is still in question, even for Kevin who probably knows more about his subject's erratic existence than anyone else now. He has traveled around the country, weaving Blaze's life from stories told by far-flung friends. Like me, each possesses a strand, whatever Blaze chose to share. We can all recall specific events—our versions anyway—but when they actually took place is often less clear. Time has a way of erasing its frame.

There I am, up on the wall from '75 to '77, and again, briefly, in the early '80s, the exact date of our last meeting in New York City still unknown. How weird to see the events of your life hung up on pastel Post-its, like underwear on a clothesline: very personal, very public.

Blaze's lyrics have become the most accurate compass for tracking his meandering life. By present count, he wrote more than sixty songs. Kevin's timeline is also an attempt to pin down when each song was written. I'd like to know their timing too, so that I might better guess which ones were addressed to me.

From the tabs on the wall, it would appear that the majority of his songs emerged in the five years spanning '75 to '79. By the early '80s, new songs were coming slower and fewer; by mid-decade, his songwriting had all but trickled away.

"So many in so short a time," I murmur. "Why did he stop writing, do you think?"

"Well." Kevin slides his eyes at me slyly. "I'm thinking that may have something to do with you."

I wince. "Don't tell me that. He had other loves," I remind him. "Before and after me."

My hand sweeps the Post-its to include Nell in his Tex years; Helen and Fifi Larue in the late '70s when he was still going by Depty Dawg. And in the early '80s, Mandy Mercier, a young singer/songwriter who knew him in Austin as Blaze.

Kevin nods sagely. "I don't doubt he loved them. It's just that—whenever I talk about heartache? I talk about the last love and think about the first."

"I wasn't the first," I protest, perhaps too much.

Kevin beckons me to follow him down the hall. On a wall in a crowded office is a scribbled history of "If I Could Only Fly," beginning with its conception in 1977. One phrase in particular gets my attention: *Sybil sacrificed for dream.*

The ground shifts again: when did I become Blaze's victim? I can't deny these words echo Grody Mike's account of the past, heard two months ago when we went searching for the tree house. I'm stubborn, I admit it; I don't want to see my own blindness. Only now that I'm back in Austin, it may be too late to look away again.

That afternoon Kevin drops me off on the drag, in front of the abandoned Hole in the Wall. The little dive is said to be one of Blaze's last stomping grounds; one of his first too, I recall. The forlorn marquee says CLOSED, the O missing, the D hanging upside down, about to fall. Peering through the planks nailed across the windows, I can feel an aquifer of regret beneath my skin, seeking release.

I walk the length of the drag in search of the Night Hawk, the diner that gave me my first job here. It's gone too, replaced by an Exxon station and Schlotzky's Deli. Most of the drag has been revamped by commerce. Where storefront head shops once co-existed beside old-fashioned barbershops, now there's Einstein's Bagels and The Gap. Only the faces on the street are familiar: college kids with more mousse maybe, and the same youthful beauty, the same slouching discontent. Bare midriffs pass by, owners engaged in charged conversations. Few seem to notice the man sitting with his back against an empty building. From the condition of his hair and skin, I imagine he's been living on the streets for years, maybe decades—a reminder that these are the sidewalks where Blaze honed his persona of the homeless troubadour, sleeping under pool tables and bridges, and in dumpsters so he said.

Gingerly I approach him. "Excuse me—did you know Blaze Foley?"

No eye contact. "He's dead."

"But you knew him?" I persist.

He stares into the street. "Foley was the Nazarene, a nobody from nowhere."

I fumble in my pocket for a bill, wishing he'd say more. We're distracted by the antics of his chocolate brown puppy.

"Half lab, half pit bull," he volunteers.

"What's its name?" I ask, stuffing a five-dollar bill in his styrofoam cup.

"No Name," he states, a reply I take as an answer, not an evasion.

That's me too. No one knows me here; I hardly do myself. Despite its changes, the drag feels strangely familiar. I have to keep reminding myself I lived here once. Austin always seemed so much more Depty's world than mine. How did I get to be the girl in this story?

Pulling away from the drag, I ease down a hill toward a park. Memory jogs: didn't we live beside a—Pease Park—that was it! Our first apartment was on Parkway; maybe it's nearby.

Today Pease Park is a strip of mowed grass dotted with merry-go-rounds, the thickets at its edge filled with twittering birds jazzed for spring. A thin stream runs along the sidewalk; up ahead, a wooden walkway curves over the trickle of water. I cross the bridge. There, at the border of the playground, is a street sign. Parkway.

Like a wanderer in a dream, I walk the lane of small-frame houses until it dips at the intersection of Parkway and Enfield. All at once it comes back to me: a century plant bloomed on that corner the spring we arrived. We'd taken its rare spike of flowers for a sign. The plant isn't there any more, but our place was right across from it—

I turn. A new, three-story, stucco apartment complex sits on the lot, but the hill running alongside it feels right; the stairs down to our basement apartment followed that same incline. Along the backyard, Lamar Boulevard is busier and louder behind a screen of tall live oaks.

Did you ever come back here, Dep? Did the past ever recede for you? Or were you pinned to it by remorse, as I am now?

Lines from his song "Rainbows and Ridges" run through my head:

> Rainbows and ridges, rhymers and rhymes
> Lovers and music all have their times
> Someone gets started; someone resigns

Blaze Foley was just getting started when Depty Dawg and I came through here in 1976. Decades later, I have to question which one of us resigned first.

> Interstate highways, buses and trains
> Only lead horses down memory lanes
> Everything passes; what's passed will remain

Images refract, like light through a prism, projecting a fan of memories, each a different color and mood: Dep at the top of the stairs, guitar case in hand, smiling down at me; the two of us sitting at the kitchen table, talking and laughing; us being squeezed together into the narrow shower.

These are what remain, these images and words—his, and mine now too— fragments of an ongoing conversation begun a long time ago. I really can't say any more when it started, or how it will ever end.

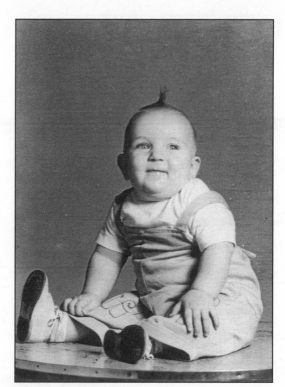

Michael David Fuller at ten months.

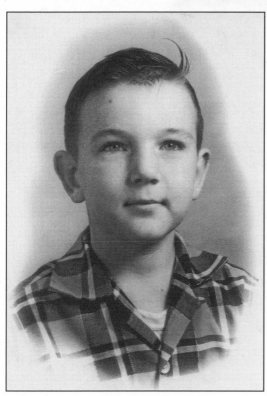

Mike at eight.

Blaze at eighteen or nineteen in his "Tex" phase. Photo taken while working for W. T. Grant in northeast Texas.

The Banning Mill Ensemble. Shot taken during a rehearsal of Anton Chekhov's The Bear, *May 1975. The same photo hung on the wall at Waller for over two decades. From left to right: Leo Sauer, Jo Giraudo, me.*

Depty and me in our first weeks together, Summer 1975.

PHOTO BY WILLIAM L. LAND.

With Billy and Margery, Summer 1975.

FROM AUTHOR'S COLLECTION, PHOTOGRAPHER UNKNOWN.

The back of the tree house on construction day, October 1975.

Snapshot taken by my father at the Atlanta airport, November 1975. The creases show where he folded the photo to keep in his wallet.

My parents Jeannette and Sam Rosen around the time they met Depty Dawg.

Grody Mike and Betsey Ross at the tree house, May 1976.

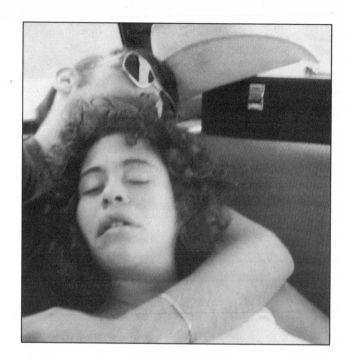

Asleep in the backseat on the way to Waller, June 1976.

PHOTO BY LINDSEY V. HORTON.

At Dog River. On our own alternative lifestyles tour. Georgia, July 1976. From left to right: Zonko Joe Bucher, me, Depty Dawg. Below: Lindsey Horton.

COURTESY OF LINDSEY V. HORTON.

Hippies with puppies. After the broom-jump, July 1976. From left to right: Billy Bouris, Grody Mike Boyle, Lindsey Horton, Depty Dawg, me, Zonko Joe Bucher.

Letter from Blaze (Dr. B. Foley). On the back he wrote, "Sybil Rosen I love you." October 1976.

Self-portrait with sheep, October 1976.

Painting of Depty Dawg by Boyle '03.

Blaze Foley and The Beaver Valley Boy. Blaze's birthday in Houston, 1979.
COURTESY OF GURF MORLIX.

Blaze in Houston, 1979.
COURTESY OF GURF MORLIX.

Blaze soon after his return to Austin in 1981.

Stacking hats in Georgia, 1983. From left to right: Blaze, Billy Bouris, Basil Bouris, Glyn Thomas.

PHOTO BY MARGERY ALEXANDER BOURIS.

Blaze's younger sister Marsha Weldon and his mother Louise Hacker, December 2003.

PHOTO BY SYBIL ROSEN.

Blaze's niece Stephanie Hardin and her two sons Jacob (left) and James (right), July 2007.

PHOTO BY MARSHA WELDON.

Blaze's nephew Paul Berry (center) and his children Carlin (right) and Luke (left), December 2007.

PHOTO BY MARSHA WELDON.

From the bird painting by Ezalb Yelof. Courtesy of Cathy Balch.

Blaze's gravestone. His image is taken from the iconic portrait by C.P. Vaughn.

31

The Live Music Capital of the World

O ur place on Parkway was in the Castle Hill neighborhood, at the foot of Austin's violet hills. In the ad, the landlord listed it as a "garage" apartment, failing to mention that it wasn't over the garage but under it.

The bleakly furnished basement room opened onto a scudded backyard with a hedge of young live oaks, a crusted barbecue grill, and what was then Lamar Avenue. Its charm was its rent, which was cheap. There were frogs in the shower and wood roaches big as my fist in the bed, crunching under us when we rolled over. Reminiscent of the tree house minus the magic, the flat had its compensations. After living for almost a year without refrigeration, the archaic Kelvinator in the cinderblock kitchen felt like a luxury.

By spring of '76, Austin was an easy town to navigate. Free bus service, courtesy of the University of Texas, connected Castle Hill to the drag. And possession of marijuana had just been reduced to a misdemeanor, thanks also to the university, since so many state politicos had their kids enrolled there.

In the mornings Dep stayed home, writing and practicing, while I put on my uniform and went to work. The Night Hawk was a large, airy diner with waitresses in red-checked dresses and lacy tiaras, a curving chrome counter, and a menu thicker than *Gone with the Wind*. In the Lone Star State, I went from being half-Cajun to half-Any Number of Genes: Mexican, Chicano, Indian, take your pick. Few Lone Stars had ever met a Star of David.

Shifting identity helped me blend in with the other waitresses, though they were less concerned with my nationality than with my inexperience. The veterans—older women who'd worked there, some of them, since the '50s—wasted no time in intimidating me. If I were idle at the coffee machine when the pot was low, someone would stand behind me so close I could feel her breath on my neck. I got the message: *Pay attention; see what's needed; take care of it.* The morning it all clicked in, I was accepted by the others and grew to love working with them, a syncopated corps of red-checked dancers in a blue-plate ballet.

The waitresses came in all sizes and colors. There was bony, tan-skinned Claris who had worked the counter for twenty-five years, knew all the regulars, what they ordered, how they tipped. That mute staggering man had been a successful lawyer till he developed cerebral palsy. And that gal who came in for coffee and a soft-boiled egg every morning, she'd lost her family in a fire caused by her smoking in bed. One day, Claris accused me of stealing the quarter a regular left under his plate. My feelings were hurt; I hadn't stolen anything since the shoplifting fiasco at K-Mart. I was moved to the floor to work the tables.

There I got to know Mary Nelle, a big blonde university student on a romantic quest. "In Search of The Big O," she whispered to me at the cash register. Sex was a constant topic of conversation.

One morning during our breakfast break, Ula, a Christian countrywoman who wore a hairnet much like the cobwebs at Waller, described how her husband had proposed to her. Apparently, he was wearing his mechanic's jumpsuit when he popped the question.

"He unzipped it all the way down," Ula related to me, matter-of-fact. "He was nekked underneath, and there was a big ole wedding ring around his gentile."

That was about the closest any of us ever got to talking about religion.

Ula had found God ten years earlier, the morning of the Texas Tower massacre. In August 1966, a twenty-four-year-old ex-Marine named Charles Whitman climbed the tower with several high-powered rifles and a sawed-off shotgun. In ninety-seven minutes he killed sixteen people, wounding thirty-three others before he himself was shot and killed. Earlier that morning he'd murdered his wife and mother to spare them the anguish of what he was about to do. An autopsy revealed a malignancy on Charles' brain, though experts could not agree if that had affected his behavior. In diaries found after his death, he had written of hating his abusive, gun-loving father "with a mortal passion." Enlisting in the Marines at eighteen, he was court-martialed five years later for, among other things, unauthorized possession of a non-military rifle. He disappeared, roaming the country in an effort to outdistance, so his diaries said, "the unbearable pressure in my mind."

Ula could still hear the blasts from Charles' rifles, see the bleeding victims running past the diner. I was sixteen that summer. The Roanoke newspaper had described the ex-Eagle Scout as "an all-American Boy." It was the first time the word *sniper*, or the possibility of random violence, had ever entered my mind.

Now, here I was, working on the same street where the tragedy had taken place. At the time it seemed to me a thing like that could only happen in Texas.

Once we were settled in under the garage, Dep went over to The Armadillo World Headquarters, the renowned counterculture music hall, to see about waiting tables there. Turned out they didn't need waiters, but they could use a bouncer, they told him, eyeing his six-foot-three frame.

"Hell," he demurred. "I can't even beat myself up."

The trip was not wasted. On the way home he was standing at a corner bus stop, with a sack of beer in one hand, his guitar in the other, and a pink bus transfer in his mouth. A manicured housewife stopped at a red light, took one look at the longhaired cowboy, and promptly locked her car door.

These lines from "Wouldn't That Be Nice?" were written a few hours later:

> Lock your door, lady, or I'll jump in your car
> I know you know how nasty we are
> Poke out your eyeballs and make you a scar
> Make you have to walk real far
> Make you do everythin' you don't wanna do
> Buy me some earthworms and smear 'em on you
> Put your fat head in a rusty old vice
> Yeah, wouldn't that be nice?

Urban life was bringing out the anarchist in him. A definite departure from the sonnets of the tree house, the mocking little ditty couldn't mask how much the incident had offended him.

"Why would anyone be afraid of me?" he asked, genuinely disturbed.

The brashness of his lyrics was offset by an ingrown reticence. He pushed himself to make contacts in Austin, and the music provided a shorthand for small talk. As Depty Dawg, he got to know the management at country venues like The Split Rail, Soap Creek, The Alamo Lounge, and Spellman's, where singer/songwriters Guy Clark, Nanci Griffith, Butch Hancock, and Steve Fromholz were taking the stage. It didn't take a monumental leap of faith to envision Blaze Foley up there with them. Only the prospect of performing in a town that billed itself as "The Live Music Capital of the World" was more daunting than he had anticipated.

He finally admitted it to me one night as we walked home from The Hole in the Wall. We'd gone there to hear a band called The Goats of Arabia. Dep had recently introduced himself to its skinny lead guitarist (who would one day take the name Gurf Morlix). The boyish musician's quiet demeanor masked a kindred maverick soul, though Depty confessed to me now that he was a little in awe of him.

"Why?" I countered, taking his arm. "You're as good as anybody here."

"Oh, sure, singing on a back porch." He sounded shaky. I was getting used to the fitful nervousness that could come over him from time to time.

"Is it like stage fright?" I'd experienced the hammering heart and urge to flee.

He lit a cigarette. "Hate to make a fool of myself is all."

"You're not going to!" Panic washed over me. "I thought that's what we came here for."

"It is." He flicked the match impatiently. "Don't rush me."

Was this how legends behaved? Dreaming was one thing, reality another.

"You're right," I told him. "Like we say at the Night Hawk: good food takes time."

We arrived in Austin with only the clothes on our backs. We had nothing in Udo either, save the moon and stars. Alternative lifestyles did not wear as well in the city. Living in a tree had been our choice, and in Georgia there was always help whenever we needed it. Here, things were different; we were very much on our own. In the glare of the streetlights, the moonlight was dimmer.

We sat at the rickety kitchen table one hot afternoon, figuring our finances. Next week was June already; for the first time since we'd been together, there was rent to pay.

My Night Hawk paycheck came to a grand total of $32.50. I shook the morning's tips from my pockets. "Plus $16.25."

Depty pulled change out his pocket. "$1.60. And a thumb pick."

"We're rich! Don't forget the guitar." We were sending Margery a small monthly payment for the Empire State.

Picking up a pen, Dep wrote down our expenses on the back of an envelope.

"Beer," I reminded him. "And Dr. Pepper. Good thing we only buy the essentials."

The final tally looked like this:

$$
\begin{array}{r}
\$32.50 \\
+\ 16.25 \\
\hline
48.75 \\
+\ 1.60 \\
\hline
50.35 \\
-\ 5.00 \text{ guitar} \\
\hline
45.00 \\
-\ 3.00 \text{ Night Hawk} \\
\hline
42.00 \\
-\ 3.50 \text{ lunch} \\
\hline
38.50 \\
-\ 2.00 \text{ cig. brownie mix} \\
\hline
36.50 \\
-\ 2.68 \text{ Ice Beer D. P.} \\
\hline
33.82 \\
-\ 3.00 \text{ Beer etc.} \\
\hline
\$30.82
\end{array}
$$

I frowned. "Thirty bucks won't pay the rent. And we got nothing worth pawning. 'Cept you, baby."

Dep's gaze moved over the bare room, stopping on the guitar. Cupping my hands like a bullhorn, I called out, "You cannot pawn something you yourself do not own."

"But say we got a good price for it, little onion," he countered persuasively, taking a swig of beer. "We could pay off Margery and have some left over to boot."

"Oh, I just hate the thought of it, Dep! You love that old thing."

"I know. Suppose we found someone who appreciated it same as us." He thought a moment, then snapped his fingers. "How about Willie?"

Mike Fuller had heard Willie Nelson sing in Marfa, the tiny west Texas town where the Fuller family had lived for a while. Even as a kid, he was impressed that a musician of Willie's stature would come to podunk Marfa to sing. Depty Dawg thought it no wonder that Willie was now close to God, at least among the fans of redneck country rock. Once a successful songwriter in Nashville, he'd come to Austin and grown his red hair long. That act alone had merged hippie and redneck music lovers into a single, large audience, lending Austin's outlaw music scene an indisputable credibility.

So I can't say I was surprised when, not long after that conversation, Depty wrangled us standing-room-only tickets for Willie at Soap Creek. At the beginning of the concert, I stood in the back with my arms folded. Despite Dep's regard, I was skeptical: Willie's deity status had to be a serious case of the Emperor's New Clothes. By the end of the first set, I'd migrated down to the stage. Charged with the task of showing Willie the guitar, that was at least part of what had propelled me forward, though mostly, I had to admit, it was the music. I was resolved not to fawn over other singers in front of Dep—I guess I had my own romantic code—and in Austin I didn't want anything or anyone to erode his fragile self-confidence. Besides, my response to Willie was feeble compared to the rows of women seated directly in front of the stage. Each seemed bent on outdoing her neighbor in lurid contortions meant to catch the performer's eye.

Oh my God, is this what I have to look forward to?

Willie seemed unfazed by their attention. Here were all these women wanting something from him, while all he wanted to do was sing. Of course I wanted something from him too. Standing at the lip of the stage, I gestured to him at the end of a song. To my amazement—and dismay—he came over.

My heart raced as his rough-hewn face bent down to me. "I—I got this guitar," I stammered.

Willie looked puzzled. "And you want me to sign it?"

"No, actually? I was kind of hoping you might—um, buy it."

He shook his head. "I don't need another guitar."

"This one's—special," I floundered. "It's really old."

"So am I," he smiled, and went back to singing.

We took that as a sign. I never disparaged Willie Nelson again, and Depty never again mentioned selling the Empire State.

At least not until the next time we were desperate for cash.

32

Good Enough for Jesus

W e wanted to feel safe in Texas, the way we had in Udo, to be deeply rooted in each other and the place. The trick, we decided, was to learn to balance stability with freedom, at the same time accepting the risks you had to take to walk an artist's high-wire life.

I thought there had to be some way to make a home for us in Austin. Since our present accommodations were shorter on beauty, I decided that what we needed was comfort. No sooner had I landed under the garage than my JAB genes began to reinstate themselves. I fell into the trap of civilization: I wanted things—not a lot, just a few, to feather the nest—a toaster, for instance. In my mind there grew this notion that we needed to own a toaster and from that rose the logical certainty that now might be the perfect moment for us to get married.

"I know it sounds cuckoo," I allowed. "But when you tie the knot, people give you things. That's sort of the point, I think. Check it out. In a single day we could amass an enormous number of items to pawn."

Depty threw back his head, laughing. "And they give you money too, right? That could be helpful. Hang on, honey, I'm starting to get a feel for this."

I giggled. "And somebody's bound to throw in a toaster."

He took me in his arms. "I like the way you think, baby doll. So sensybil."

The idea of getting married was not new. We'd talked about it often, especially since the abortion. We wanted to be together, *for always* we said. Now it was just a matter of time and a toaster before we took care of it.

In June I wrote to my parents about our decision. A week later, we received two handwritten, special-delivery letters from Daddy—one to me and one to Deputy.

The letter to me is reprinted here, word for word.

June 14, 1976

Sybil Dear:

   Your letter was a startling surprise to Mom & me. In our mind we felt you were very serious about Deputy and we thought you might want to marry him someday. I had hoped your interest in Judaism some months ago was intended to possibly influence him to convert, if you decided to marry.

   While we like Deputy as a person, we are a Jewish family in a Jewish home. To us that means we want our children to marry in the Jewish faith and a marriage here in Roanoke, by you to Deputy, as a non-Jew, would not be proper or acceptable to us. In as much as Deputy has no religious affiliation, how difficult would it be for him to convert to Judaism, even by a reform Rabbi, not Conservative, if he knew how strongly we feel about this?

   Sybil dear, we too want to share your happiness, and while we know you and Deputy may have a struggle, our feelings about Judaism and our children are too deeply rooted to put aside without a serious traumatic effect on us. Ever since you were a child, we dreamed of the happy day when you would marry a fine young man who loved you, and we could share this happiness sanctified with a religious ceremony. You have found the man and now you want to rush into this very important event of your life.

   In the eyes and mind of this Jewish family, your marriage to a non-Jew would not be valid according to the Jewish tradition, which we have been taught to believe is the basis of an ethical, good and happy life. If Deputy should decide to convert to Judaism, Mom wants you to know that we would have a small wedding with just our closest relatives & friends when the time came.

   We have always loved you and tried to do whatever we could to make you happy. We hope that we will always share the deep love and camaraderie we have had in the past.

All our love,
Mom & Dad

I had expected something like this. A certifiable late bloomer, my adolescence was occurring now. Introducing Depty Dawg to my mother had been my most rebellious act; marrying him would be a supreme declaration of independence.

There was no mistaking the conviction of my father's letter. Years before, my parents had insisted that my older sister Susan break off with her Episcopalian boyfriend until he agreed to convert. That marriage had blessed them with two Jewish grandchildren, and no doubt they felt it only fair—and possibly productive—to take the same stance with me.

I couldn't really blame them. Thirty years had passed since my father had fought in the war against Hitler, its victory clotted by the terrible disclosures of eleven million Jews and other victims murdered in Nazi death camps and gas chambers. I was a little girl when Michael Topiol, a fifty-year-old German-Jewish survivor of Auschwitz, had come to live with us in Virginia. One night I woke to the sound of crying somewhere in the house. Getting out of bed, I followed the sobs to the kitchen. Michael was whispering feverishly in Yiddish to my parents, who were weeping profusely. I didn't know then what was being said, only that it was so painful it had to be uttered standing up in the dark.

In the face of incalculable loss, Jewish couples were encouraged to procreate. My parents were not going to lose their offspring to assimilation, which is what marriage to a Gentile equaled to them. True, Depty had disavowed his evangelical upbringing much the way I'd distanced myself from any religious observance of Judaism. If anyone had asked, we would have said that our religion was Beauty, and that we believed we'd found Its most intimate expression in the woods and streams of Udo. But nobody asked.

Daddy had signed the letter *Mom & Dad*; for me it resonated with her absence. I suspected she'd taken to her bed until she received a reply from me she could live with. I pictured her getting up in the morning red-eyed and mute, going off to her job as a bookkeeper, and returning in the evening to her locked bedroom. Her seclusion had put a stone in my stomach whenever I lived at home. I could feel its weight even now, a thousand miles away.

My father's message to Deputy was shorter and gentler. He'd worked hard on it, I could tell. Daddy often wrote three or four drafts of a letter that mattered to him.

June 16, 1976

Dear Deputy—

Jeannette & I have had some serious and emotional moments since Sybil told us of your plans to get married. We feel that we want to be able to welcome you into our family—not just as a son-in-law, but more like a son. Obviously your marriage and its success will depend on you and Sybil, so we really don't know how you feel about being a "son" in a Jewish family.

A son of course in this case would be a converted one—accepting Judaism at whatever level you find it has meaning for you. The conversion process is a form of study & learning and I earnestly hope you will decide to follow this course.

Please let us know how you feel about this before making any definite plans.

> Affectionately,
> Sam Rosen

P.S. Please understand that all expenses incurred in converting would be taken care of by us. SR

Whatever else I'd expected, it was not this. Nor did I foresee Deputy's response. Daddy was inviting him to be his son, touching Mike Fuller in the festering place left by his own father.

He gazed up from the letter, eyes glittering. "What the heck. If it means that much to them. It was good enough for Jesus."

He winked. "Better reason than a toaster, if you ask me."

The stone in my stomach began to vaporize. Leave it to Dep to come up with the one possibility I'd never imagined.

"Look." I was incredulous. "You have to do what feels right to you."

Taking his hand, I held it to my heart. "No matter what, remember?"

He leaned back in his chair. "Be kind of nice, wouldn't it? Have a real wedding with all of them there."

"Oh, yeah, I can just picture it. What would we sing?" Tipping him forward, I climbed onto his lap. "Your family wouldn't come, would they?"

"Marsha might. Don't know about the others."

I twined my arms around his neck. "Well, if they do, you can just tell them I'm half-Baked."

He grew thoughtful. "Do I got to wear one of them marmadukes?"

Palms down, his hands formed a skullcap on the top of his head.

"Yes, De-pu-tee," I snickered. "And it's called a *yarmulke.*"

"Already got one," he clowned. "Call it my *palmulke.*"

Reaching under his belt to tickle him, I remarked absently, "You know I think you'll probably have to be circumcised."

His hands stopped me. "Ooh. Really?"

I always wished afterwards that I hadn't said that.

Through Hillel—the Jewish youth organization at the University of Texas—I got in touch with a rabbi. He agreed to meet with us on campus in a subterranean cinderblock office lined with newspapers and books. It was a little surreal, seeing mustached, cowboy-hatted Depty Dawg shaking hands with this wan, bearded scholar in a skullcap and prayer shawl: Grand Ole Opry meets *Fiddler on the Roof*.

I wondered if the rabbi would try to talk Dep out of his decision. From my brother-in-law's conversion, I knew he was mandated by Judaic law to test the seeker's commitment. This rabbi didn't do that. He simply presented the work necessary, handing Dep a pile of Jewish authors to read: Martin Buber, Theodore Herzl, and several thick commentaries on religious codes and commandments.

My heart sank. Depty read the newspaper everyday; he was uncannily aware of what went on the world, but I'd never known him to read a book. The thought of his slogging through Jewish intellectual philosophy for the sake of a gadget went way beyond the call of love or duty. If this was the rabbi's test, it was very effective.

Dep didn't hesitate. He put the books resolutely under his arm and invited the rabbi to join us for breakfast at a fast food joint on the drag. The rabbi's consent impressed me too; seemed like he was making a sincere effort to get to know us. It wasn't until Depty ordered sausage with his scrambled eggs that I saw what the rabbi must have known all along: this wasn't going to happen.

We would get married sooner or later, that much we knew. And we would deal with my parents' objections then.

I was going to have to survive without toast.

33

Jumping the Gun

L ater came sooner than we expected. At the end of June, we drove back to Georgia with Lindsey and his wife, the couple who had taken us in when we first arrived in Austin. We were homesick for Whitesburg and not about to miss the Fourth of July festivities at Waller, especially on the country's 200th birthday.

Lindsey's icicle blue eyes glimmered against his long, red-gold locks. He and Depty Dawg had picked up their friendship from the days they had bonded over music and weed in the Sears parking lot in Irving. Lindsey had known Dep both as insecure Mike and motorcycle Tex. Reunited in their mid-twenties, their mutual inclination for raising hell had matured; it was unnerving how much ruckus they could make in a bar. They had taken a vow: whoever died first, the other would return to his grave and pee on it. Lindsey would fit in well at Waller.

His wife was a tall sturdy blonde with the prestige of being the first female telephone lineperson in Travis County. It was a trip to track her down at work, high among the poles and wires, waist-length yellow hair tucked under a hardhat. To my mind, she and Lindsey could be the poster couple for the hearty-partying duos the Lone Star State seemed to grow like wildflowers.

In Georgia, Waller was abuzz with news. During our absence, the hippies on the river had carried out a boycott of Whitesburg. Their point had been well-taken: Big Chief Hightower was out, and Tony of Punk Patrol fame would soon be in as Mayor. What a country. Even better, a peanut farmer from Plains, Georgia, was running for president.

The Texas Four slept on Bubba and Helen's living room floor. We *oohed* and *aahed* over the sweat lodge they'd built beside the lake, and marveled at Seth who had recently taken up English. Conducting our own alternative lifestyles tour, we took Lindsey and his wife first to Udo—where Grody Mike was in residence with the dogs and the jasmine had taken root—and then on to the plastic house and the teepees by the creeks.

One night we dressed up and went to Banning Mill, which was still operating as a restaurant and bar. Depty went incognito in cape and football helmet, and Lindsey's wife beat every guy in the bar at arm wrestling.

On Old Black Dirt Road, Margery and Billy's sheep herd had tripled, the blueberry bushes were fruiting, and Basil was already three months old. Cradling the cooing infant in his arms, Depty suddenly looked up at me.

"Let's do it, Vidalia," he whispered. "Let's get married. Right now."

I stared at him. "What? You mean here?"

"Right here. We'll tie the knot at Waller. With all our loved ones present." He held up Basil. "Party guaranteed."

Word of our nuptials spread through the county. More than one hundred people gathered at Waller on the Fourth of July. In the bathroom I slipped on a bleached T-shirt donated by Sas. What would Momma say if she knew I'd made it to white after all?

"Aww," murmured Sas, coming in to check on me. "Nothing like a bride." Her tapered fingers smoothed the shoulders of the cotton shirt. "That takes care of old and borrowed."

"And it's new to me," I reminded her. "So's there's that."

"You got to have ritual." Sas' brown eyes were mischievous. "I mean how often does a girl get married in her life? Two, maybe three times?"

Blue would be a hydrangea blossom cut for the bride's bouquet. Clutching the puffball of flowers, I walked out onto the porch to join Depty Dawg waiting for me by the railing.

Does this really count? I wondered.

The porch was crowded with friends, overflowing into the yard. Dep and I stood with our backs to the river, while the Elders of Zion—Glyn and Billy—officiated. The ceremony itself is a blur in my memory, though I do recall that after the kiss a lot of brown rice got thrown.

Sas came up with the idea for us to jump the broom. She grinned wickedly. "Though they ought to call it 'jumping the gun.'"

It was, among other things, an Appalachian custom from those isolated mountain passes where the traveling preacher came by only once in a blue moon. Chaste but impatient lovers could unofficially marry by jumping over a broom handle, signifying a vow to get it done proper when the minister finally showed. The leap of faith magically bestowed all conjugal rights then and there.

In the yard above the flood plain, Billy and Glyn held a broom length-wise off the ground. A thick circle of friends formed around us. Depty Dawg and I took hands, counted to three—and leapt.

A spontaneous *oohm* rose from the ring of onlookers, swelling into a vibrant hum that lasted a minute or more. How far the sound carried was not for us to know, but it buoyed us into the night with the unshakeable feeling that we were bound forever.

Footnote to history: we spent our honeymoon in the spare room on Old Black Dirt Road. To make our boudoir more romantic, Margery put a potted blue hydrangea beside the bed. When one of their dogs peed on it, it had to be moved outside.

And so we had pledged ourselves, each to the other, on the back porch at Waller. But already, since leaving the tree house five months ago, our expanded universe had begun to wobble on its axis. For one thing, in Austin there were bars to frequent, some of them within walking distance.

Unlike Depty Dawg, I wasn't used to bars. The evenings we spent in them always began brightly, though usually I wanted to call it quits long before he did. By the time he was ready to go, he'd be reeling, and it'd be up to me to steer him home. Partying in Austin was not the same as at Waller, where we had Ethyl, and Grody Mike or Glyn to propel Dep toward her. Nearly everyone here was still a stranger, and it seemed to me that Dep's drunkenness had acquired a new edge. Either he was losing his fine ability to read people's responses, or the extra beers made him care less what anybody thought. Drunk, he had no natural brakes or boundaries, no inclination to curtail his humor, or the wild physical flinging that drew angry attention. The hostility he invited often fell on me, and I had no other response but to take it personally.

"Get him out of here," a bouncer would scowl.

"I'm trying," I'd answer, scalded with good-girl humiliation.

So I began using the excuse that I had to be at work at six in the morning, staying home some nights while he went out alone, a thing we'd never done before. He'd hook up with Lindsey and come home around four, slipping into my arms, wishing he could be in two places at once. At dawn, he'd wake up anxious.

I tried to reassure him. "I know you need to be out there, Dep. I can't ask you not to go."

His hair hid his face. "I'm working hard as I can." He still didn't feel prepared to perform in public. Pulling me to him, he gruffly asked, "You trust
me, don't you?"

"Yes. Only when you're gone all night, I can't sleep. And then I have to get
up and go to my job."

I wished I didn't sound so whiny. These were new feelings between us, and
I for one didn't have a clue how to navigate them.

"I Should Have Been Home with You" was written that July. He'd stayed
out all night again, staggering in as I was getting dressed for work. Leaning
against the door frame, he slurred an explanation. "I had to wait for Lindsey,
he's the one with the wheels—"

Raising a hand to shush him, I slipped out the door without a word. It
wasn't a game of silent treatment, more that I had no way to express the feeling of abandonment the night had brought on. Even if I had found the words,
it wasn't in my nature then to confront him.

When I came home from work that afternoon, these verses had been left
on the kitchen table:

> Saw a dancin' young lady who worked in a bar
> A dozen lone rangers don't know who they are
> The waitress was spinnin', my head was ajar
> I should have been home with you
> Saw a reelin' old drunk man dancin' around
> Thought his gray whiskers still must have been brown
> Ida Lupino couldn't keep her dress down
> I should have been home with you
> The band rock and rolled but it wasn't the best
> And nearly all of 'em all sound like the rest
> Some girls looked pretty but you were the best
> That's why I came home to you
> Got home about daylight, I been gone too long
> Woke up at eleven and saw you were gone
> So I drank lots of coffee and wrote you this song
> Wish I'd have been home with you

He was lucky; he had music to shape his confusion. I envied his ability to
spill his emotions of the moment onto paper and melody. When he sang the
song for me that night, I could hear unfamiliar dark notes. As if he could see,
better than me, where this new disconnection might leave us.

It was a momentary stumble. The skies over Austin were bright and clear, and there were lots of things for us to do together. We chewed peyote buttons and lay in our backyard, howling at the moon. We barbecued hot dogs on the grill with Lindsey and his wife. One afternoon, the four of us drove into the Hill Country west of Austin, to leap from the brown cliffs above the Pedernales River. That is, three of us jumped; Dep sat on the bank, laughing. He couldn't swim, had a fear of water, and was, I think, too modest to put on a bathing suit.

He left for Georgia again in August, this time alone. Still convinced it was too soon to make his mark in Texas, he figured he might get some necessary experience playing in clubs between Carroll County and Atlanta. In the age-old tradition of female philanthropy, I would stay in Austin, to keep working, and send him money. He was hopeful he'd get noticed in Georgia: good reviews in local papers or, even better, some interest in recording his songs. And bringing that recognition back with him to Texas might help grease Blaze Foley's entrance into Austin's outlaw music scene.

Or maybe he was just getting restless.

34

Letters from Blaze

We had been each other's constant solace for over a year. During our first time apart, Depty would complete a short version of "Cold, Cold World" Months later, he would add a final verse. But this was another of those early songs that had been churning in him for years:

> I've tried for a long time
> But I think I can't win
> I could do it all better
> If I could do it again
> Wherever I'm goin'
> It's the same place I been
> Ain't it a cold, cold world?

He returned to Austin at the end of the summer, ragged and edgy, full of ancient sorrows. He didn't talk much about his experiences on the road, but the lyrics spoke for him. The perennial wanderlust was surging once again:

> Can't get no job
> And I can't get no rest
> Started out east
> But I ended up west
> And I'm so glad to be here
> I'm sure I would guess
> Ain't it a cold, cold world?

His ambivalence about performing had not gone away, and so soon after his return, he turned around and went back to Georgia, this time determined to accomplish his aims. It would be our longest separation. By then, we'd upgraded from Parkway to a furnished flat on Castle Hill Road. The new place was in a row of ticky-tack apartments with the square impersonality of a dingy motel room. It had a small separate kitchen and no amphibians in the tub. A calico cat with mismatched blue and green eyes decided to live with us there. Melissa, we called her, was good company when I was alone. She would sun with me on the concrete breezeway outside our front door as I waited for the mailman to deliver letters from Blaze.

I'd quit my job at the Night Hawk and was holding down two more: the morning shift at Les Amis, an outdoor café off the drag, and alternate nights were spent at a Mexican restaurant, La Fonda de la Noche, around the corner from Les Amis. The diner had been good training, but the new jobs didn't require a tiara. I could show up in whatever I put on that day, and the less the better. The women I worked beside now were artists, hippies, and students from the university, all trying to make a living as painlessly as possible. The revelation—and revolution—of these jobs was that the management actually stood by its staff. We were encouraged to complain if a tip was too small. It wasn't unusual for a waitress to throw chump change at a departing cheap-skate. Customers, I decided, want from their waitresses what they didn't get from their mothers, that is, your complete and instantaneous attention. We deflected their demands by getting stoned in the alley, or eating mushrooms before going out on the floor. At times this backfired. We had no trouble re-lating to the customers, but in the kitchen the cooks were hallucinating and service could be slow.

After work, I'd hurry home to see what the postman had brought. I'd only heard from Depty once by phone, and I was getting concerned. Finally, a let-ter arrived, postmarked September 22 and mailed from Atlanta, addressed to "Little Sybil Rosendawg." The envelope was from Allgood Music Co., a store in north Georgia where the Ralph in the letter worked. He was a musician with Buzzards Roost, the band that had christened Depty Dawg. Ralph had never seen his former roadie skinny. Dep was reintroducing his new self to old friends.

For the return address, he'd written "Blaze Foley and the B.V.B's." Another Foley inner prize: to be backed by an all-girl band named The Beaver Valley Boys.

Here is his first letter as I read it then, misspellings and all.

Tues. nite

Dear Sybil,

I guess your pretty upset because you haven't gotten a let-ter from me. But you know how I am. I'm on the bus now from Rockmart to Atlanta. I spent last night with Ralph & all day at the store. We must have played for 6 or 8 hrs. I really enjoyed it. Ralph seemed to enjoy it too. I have never really played in front of any of Buzzards Roost but I wasn't nervous at all. It sounded good. I am going to get a tape [made] Friday night in Underground. Ralph is also going to help me get a P.A. & maybe a little loan. I haven't gotten to talk to Bubba & Helen yet.

I have had a real good visit with Joe. Waller is fine. Haven't really seen Bill & Marge yet, but I'm going back to the county tomorrow and work with Joe.

Sybil, I want you to think about yourself & not worry about me so much. We are doing this for many reasons. I think it will make us both stronger individuals. I think for now we should really explore our deepest selves & our wants, career goals, life goals etc. You have taught me many things about understanding ones self. Im beginning to see that I can understand myself.

So please don't just sit around worrying. We will always be together in one way or another, cause you are truly a part of me. I will be back as soon as I think I have accomplished what I need to or at least what I can. I am going to have to devote all I can to my music. Im sure everything I put into it I get back just as much in different forms & ways.

I think you should apply all you need to your acting also. We must do it now cause time just eases by everyday. I am going to set aside a couple of days to do nothing but work on my music in the treehouse. I plan to finish several songs in those 2 days. Anyway I want you to think about your acting, your self, your heart mind & soul more because all of you is truly fine.

I love you, I'll see you soon, I miss you. You are part of me & my music. Take care, and if you feel the need to fulfill your physical needs do, just be careful.

Bye for now

Love Blaze

Remember you make songs in me.

35

Dear Blaze

In love stories, the characters write letters to each other whenever life conspires to keep them apart. Mail is the consolation prize for absence. No doubt it would be helpful to slip into these pages the letters I wrote to Depty Dawg that autumn. Except I don't know what happened to them, if they got lost in his wanderings, or if he kept them a time. It occurred to me they might show up when I returned to Austin, just as Margery's recording had resurfaced in Whitesburg. Through the grapevine of Blaze's friends here, I've learned that his attaché case was discovered in his room after his death, filled with lyrics, notes, and keepsakes; someone else told me for certain the items were in a paper bag. Not that it matters: the basement where the contents were stored flooded in the mid-'90s, washing all his mementoes away. Thank God I kept his letters.

I don't dare try to recreate mine. My attempts would be too self-conscious for a history of this kind. I can only imagine that they were a lot like his— chatty, ardent, full of heartfelt encouragement and pieces of news. Revisiting the Castle Hill apartment yesterday, I had this sudden recollection of opening his letters, the excitement of doing this hard thing together, enduring separation for the sake of art. That may be the optimist's view, but at the time the notion tinted my solitary life in Austin with a wash of dedicated purpose.

He had signed the letter *Blaze*; that may be a first. At last he seemed ready to transform himself in the eyes of the world, and in his own. I didn't understand why we had to be apart for this, but that was the way things were. I was glad he was back with friends in Carroll County, but envious too: what was I doing in Texas when he got to go back to Georgia?

The thing was, I wasn't as lonely as I thought I'd be. When you're a nomad, you're always sleeping on someone else's floor. I'd never lived alone before, and I was surprised how much I liked it.

Reading through Dep's letters twenty-seven years later, I recognize enduring aspects of his character that have been embroidered into his legend. His generosity is a binding thread of his legacy to the musicians in Austin. His sincere encouragements helped me then too, though I'm not sure I fully understood their value, or their rareness.

I picture me writing him back, telling him he shouldn't worry either. That I'd bought an old manual typewriter at a yard sale, that I was spending the afternoons in the kitchen on Castle Hill, struggling to put my escapades as a waitress down on paper. It's curious that I never thought then to write about Depty Dawg, or our off-beat love. He could crystallize his immediate feelings and observations into a song; it would take years of reflection before I could write about mine. Odd, too, how it hasn't gotten any easier.

I sent him money when he asked, which wasn't often. We agreed it'd be more practical for me to hold onto my pennies, and save up for plane tickets to come see him. I was also hustling. That summer Jean Carlot had supporting roles in two student films at the university, and a cameo in a docudrama for the Elizabet Ney Museum. Depty's absences were teaching me self-reliance, an insight I've only had in hindsight.

There was probably a lot I didn't write to him. A response, for instance, to the comment about me fulfilling my *physical needs*, as he so delicately put it. It wasn't something I was inclined to do. I've never really gotten the concept of casual sex; isn't that an oxymoron? Even the times I thought I was having casual sex, turned out I wasn't.

At Les Amis, a wiry, young writer named Matt was pursuing me fairly persistently. Nothing like an absent boyfriend to make a woman more attractive. There's an implied vulnerability, easy to manipulate, as in *how could he leave you alone?* It's possible I'd started to wonder that myself.

I agreed to go out with Matt in the illogical hope that one date would make him want to go away. I brought him back to Castle Hill, but I wasn't destined for infidelity. Too nervous that Dep would show up unexpectedly—since I never knew when he was coming home—I let the thought of his finding me with Matt squelch any physical desire in need of fulfillment.

Whenever Depty brought up my needs, I had to wonder whether he wasn't talking about his own. We hadn't discussed what could happen to him on the road. I doubt he'd have volunteered to tell me he'd been with other women. Observed through the long lens of decades, clearly it was bound to have happened. For one thing, there was his well of loneliness, not to mention his appeal as a man and the charm of his music: I knew how that worked. Add alcohol to the mix, plus the fact that he often had no place to stay. Maybe, too, he was making up for lost time from his fat-boy days.

Honestly, I don't remember dwelling on it. I believed him when he said I was a part of him. His heart was trustworthier than mine.

An irrational equation: lack of jealousy equals lack of love.

36

Artist at Large

The second letter I received from Blaze that autumn was addressed to "Mrs. Little Sybil Rosendawg Foley." The return address read "c/o Old Black Dirt Road." Inside were two pieces of paper, one a drawing of himself. Alongside it, he had written:

> This is a self portrait of me nude, (from the rear) in boots & hat, with sheep. (Nice sheep I met at Billy & Marge's) Her name (if you're interested): Vidalia Onion. (Not her real name but that's what I call her) She's O.K. But don't worry. It's not the onion I want.
>
> Love
> Blaze "Picasso" Foley
> Artist elite
> (at large)
> [or something of that nature]

Across a smaller scrap of paper he had penned *Sybil I love you always Depty.* It was an echo of the inscription my mother had engraved on my father's bracelet more than thirty years before, the one we'd lost last summer.

Everyday now I received a letter, sometimes two or three. He was going back and forth between names, sometimes signing *Blaze*, other times *Depty Dawg*. Changing coats like a chameleon, he was flip-flopping between identities, ending the day as *Depty* and waking up as *Blaze*. At times he was both at once, signing *Dep/Blaze*.

In between letters, we were talking on the phone. We couldn't afford a line at Castle Hill, so he'd call me at La Fonda at the end of the night. He was already thinking about going somewhere else, and wanted me to meet him there. An alternative country music scene was emerging in Chicago, and Dep thought it likely a big city would have more professional theater opportunities for me.

Meantime, he had good news. Blaze Foley had begun to perform in clubs in and around Atlanta. Depty was encouraged, even as the experience was proving a mixed bag. In early October, he wrote:

> I have so much confidence now, more than I've ever had. So much thanks to you. Anyway, James at Good Ole Days isn't the Cracker Jack I thought. He had me booked all right, opposite some turkeys. For $5.00 per night & tips and I have to pay for my own beer. But that may be only one of my many disappointments.
> I was able to swallow it & look on ahead. I've got other things working & Joe & me can do it to it.

Zonko Joe was back in the county. He and Depty Dawg were hitting the music venues as a medical team. Dr. Blaze Foley BAMAPHD, an unpunctuated spoof on the erudite, wore a stethoscope around his neck, using it to tune his guitar. After a song, his associate, Dr. Whiplash Brubaker, would check the audience's vital signs to measure its effect.

In mid-October, I flew to Georgia for a brief reunion. It was good to see our friends again, to fall asleep in Depty Dawg's arms. We never made it to Atlanta to catch Blaze Foley in action, but he did sing some new material for me. He was putting words to an instrumental that would become "Election Day," lines of which he had already included in a letter to me: *My luck's been bad, the telephone just took my only dime.*

Three days flew by. Too soon, we were hugging at an airport.

"And why am I going back to Texas?" I asked myself, and him.

"We'll go to Chicago together," he answered. "Soon, I swear."

I threw my arms around him. "Please don't remember me with tears in my eyes."

He held my face in his hands. "There are no good-byes. Just see you laters."

He was concerned our farewells were becoming too painful. It hurt to leave him with lingering doubts. As soon as I landed in Austin, I called him from the airport to reassure him that, together or apart, our love could survive distance and time.

In answer I received from him the longest letter he would write. The following excerpts reveal the weight of his worry. I understood that desire to stitch the pieces of his life together, even as I underestimated the inadvertent hints about the depth of his despair:

The first time I left I felt that what I wanted to do musically would mean losing you forever. I couldn't have gone on thinking that . . . What I'm doing is for you and me. I want you to believe in me. I won't do anything that doesn't include you. I can't. The first time [I left] I had kind of lost hope because of the waste [*sic*] deep pessimism that covers the world. But now I try to walk above it because of the feeling you give me . . .

Sybil, please don't feel like I picked music over you. I couldn't do that. I would give it up now and become a salesclerk. But I'm not a salesclerk, I'm a salesman of songs right now. I know someday you want to be able to have a home on some land and children and so do I. I want you to be the mother of my children more than anything. But I want those children to be well provided for and loved . . .

Sybil, don't feel lost, alone, or reckless. I love you, I love you. I wish I could kiss your beautiful self right now. I'm so glad we talked, I feel like living now.

37

Address Unknown

D earest Dep/Blaze,
I know I said I wouldn't try to recreate my letters to you, only
I need some intimate conveyance, a way to reach you, to tell you
what your letters mean to me today. Your tenderness and concern
are the sweetest gifts of this long-delayed reunion.

The seeds of our sorrow are in these letters too. We were so
young, honey, so ill-equipped to mend the fissures absence and
uncertainty were creating. Yes, conventional wisdom says that you
can only save yourself, but we're alike, you and I, undying romantics, and I can't seem to throw away the certainty that love can
transform: it can bring out music; it can bring back the past.

I've come back to Austin to reclaim the girl I was. I don't like
having to acknowledge the doubt that pulled at me each time you
said, *See you later.* Your disappearances collided with my insecurities, eroding my shaky confidence: maybe you didn't love me after
all. You understood this better than me; your letters are rife with
reassurance.

I'm trying to see you clearly too. You were working so hard, and
for such good reasons. I don't think I really grasped what it cost
you to get up on stage and perform. You had made a brave step.
The time in Georgia was important for you, just as my solitude
in Austin was for me. In your letters, you sound mostly buoyant
and unstoppable; maybe you just didn't want me to fret. Of course
now I have a clearer picture of what your life on the road was
like. You left a zigzagging trail of clues, didn't you, Dep? This one
was embedded in two verses of a song you would write that fall—

another tune I wouldn't hear for twenty-six years, thank you very
much, "Baby, Can I Crawl Back to You?"

> Sittin' in a barroom countin' my dough
> Runnin' out of money and places to go
> Sittin' in a barroom drunk at night
> Won't get to sleep till the first daylight
> Baby, can I crawl back to you?
> Sittin' in a jailhouse countin' my dough
> Ran out of money but I found a place to go
> Ought to be leavin' in a day or two
> Get myself together, can I come back to you?
> Baby, can I crawl back to you?
> Baby, can I crawl back to you?

The man you were away from me was not the one I knew. The
tree house had suspended your rogue self, or maybe you suspended it for the tree house. You tried to keep it separate from our
life in Austin, but in the end you couldn't. You had started to live
two lives. Maybe that's why you had to keep leaving; your comings
and goings were intended to protect me from what you had to live
out, one way or another.

Lovers and music all have their times.

You were already seeing the two as separate, weren't you, Blaze?
As I write this, I realize that my deepest regret is that you didn't
feel you could trust me with all of you. Maybe that was because
you knew, better than anyone, how fragile I really was. If only I'd
been strong enough to hold on to the you I had.

I love you. I miss you. Please send me your current address.

Sybil

38

Postcards from the Road

He was bouncing between venues in Carroll County and Atlanta, learning the ropes the hard way. His letters are chronicles of the difficult task he'd set himself.

Often he was able to meet discouragement gracefully. One afternoon while waiting to perform at Good Ole Days, he wrote me tongue-in-cheek: "I'm going to play again to a totally empty house. But the people that work here are a good audience, both of them." Being his own manager meant having to promote himself, offstage and in print. Sometimes the results were maddening. When a local gazette incorrectly printed an announcement of his act in Atlanta's Underground, he fumed: "They missppeelleedd my name again in print. Blaze Folley? Blaze Foley!!"

Despite these setbacks, he was finding time and space to write. The snatches of lyrics he included in his letters give clues to his frame of mind. Like this first glimpse of "Rainbows and Ridges":

A chair got knocked over
I got the Blues
Some don't get any
Some get to choose
Some days you'll win
Some days you'll lose
And tears
They just fall to the ground

On postcards sent in the span of a week, he mixed identities playfully, signing himself *Blaze Dawg* and *D. Dawg Foleywoley*. He was on an emotional roller coaster, some days up, some days down, but his music was beginning to receive positive responses, and that was all that mattered. A letter penned in mid-October contained this hopeful news:

I did some Previously Unreleased Dawg last night. It went over real well . . . A guy from B.F. Deal records is coming here from Austin. Some people here told him about The Armadillo Song and he's interested. Keep your fingers crossed.

"The Armadillo Song" was Blaze's response to Texas' love affair with itself. The docile armadillo had once been a symbol of the anti-war movement; more recently it had been shanghaied by a posse of rhinestone cowboys in a series of Lone Star-struck tunes. Blaze's song was meant to be the ultimate antidote to self-adoration. The refrain went:

> I want to go home with an armadillo
> Spread her little legs
> And try my best to thrill her
> To her very soul
> With my cowboy pole

You get the idea. It was a little weird being the girl of the guy who wrote those sentiments. If Depty sang them when I was present, inevitably some drunk would turn to me and ask, "Is that about you?" Another example of muse status gone awry.

His hopes for "The Armadillo Song" never materialized. Dep was determined now to go north. Scott, a Zonko-ite formerly of Waller and currently of Chi-town, had invited us to stay with him when we arrived. We'd written back to say we were definitely coming, we just didn't know when.

Across the fold of a letter dated October 27, Depty wrote, "I love you, little onion, you make my eyes water." He was lonely in Georgia, and no longer writing about me fulfilling my physical needs elsewhere. "Big Woo" is an expression from our private lovers' lexicon:

> I don't know how much longer I can stand this being away from you. I still have the first glimpse of you in the airport, along with many more glimpses of your smile, your lips, your hair, your body naked and close to mine, holding you and kissing you, giving my seed to you.
>
> How is your Libido? I'm sure you must be in need of some kind of fulfillment. I know we talked about that. I hope you will wait for me to fulfill you. I will not fulfill myself in any way but with visions of you. (How about a big hand?) OK (Get it?) Big Woo.

By the end of October, we'd come up with a plan: rendezvous in Virginia for Thanksgiving and go on to Chicago from there. A few nights before I was to leave Austin for good, Dep caught up with me at midnight on the restaurant phone.

"Just hearing your voice puts goose bumps all over my body," he whispered.

I ducked behind the counter to hear him. "How's it going, honey?"

"Miserable." He cleared his throat. "I was hoping to get another letter from you by now."

"It's been so hectic," I hedged. "Getting ready to leave and all. Besides, I'm never sure where to send them."

"I know." He sounded chastened. "I do get around."

"I'll just be glad when we can resume as one," I consoled him. "I'm starting to feel like a country music widow."

He grunted. "That'll be a song someday." The silence ended with his sigh. "Don't mean to complain about them letters, little onion." His voice cracked. "I just love getting them is all."

He began to cry. "My daddy wrote me, did I tell you that? I can't find his letter anywhere."

39

Postage Due

Dearest Blaze,

This is the letter I never wrote you. I didn't want to tell you that night on the phone, but the reason I hadn't written was because I'd been crying for three days. You weren't the only one in hiding, honey. In your absence the depression that had stalked me for years had begun to show itself. There were times on Castle Hill when I couldn't get out of bed, a condition so like my mother's it made me nauseous with fear. That feeling of no face was becoming less a metaphor and more a physical sensation, terrifying and tenacious.

The life we had chosen was cracking us wide open. We were impatient for something to happen, some sign that our efforts were not in vain. I was afraid you'd get discouraged and give up; maybe you were scared the same thing would happen to me.

I wanted good news from you to deliver me from myself, and when that didn't come, I began to read your letters critically. Your misspellings and mixed-up grammar grated on my nerves. I was confused. I never stopped believing in your gift, and I still wanted to believe in us.

Maybe you were right: Chicago was the answer. I was ready for you to come home.

Big Woo,
Little Sybil

40

On the Road Again

November '76 brought us things to celebrate. Jimmy Carter was elected to the White House, and Depty Dawg, despite his frustrations, could still write letters that held glimmers of hope. In a note written on Election Day night, he listed the acts playing in Atlanta that evening:

Marsha [*sic*] Ball & The Misery Brothers are at Rose's [Cantina] tonight, Willie [Nelson] & Co at the Omni, & Dr. Blaze Foley at Good Ole Days (still $5 plus tips) and Underground (tips only).

At the end of the month there would be our long-awaited reunion in Roanoke, dampened only by the fact that my mother put us in separate rooms again. This time I didn't object. By silent agreement we all steered away from the subject of marriage and the ill-fated conversion attempt. Daddy still had our picture in his wallet, and Momma seemed resigned; at least my clothes didn't smell of wood smoke any more.

Desperate to be alone, Dep and I borrowed their Dodge and drove up the Blue Ridge Parkway, rolling down the windows so the car wouldn't smell of weed. Fiery leaves clung to the hardwoods, the fading fields brightened by the last goldenrods and asters. We found a secluded pull-off where we could make out; we would never master making love in a car. Besides, we had things to discuss.

My parents had offered to buy us two one-way train tickets to northern Indiana. There we'd be able to stay with my older sister, Susan, before going on to Chicago.

"They're shipping me out," Depty declared. "Probably wondering why I ain't made an honest woman of you yet."

"Please," I insisted. "If I was really honest, I'd tell them we jumped the broom."

He buried his face in my hair. "Cold up there in Chicago right now, Vidalia. Brrr! Newspaper says minus below."

"But you still want to go, right?"

"Oh, sure. Just pray we got money enough." He lit a cigarette, making circles with the exhaled smoke. "Austin's cheap compared to Chi-town."

"Thank God for Scott." Our friend had written to say we could stay with him in the suburbs as long as we needed.

Depty frowned. "We got to be close to the music. We'll need a place in town. And a telephone and—"

"Dep. Stop. I know where this is going. We're not selling the Empire State."

"Just to pawn, little onion," he insisted. "First paying gig in Chicago, I'll come back and get it."

"Great. You're already talking about leaving again."

"Tell me something. How much we got?"

Sighing, I started the engine. "Fifty bucks."

The owner of the downtown pawnshop was a member of my parents' synagogue; in high school I had briefly dated his son. Coming into the store with Depty Dawg and the guitar, I spotted him behind the cash register, a soberly dressed, southern businessman with neat '70s sideburns.

Before I could say hello, he'd already taken in Dep's long hair and pierced ear, and was coming around the counter toward us.

"Get out of my store, you scum," he yelled.

It made no difference that I was with Depty; we were *both* being shown the door. Here it was again: every time I brought him into my world, seemed like there was always someone to judge him by appearances. Fleeing the shop, I glanced back at Dep; there was no mistaking the fear on his face.

Out on the sidewalk, catching our breath, we laughed about it—but it had cut deep. That might mark the moment we started running from each other.

Thanksgiving was subdued. Dep was anxious to get on the road; I wasn't sure what to be grateful for. Two days later, my father put us on the train to Indiana.

Settling into our coach seats, Depty tucked the Empire State under his feet.

"Can't seem to get rid of this ole thing," he murmured. "Must be a sign."

The train chugged west into the mountains, curving around a bend. From the window we could see the length of cars following the locomotive up into a craggy ravine.

"I need a long rest in your arms," Dep breathed, eyes looking out.

He turned to me, frowning. "Don't know how long I can do this for, little onion. It's too hard. Too lonely. Ain't how life's supposed to be."

I took his hand. "We're together now, doesn't that help?"

He threw an arm over me. "Think I'll just hang out with you and chase songs all day."

"No legend?"

I closed my eyes. The clacking of the wheels eased the worry from my mind.

He pulled me close. "We'll let the words take care of that."

Our train ride ended sixty miles east of Chicago, in a little mill town on the shores of Lake Michigan. I'd never seen anywhere so gray. Susan picked us up at the station. She, too, was dismayed by my hillbilly boyfriend, but she did let us sleep together on a fold-out couch in her basement. Her four-year-old son, Jason, and toddler daughter, Jessica, thought their aunt's big singing cowboy unquestionably fascinating, especially after Dep agreed to go outside with them and make a snowman in a Stetson.

We were unused to the steely air, the raw wind gusting off the lake. The following day, we took the train into Chicago, only to learn on our arrival that its legendary Mayor Richard J. Daley had died, and the city had closed down to mourn him.

41

Cold, Cold World

Our first frigid days in Chi-town were spent numbly watching Mayor Daley's funeral on TV. Scott had a brick house in Evergreen Park, a well-appointed suburb north of the city. Once a hardcore hippie, lately Scott had traded in his Harley for a three-piece suit, and a job with his father at the stock exchange downtown. Dep and I slept in his attic, clinging to each other, wondering how the hell we were going to make it. We had forty bucks to our names.

For Christmas-slash-Chanukah, we agreed to spend one dollar on a gift for each other. In a used bookstore Depty found a thick worn volume of Shakespeare's *Collected Works*. Inscribed *To Little Sybil from Big Depty 12/25/76 With love & everything D. Dawg*—it was his gift to me in a year that had taken us from Georgia to Texas to Illinois. With my buck, I bought him a second-hand woolen cap and a pair of heavy gloves. He was going to need them.

We celebrated Christmas Day at Scott's parents' swank apartment on Chicago's Gold Coast. High above Lake Michigan, the wind blustered in rattling squalls against a tall bank of windows overlooking the gray water. House rules required the men to wear jackets for dinner, so Scott had provided Depty with a green sports coat.

"I feel like the doorman," he whispered, seated beside me at the elegant table.

We clinked glasses of champagne. Depty kissed my cheek. "Merry Christmas, little darlin'. We done made it."

New Year's Eve came and went quietly. We spent the evening lolling around in Scott's attic. On the second day of '77, Dep donned his new hat and gloves, and we ventured into the frozen city to look for an apartment and check out the theater and music scenes. Scott had told us about Kiley's, a bar on the North Side known to book country rock bands, and Dep knew of another venue on Lincoln Avenue, Somebody Else's Troubles, where folk legends Phil Ochs and Steve Goodman, not to mention John Prine, were often on the bill.

On our way home I picked up a neighborhood gazette in a grocery store one block west of pricey Lakeshore Drive. Back at Evergreen Park, I answered every ad, looking for work. There were five or six requests for dog sitters and pedicurists; only one looked really promising: "Housekeeper/nanny wanted. Good hours, good pay."

Dialing the number, I spoke to a woman with a familiar Brooklyn accent. She was funny and warm, not at all the chilly upper-crustacean I expected her to be. I made an appointment to be interviewed at her Lakeshore Drive apartment in a few days' time.

Meanwhile, we found a cheap tenement apartment on the city's North Side. The chipped plaster walls stank of mildew and neither of its two dreary rooms was a bath. We'd have to share the facilities in the hall with the other tenants on our floor, and the homeless men who slept in the vestibule. Its charm was its rent, which was weekly.

The night of my housekeeper interview coincided with our move to the slums. We agreed that I'd go to Lakeshore Drive first, and meet Dep afterwards at the new flat. The doorman announced my arrival. I rode the ornate elevator to the twelfth floor.

Duct-taped suitcase in one hand, I lifted the other to knock at the apartment door when suddenly it opened a crack. There stood a tiny Jewish faun, a boy of four-and-a-half with dark hair in close ringlets. Taking in my mended bag and ragged bellbottoms, he closed the door in my face. I knocked again: this did not bode well.

The woman on the phone came to let me in. I knew her immediately as the faun's mother. At thirty-four, she was small and fairy-like, with pale inquisitive eyes and amber curls. She was bemused.

"That was James, by the way. He thinks you're already moving in."

She led me through the spacious living room. A black marble fireplace graced one wall, while a mahogany baby-grand piano filled an entire corner. A long row of bay windows looked out on the lake which, in January, was an expanse of colorless ice stretching bleakly to the horizon.

In the chandeliered dining room I was introduced to the woman's husband, still seated at the dinner table, sipping brandy and smoking a cigar. Trimly dressed in a pale blue shirt, thin suspenders and sharply creased pants, he looked like an elegant, small-time gangster. In reality, he was a research psychiatrist working with the criminally insane. Standing politely, he closed his eyes when I shook his manicured hand. James was nowhere in sight.

The woman brought out a tray bearing a silver tea service and a plate of thin chocolate cookies, and whisked me back to the study. In her book-lined office, a fat tabby named Scooter was perched on top of a bookshelf, a gray-suited Cheshire cat in a leather-bound wonderland. It turned out that James' mother was an adjunct professor of women's studies at a local university, and that she'd recently co-edited a compilation of women's writings from Sappho to Doris Lessing. It didn't matter that I'd never heard of either: I was impressed.

She poured me out a cup of tea and asked about my life. I told her about Depty's music, my desire to pursue theater, our reasons for coming here. Then the professor turned to business. The job would be cooking and cleaning and, most importantly, looking after James. The hours would vary, according to their schedules. They were going on vacation in St. Lucia in February; I could come if I chose, or that could be time off. The pay was okay—not what I'd hoped—but it would increase if things worked out. The job was mine if I wanted it; she knew she was going to hire me after hearing my voice on the phone.

Depty and I could use steady money, that was obvious. But the work would be demanding. I didn't want to be away from Dep any more than necessary, or be distracted from auditioning for acting roles. Lakeshore Drive was a very different world from the one we occupied. Frankly, the professor and her work interested me more than the job itself. I wasn't sure what to say.

Then James came into the room, naked, with a blue baby blanket thrown over his head—and the decision was made for me.

I was right; the job was challenging. It required me to run a busy household of complex people and so my education picked up where the Night Hawk ladies had left off. Cooking, cleaning, shopping, and making lists were time-consuming elements of my duties, though mostly I just hung out with James.

From the first day, he and I grappled with the question: who was boss? James was a brilliant kid, like his father, an emperor by inclination. When I balked at his imperious commands, the four-year-old informed me, "My parents got you for me."

One afternoon he demanded I switch off the light in his room, something he was capable of doing himself. After fruitless argument, I wrestled him to the ground, yelling into his face, "I am not your slave!" We were crazy about each other.

Together for hours every day, we walked in the morning to the neighborhood preschool, where I would return to pick him up at noon. Running home, we'd open our coats to make wings, catching the gales that whooshed off the lake and sent us tumbling backwards. Many afternoons, Dep came over to play with James while I made dinner for the family, which often included us. James told Depty all about Ralph: a character I invented who'd taken up residence in his ear, offering commentary and advice.

Over time, James came to speak to me in a tone resembling respect. And he, in turn, taught me not to take myself too seriously. He had nicknames for me too: Ish Kabbible for one, Old Wide Face for another. Sometimes for a treat, James and I had lunch at a Greek restaurant near his school. It became our tradition to order a salad and divide each morsel equally, including the anchovy. Once I returned from the restroom to find that James had eaten the entire slimy fish.

"What's the big idea?" I scolded him. "I thought we were sharing that."

"Ish," he admonished me grandly. "It's only food."

I had much to learn from them all. The professor had an inspiring intellect with an abundance of creative energy. She got me reading Virginia Woolf, Jane Austen, and Doris Lessing. Borrowing from her extensive vocabulary, I imitated her language and gestures, trying on her manner as my own. In time, we became confidantes, talking at length about our mothers and our men.

The professor regarded her husband as a man of rare integrity, a modern-day hero. The household revolved around his brilliance, and his caprice. The doctor, as Dep and I came to call him, insisted that the seeds be picked out of his watermelon, a laughable affront to us seed-spitting hicks. His demands were offset by a warm silly humor and often startling insights. Misquoting the English poet Alexander Pope, the professor described their marriage as "the feast of reason and the flow of souls." Depty's and my souls flowed, but we hungered for reason. It was hard not to covet the glamour and sturdiness the professor and her husband seemed to project.

"How will we ever find our way?" I asked her once, during an afternoon chat.

"Things are always becoming," she answered thoughtfully. "If you can learn to live with uncertainty, you'll recognize the truth when it comes."

Our friendship electrified me. The doctor was more elusive. He'd grown up tough and poor on the streets of New Jersey; his keen mind and a driven need for stature had gotten him to Lakeshore Drive. It was hilarious to see him in his cufflinks and suspenders sipping port with Depty Dawg in a tie-dyed T-shirt and earring. Each, in his way, was a maverick. The doctor had already reinvented himself several times over, and he, too, had torments he would not be able to escape.

James flat-out adored Depty Dawg. Dep was cowboy and pirate, rocking horse and clown. I'd hear them giggling in James' room for hours as I went about my chores. They sat on the floor playing games or watching TV. *Sesame Street* was a favorite; they could mimic the Muppets to a T. Then came the morning James declared the show too babyish for him to watch any more.

"What?" Dep and I exclaimed in unison. We were crushed.

To comfort himself, James still drank chocolate milk from a bottle. The sugar had rotted his front baby teeth, so the dentist had recommended they be replaced with metal studs till his permanent set came in. The surgical procedure required an overnight hospital stay. I spent the day of his operation in the waiting room with his mother. James was groggy when the orderly wheeled him into the room he would share that night with other kids recovering from routine surgeries.

Cranky and self-conscious about his new metallic bite, James' smile flashed silver when Depty Dawg came in toward evening, and proceeded to tease him about his new *bionic* teeth. The professor and I looked at each other: that's what we would call them; that would help.

Dep took out his guitar to sing for James and the other children. The nurses wandered in, one by one, to listen. He played till every child had fallen asleep, and the room was perfectly quiet save for his fingers moving on the strings.

Moments like these made our reasons for being together so desirable and—so I believed—still possible.

42

If I Could Only Fly

Now *I* was the one leading a double life. Immersed all day in the rhythms of James and his parents, I was riveted to them by my affection—and by my appetite for my ongoing feminist education. By early '77, the women's movement was in full cry; I had no idea how thirsty I was for stories of heroines claiming their own lives. Every day I drank in women's literature and history, imagining myself a learned lady like the professor, or a warrior maiden of Sas' ilk. Then at night, I'd take the train home, smoke a joint, and head out to the bars with Dep.

He'd already introduced himself to a country rock band at Kiley's. Sometimes they backed a raven-haired fiddler named Betsey, the daughter of Bill Redhed, proprietor of Somebody Else's Troubles. Betsey and her green-eyed sister, Cassie, set out to befriend Dep and me. He began to play the occasional set at Kiley's.

For the first time I was watching Blaze Foley onstage. It was thrilling to hear the response his songs received, unsettling to realize he was usually drunk by the time he got up to sing. I knew performing was hard on him; he was so emotionally naked under the lights.

One night, as he launched into the "Fat Boy" song, the bartender began talking loudly across the counter. I watched Blaze's performance deteriorate. Distracted and agitated, he finally stopped singing altogether.

"Excuse me?" he snarled in the direction of the bar. "Is my music interrupting your conversation?"

"Shut up and sing," the man yelled back. "Or better yet, get off the stage."

His insult was followed by light applause. Blaze bowed and left the building and the song unfinished.

"Maybe you shouldn't insult the management," I suggested meekly, out on the street with him.

"I don't care," he scowled. "It's rude to talk when somebody's singing."

"I agree, but you know what? You're not in church any more."

He glared at me. "And you're turning into a snob."

We stared at each other. I took a breath. "You're only hurting yourself." His indifferent shrug stung; this was a betrayal deeper than any infidelity.

"I guess I just don't get it," I conceded. "What have we been doing all these months? This is your music, Dep, your beautiful music. You got to take care of it."

"You're right," he snapped. "You don't get it. We're not in the tree house any more."

I turned and walked away; I didn't want to be reminded of Udo. Those faraway days seemed like child's play, and I was trying so desperately to grow up. I needed to believe that freedom and responsibility were not necessarily opposed, that there could be freedom in taking responsibility, especially if it allowed love and creativity to flourish. That's what I wanted for us, and I didn't want to see my efforts squandered.

Espousing like a petticoat feminist in a honky-tonk novel, I couldn't quite keep up with the plot. So naturally I was caught off-guard when, at the end of January, Depty quietly announced that he was going back to Texas.

"What?" I was stunned. "I thought we came here to be together."

"We did," he sighed. "I just don't see much chance for me in this town."

Chicago was urban and midwestern. Depty Dawg was a country boy with a Mardi Gras soul. Besides, it was too cold here.

I sank on the bed next to him. "We just arrived."

"I know." He put an arm around me. "And you found something you love."

"You mean my job?"

"I mean James."

I burst into tears. "I love you," I insisted. "Only I've got to put down roots, Dep, if I'm going to grow wings."

"I wish I could," he cried.

"When will you be back?" I whispered.

He took me in his arms. "I can't say."

And so we said *See you later* once again, this time in a jumble of confusion and relief. I was living in a flat I was afraid to come home to; I couldn't understand how he could leave me here with no big-city experience. Yet I didn't feel I could ask anything of him. He was an artist: he would do what he had to do to make his music live. And secretly, part of me was glad to see him go.

Our commitment was being sorely tested, and all my old instincts for flight were suddenly airborne. It was easier to let him go than to try and confront his pain—or mine. We couldn't have taken on each other's suffering then; I couldn't certainly, not with my own waiting impatiently offstage to make its full-blown entrance.

This time I was ready. In his absence, a voice opened up in me. I began to write with the same explosive intensity that had overtaken him in the tree house. Now, while James was in school and his mother away teaching, I sat at the typewriter in her office, composing first a smattering of poems, then a short—very short—story for kids.

The professor read my tentative attempts. She responded, "You're a writer," and got me penning sonnets with their intricate demands of form and rhyme, three rhyming stanzas with a couplet at the end:

Still the muse is not betrayed by rapture;
I am myself resonant in capture.

Sometimes now I stayed with Betsey and Cassie at their mother's townhouse near Somebody Else's Troubles. Our North Side hovel still unnerved me, but at least there I could be truly alone. I was filling empty spaces with sonnets of my own.

It was a windy and stunningly cold day when Depty Dawg returned to Chicago a month later. The thinness of his coat dismayed me. He didn't care; he was excited. He had brought a new song to play for me.

He'd gone to Mardi Gras again, this time with Lindsey, his Texas running mate. By the end, they found themselves drunk and stranded at the airport. Clinging to the chain-link fence, they watched the planes take off and land. Lindsey had murmured, "If we could only fly home." And from that wistful comment, a song had emerged.

Dep and I sat on the end of the bed, tears sliding down both our faces as he sang:

The wind keeps blowin' somewhere every day
They tell me things get better
Somewhere up the way
Just dismal thinkin' on a dismal day
Sad songs for us to bear
If I could only fly
If I could only fly
I'd bid this place good-bye

To come and be with you
But I can hardly stand
Got nowhere to run
Another sinkin' sun
And one more lonely night
You know sometimes I write happy songs
But then sometimes little things are wrong
You know I wish they all could make you smile
Tomorrow maybe we can get away
I'm comin' home soon and I want to stay
I wish you could come with me when I go again
If I could only fly
If you could only fly
If we could only fly
There'd be no more lonely nights

I should have known then that with this song he was saying good-bye. When I saw the lyrics scrawled in his familiar print, these words came into my head: *he doesn't need me any more.* We both understood that he'd made a quantum leap as a writer, giving voice to the paradox of the boundless heart enslaved to freedom. We didn't talk much about it; we didn't have to. Clearly he knew now that he could do this; he had only to really want Blaze Foley to make him come true.

That bittersweet visit was marked by a long-awaited event in Chi-town: Blaze Foley jammed with little James. Several weeks before, my charge had come with me to Betsey's house. After hearing her on her fiddle, he decided that he wanted to learn to play too. His mother found him a teacher and twice a week now I took him uptown in a taxi for violin lessons. The teacher, an ancient wrinkled Chinese musician, had given him a pint-sized Suzuki violin to practice on at home.

Every day James had asked me, "When is Depty Dawg coming back?"

"That's what I'd like to know." He hadn't written any letters this time.

That March, James got his wish. Standing in the kitchen with the tiny fiddle against his shoulder, he squeaked the bow against the strings, a sound much like tooth-drilling without Novocain. Depty sat in a chair, strumming and trying not to cringe or laugh, while I stood in the doorway, unnoticed by James, doing both.

Dep left again soon after. Our universe had broken apart, leaving us on separate fragments. I couldn't give him money for beer any more; my feminist education had taken care of that. There was rent to pay, food and type-writer ribbons to buy. We were disconnecting—or trying to anyway—though our bodies kept telling us otherwise. We were bound by invisible threads we could only see through touch.

For all our confusion, we were still the other's biggest fan. Depty was excited to read my first efforts. He was writing too. That visit he added the final verse to "Cold, Cold World":

> I might have to leave you
> I think's what she said
> Wish I could sleep
> 'Stead of tossin' in bed
> I could find myself thinkin'
> That I'd rather be dead
> Ain't it a cold, cold world?

43

My Reasons Why

My memories of Chicago remain more elusive than those of Georgia and Texas. And maybe that's due to the gap between what I thought was happening—and what was really going on. The new verse to "Cold, Cold World" expressed Dep's fear that I would leave him, when in fact he was already gone. All these years I believed I broke up with him; in hindsight I can see that he made the break himself when he left in January. Seems like I'm always the last to know anything.

In "Rainbows and Ridges" he would write: *Someone gets started; someone resigns.* By Chicago, each of us was getting started. Does it really matter any more who resigned first?

He would come back to see me several times that spring. His second visit, it was already April. I was no longer at the North Side flat. I'd moved in with Betsey and Cassie until I could find a safe place I could afford. Writing in earnest now, I'd also been cast as the teenage heroine of *Hothouse*, a play by Megan Terry. We rehearsed nightly in the Jane Addams Theater, right around the corner from James' lakefront apartment. My own dreams had begun to move in me again. Alone in Chicago, I'd discovered an alternative lifestyle my heart leapt to embrace: quiet contemplation in a room of my own—the life I believed I needed to nurture the writer I wanted to become.

These recollections did not all return on their own. It would take Blaze's lyrics, heard decades later, to bring our last months in Chicago into sharper focus. Though I'll probably never know who he had in mind when he wrote "My Reasons Why," his lyrics speak of diverging paths and the hope of a timely reunion:

> If only we could read between
> The lines that we have drawn
> Would we find each other waitin' helplessly?

I only hope that time will last
And this won't take too long
And we find each other waitin' patiently

By the time we got to Chicago, Depty Dawg had to know what it was going to take to become the legend he envisioned: lots of drinking, lots of women, being subversive, going to jail. It would be hard to reconcile that with old-fashioned love. If he couldn't, then at the very least, he wouldn't put me through it. I can believe Depty Dawg was capable of that kind of sacrifice.

And maybe that's what he was trying to tell me later that spring, when he cut off his ponytail and gave it to me, not long before leaving Chicago for the third time.

"You're a part of me," he whispered. "No matter what."

Placing the coil of hair in my hand, he was ensuring that some part of him would always be with me.

Weeks passed; spring careened into summer. The longer he stayed away this time, the stronger became my resolve to reinvent myself: I wanted my freedom now too.

Late one June afternoon, he showed up at the Lakeshore Drive apartment for the last time. I left work early. In a small garden park by the water, we sat across a picnic table from each other. He looked seedy and weary. My mind had begun to persuade my heart against him, to judge him as others had as drifter, drunk, and ne'er-do-well.

"I need to be on my own," I told him. "Just me, alone."

The flat pad of his thumb brushed under his eyes, erasing each tear before it fell. I was numb with the determination to let him go, unable to acknowledge—to him or to myself—the true-hearted poet I was about to give up.

For his part he didn't say much. He'd come back again and again through the spring, waiting for me to say the words he'd already written. I was the one holding on.

And for a very long time, that was my last image of him: walking away from me with his guitar case in hand.

He didn't look back and, for years, neither did I.

Part 3

Country
Music
Widow

44

Scavengers

Twenty-six years after I said good-bye to Depty Dawg in Chicago, I'm wandering around a deserted graveyard outside Austin looking for Blaze Foley's grave. No one here can tell me how to find it; you have to let him guide you, his friends all say.

The entrance to Live Oak Cemetery is marked by a sprawling grove of ancient oaks whose leathery leaves are evergreen; they don't fall in autumn. Live oaks can defy the seasons for hundreds of years, and here their sprawled branches cast a dense canopy over the sun-baked Texas plain. Under the great trees, gravestones—some of them dating back to the 1800s—are nestled comfortably, tilted with time, the etching on the rough granite almost worn away.

It's the beginning of February, a few days after the fourteenth anniversary of Blaze's death. The weather in Austin has been surprisingly warm; only yesterday it shifted, turning cold and raw. I've been walking under the old oaks searching for his gravesite for over an hour, and I'm starting to shiver. Beyond the massive grove, the burial grounds open onto a barren field where neat rows of young trees have been planted. I move into the sunshine, but the wind blows unhampered here and if anything, it's colder. The gravestones beside the smaller oaks are more recent; exposed to sun and wind, they feel forlorn, less settled than the ones whose names are no longer recorded beneath the shaded stand.

Chain-link fencing encloses the entire two-acre graveyard. On the other side of the fence, horses and longhorns graze unperturbed by their silent neighbors. Mostly it's quiet in the field beside theirs, though some days are busier than others, and every once in a while a car comes in at night. The cemetery is a private place for lovers who don't get easily spooked, or are just too horny to care.

In the windswept field, a faint pealing of bells draws me to a slender oak hung with chimes and Christmas ornaments. I follow the sound. Suddenly I come on Blaze's grave. The black stone slab lies flat to the earth, disappearing in the gray light, so that my foot is almost upon it before I notice it. I look down: his bearded image, etched in stone, has my astonished face mirrored behind it—as if we had never been apart.

The mirror rises toward me; I've fallen to my knees. Blind fingers seek the creases of his likeness.

Depty, I'm so sorry I stayed away so long.

My tears pool in the seams of his epitaph:

BLAZE FOLEY
Poet—Songwriter—Musician
1949–1989

I love that *poet* is his first description. Across the black surface, a line drawing of a guitar bears the titles of his songs in various handwritings, and this verse from "Big Cheeseburgers and Good French Fries":

I like to drink beer, hang out in bars
Don't like buses and I don't like cars
Don't like presidents, don't like stars
Never had stitches, but I do got scars
Love to go to parties and I love my friends
Got no books, just got bookends
Think I'm crazy but that depends
Don't seem that crazy to me

I lay my cheek against his stone-cold face.

Was it worth it, Blaze, all your sorrow and sacrifice?

The wind howls; the chimes clamor. I join them, wailing, and as I do, the grief opens unexpectedly. I find myself going beyond guilt and blame, beyond my fault, his fault. I see that we are in this together, inseparably, carried along a river of circumstance whose headwaters begin far back in the past, before either of us was born. The river extends before us too; in time it will wash away completely the traces of our lives. We'll disappear into the waters of a vast ocean, reappearing as clouds and falling as rain, nameless and plentiful.

Whatever has propelled me here—be it loss, compassion, or the need for forgiveness—whatever I want from him, I must extend to myself too, to the faceless girl I used to be.

He mourned for us then; I mourn for us now. If timing is everything, is my sorrow any less true for being delayed?

My coat is too thin to keep out the wind, so at times I have to get up from Blaze's grave and walk the fence line to keep warm. The horses lift their heads, ears twitching madly, then go back to grazing. Hands in my pockets, I roam the open grounds. The gravestones read like novels in haiku form, lifetimes distilled in a few precise phrases. Fathers and grandmothers are buried beside day-old children, and the graves of veterans are heralded by tiny weather-worn flags.

Coming here has made his death real at last. I can let it in now: the bullet boring through tissue, parting muscle and bone. For years I thought he was killed breaking up a barroom brawl; the truth is more complex. His death is the glue of his legend here in Texas where it's said he died a hero, shot down protecting an old man, a neighbor he'd befriended. His killer, the old man's son, was acquitted on a claim of self-defense, the final irony in a myth fraught with paradox.

The self-sabotage I glimpsed in him in Chicago had gathered strength in Austin. The urge to self-destruct was wily; it had convinced him to let love go, a tactical move designed to preserve itself. Unchecked, the impulse would work its way into the recipe of his legend, the yeast that would cause it to rise.

The wind hastens me back to his grave. Under the young oak is a spigot and hose, so I wash away the dirt collected in the stone's seams. The black granite shines like patent leather for a few seconds, then the wind dries it and the stone is cold again.

Vultures glide above us, wingtips splayed like fingers in ecstasy. Buzzards over a bone yard can produce a chill. Scavengers with six-foot wingspans, they're the heavyweights on death's clean-up crew. In the air their masterful soaring is admirable, even enviable; on the ground we avert our eyes from the sight of one plucking an eyeball out of fresh road kill. No one wants to be reminded that death is messy; life is sordid enough.

I've become a scavenger too; I feed off the dead, a thief of flesh and memory. Only I'm more like a pack rat, picking through the details of other lives and carrying them back to my own. Five months ago, I knew almost nothing about Depty Dawg's last decade as Blaze Foley. Now I've vowed to learn all that I can about this life that keeps colliding so intensely with my own. Yet even as I do, I know the goal is unreachable.

For nothing I will discover can ultimately recreate Mike Fuller's experience of his own life, how he might remember it or what he would say about it now.

45

Lone Stars

B y the time I encountered Depty Dawg in Georgia, Mike Fuller's life was already half over. When we parted in the summer of '77, Blaze Foley had little more than a decade to live. It would be several years before I saw him again in New York City sometime in the early '80s; the date eludes me still.

Placing myself on the sidewalk outside The Lone Star Café on lower Fifth Avenue, I can summon only the bitter cold and there, beside the door, a poster announcing "Blaze Foley Opening Tonight for Texas Songwriter Kinky Friedman."

And now here he comes, listing up the avenue with his unmistakable gait. It's got to be at least four years since I saw him in Chicago, yet he doesn't seem all that changed. A guitar case still dangles from his hand—a permanent appendage—and under a battered cowboy hat, his hair sways with each tilting step.

Eyes glistening, his face crinkles in a smile when he sees me. "Little Sybil."

He sets down the guitar, bending to take me in his arms. His hair brushes my cheek. Through his thin coat I feel his body trembling.

"It's good to see you," he says.

"You too." I cover my eyes as if the wind had produced these sudden tears.

He shivers. "You look great."

"You're cold. Can we go inside?"

"Don't see why not." In late afternoon The Lone Star is still closed. Depty peers through the window. "Ought to let me in, don't you think?"

He raps on the pane. Moments later, we're sitting at a table before an empty stage. He locates a Kool, searches for matches. His hands are shaking, whether from nerves or the cold or the night before, I don't know. He's less thin than I remember, but then so am I; we're in our thirties after all.

Finally he pulls matches from his back pocket. "Vy-ola!"

"If you was a snake, you'd have bit them," I murmur.

Dep keeps his head down, laughing the same gleeful riff. That may be the closest either of us comes to mentioning the tree house.

Opening the guitar case which, I note, does not hold the Empire State, he takes out a 45-rpm in a white paper sheath. "This is for you."

He finds a pen and inscribes the cover: *To Little Onion from Old Big Foot, Love, Blaze.*

It's a Blaze Foley single of "If I Could Only Fly," released by Zephyr Records in Houston in '78. Smiling, I turn it over. On the flip side is the mock-gospel tune "Let Me Ride in Your Big Cadillac," one of his early tree house songs.

I blink away tears. "Thank you." I kiss his cheek. "I'm so proud of you, I mean it."

He shrugs. "They're playing it on jukeboxes in Houston is all."

"But opening for Kinky too? You did it, Dep. I knew you could."

He stubs out the cigarette. "What you been up to?" he asks, taking out the guitar. Dep never did like to talk much about himself.

I may have told him I was living in Greenwich Village and working as a waitress in Queens. Maybe I told him that I'd started writing plays. Probably I didn't mention the different men I was seeing, or that I was in therapy for depression. I don't remember what I said.

Maybe he told me he'd been traveling between Austin and Houston for the past few years. We'd become urban dwellers, both of us. It's possible he caught me up on the news from Whitesburg. I don't remember what he said.

All I can recall are his fingers picking at the strings, playing melodies I'd never heard. Not once does he sing for me; not once do I ask him to.

Outside, night falls early. A young man in a baseball cap sweeps in to wipe down the tables. It's time for me to go to work. Promising to come back and hear him sing one night soon, I hug him and leave. There is so much to say and no way to say it.

A few nights later, I returned to The Lone Star before his set began. I'll never know if he saw me come in. I was glad to see he was wearing a warmer coat, a long trench coat, though it did look odd beneath the cowboy hat. He'd been drinking, I could tell. The technicians were doing a sound check, and he wasn't cooperating. Sitting on a stool on the stage, he taunted them in front of the audience that was already there.

It was too painful to watch. Nothing and everything had changed. He'd come this far and here he was, still sabotaging himself. I left before his set began.

Years would pass before I learned that Kinky Friedman fired him from the stage that night.

Or that I would never see him alive again.

46

Texas Troubadour

Decades later, I'm tormented by what I don't know. I want to unravel the rest of his story, to see if and how our paths entwined beyond our last good-bye. Fleshing out his life, I take the torn shreds of fact I find and tack them onto our tattered history. Like Blaze, the truth is hard to pin down, and my efforts are confounded by his myth, of which he was the chief contributor. For instance, he liked to say he was born in Marfa—partly for the way it sounded, mostly because it made a better story for the hillbilly kid from Malvern, Arkansas, longing to be a Texas troubadour.

Mike Fuller's fully fledged flight as Blaze Foley would occur in Houston in the late '70s, in tandem with Gurf Morlix. The two musicians had introduced themselves by other names at The Hole in the Wall in the summer of '76. Dep had been intrigued by the name of the young guitarist's band, The Goats of Arabia, as advertised on the dive's marquee. Two years later, they would migrate together to Houston in a musical partnership that lasted three more. Since then, Gurf has gone on to produce albums for Lucinda Williams, Ray Wylie Hubbard, and Mary Gauthier, not to mention his own, and his wide-ranging virtuosity is also the stuff of legends.

These days Austin offers a Sunday phenomenon called gospel brunch, where musicians sing hallelujah before a restaurant's breakfast crowd. This morning a gospel brunch is taking place on the patio of Maria's Taco X-press on Lamar Boulevard, and Gurf Morlix will be playing there. I don't guess we've seen each other in at least twenty-five years.

We meet again on the sidewalk outside the café. Still boyish despite the gray hair falling to his shoulders, Gurf peers at me as if reorganizing his memories to fit the person before him. Reflected in his face is the possibility that he doesn't remember me at all, but that matters less than the fact that we both knew and loved Dep, as he still calls him.

Gurf can recall Dep's first gig in Austin. It was in the summer of '77, just after Depty Dawg came back from Chicago for the last time, at happy hour in a disco behind The Hole in the Wall. As the intro to "I Won't Be Your Fat Boy Any More," Depty passed around a portrait from his Tex days at Sears. Gurf was impressed; Dep's Blaze Foley was funny and touching, and his songs were good.

"So when I went to Houston the following summer," Gurf reminisces on the patio before the gospel brunch begins. "Dep just came along."

Gurf is the only person I've ever met about whom you can use "grin" and "terse" in the same sentence.

"He attached himself to me." Gurf grins tersely. "I don't know why."

I think I do. Gurf would provide ballast for Blaze's mercurial emergence, and Blaze, in turn, offered his new partner an expanding bag of original tunes. Houston was an enticement too. Spurred by Willie Nelson's Texas-music revolution, the oil boomtown had become a haven for other gifted performers, like Lucinda Williams and the late Townes Van Zandt.

Riding that creative wave, Blaze Foley's prize band—The Beaver Valley Boys—became a reality at last. It wasn't an all-girl band as Dep had envisioned in the tree house; nor did the players remain the same gig-to-gig. When he and Gurf played alone, Blaze would introduce his partner as The Beaver Valley Boy.

Performance art was the heartbeat of the legend he was hell-bent on creating. He and Gurf invaded junk stores for outrageous wigs and costumes. During a show, Blaze might read the instructions off a tampon box, or expound from medical encyclopedias on hallucinogenic drugs. His sense of style was evolving too. Shedding the cowboy hat for a bowler, he wore button-down shirts, colorful ties, and suspenders. His intricate finger-picking grew stronger, more skilled, and he was composing from morning till night.

The new improved Blaze Foley caught the eye of some Texas oilmen with money to burn. Bankrolling a musician seemed like a groovy idea, so they formed Zephyr Records with Blaze Foley as their major investment. Under Zephyr's banner, he and The BVBs opened for headliners or played to packed houses in Houston and New Orleans. Zephyr provided Blaze with a green "woody" station wagon to get to his gigs, and released the single of his signature song "If I Could Only Fly." It could be played for a dime in juke joints from Houston to Austin.

Taking in Gurf's description of Blaze in Houston, I feel like Moses at the border of the Promised Land: seeing its milk and honey from afar and never getting a taste. I'd like to erase the past and redraw myself as Mrs. Rosendawg-Foley in Houston, a fantasy that somehow always includes a miniskirt. Hem to my thighs, I picture us reuniting at one of Blaze's shows. Coming into the club unnoticed, I stand in the back listening as he sings from "Anything Less":

> I was stranded down in New Orleans
> I was wanderin' through the streets alone
> You know I wish it could be just a bad dream
> 'Cause I'm about to chew my fingers to the bone
> Take me back the way I am
> 'Cause you can't change me
> I can't even change myself
> I know. I tried
> But I've looked around
> And I don't think that I can settle
> For anything less
> For anything less

When the band takes a break, I go down to the stage.

My daydream is transparent; I want to make the past turn out differently. Fantasy may be the balm the mind secretes to leach out regret, but the fact remains that in the summer of '78, around the same time Blaze Foley hit Houston, I, too, was in transit.

The year spent as a single girl in Chicago had been fruitful. Tucked into a snug apartment with a typewriter of my own, I had young James to love, and a variety of musicians at Kiley's to fulfill my physical needs. Now James' family was moving to Westchester County, north of New York City, and I was following them east.

They had purchased an old rambling lodge in Briarcliff Manor, high on a manicured hill. There I had two small rooms above the kitchen as my own. My desk looked out on a sloping lawn fringed with a grove of pink and blue hydrangea.

Udo pursued me here. Like C. S. Lewis' mystical Narnia, the universe of the tree house had become a world apart, tucked behind a portal I could no longer find. Still, it moved in me. Imagining it as the setting for a children's picture book, I created a hidden land where a chipmunk named Bissel (Yiddish for "little") lives in a tree with a spider called Gwad (Dawg backwards), celebrated for the music he makes on the strings of his magical web.

When asked how she came to live in Udo, Bissel muses, "I don't know really. I fell out of a dream and when I woke up, I was here."

One day, as she grieves for a cousin crushed by a tangerine, a single tear falls to the floor. Later, while she sleeps, Gwad creeps from his corner, takes Bissel's tear, and hangs it on his web. He'll pack up his strings—and the tear—when he and Bissel decide to leave Udo forever.

Two-and-a-half years after our exodus from the tree house, I had included sorrow in my first revision of the past. I was still weaving fairy tales. Make-believe was easier to deal with than my present reality: James' parents' marriage had come apart at the seams.

My romantic vision of their ideal marriage was blindsided by its demise. The doctor had begun to drink heavily in the evenings. Often the target of his anger, the professor stayed away from home, working in New York City. Left to keep the household together, I was torn between my loyalty to James and wanting to bolt. One night the doctor came to my room seeking comfort. When he saw how frightened I became, he did not pursue it. Soon after that I was packing my bags. Even James sensed it was time for me to go, though I would mourn his absence for months.

Alone and in self-exile, I headed for the Big Apple. By June of '79, Manhattan was no longer a chimera. Since arriving in Westchester, I'd been commuting to the city every Saturday to attend an acting class. Now my teacher had offered me a room in her downtown flat.

Unfamiliar with the Village, I had the taxi drop me off blocks from my new home. As I crossed Seventh Avenue, my suitcase suddenly popped open, and I watched my clothes blow in slow motion down the lanes of traffic, trampled under wheel. Perhaps this was a sign of what the city had in store for me.

That same year Gurf and Blaze went into a studio in Houston to record eleven Blaze Foley songs. The next winter they would record seven more in a backyard studio at Loma Ranch in the Hill Country west of Austin. With these reels, the partners hoped to release Blaze Foley and The Beaver Valley Boy's first LP.

"Why didn't you?" I ask Gurf on the deserted patio after the gospel brunch.

"The master tapes were stolen out of Dep's station wagon," he states from behind his shades. He still can't figure out why Dep insisted on carrying them around in his car, instead of leaving them in one safe place.

"I asked him if he knew why anyone would steal the reels," Gurf goes on.

He scratches his head in answer, an uncanny imitation of Dep: "'Aw, 'cause they was shiny, I guess.'"

We grin tersely at the irony of that.

Then, out of the blue, Gurf is reminding me that he and Dep came to see me in a play I performed in a church in Manhattan.

"What?" I'd totally forgotten.

"Yeah," Gurf replies. "And you had this one line—"

"Asshole!" we shout together, memory complete.

Gurf laughs, a whole sound this time. "And Dep said, 'Well, if you got to say one word in a play, that'd be it.'"

Vaguely, I see myself talking to them backstage, Depty towering over us, me in the gold lamé jumpsuit with the sagging butt I wore for my five-minute walk-on. I don't know if this is real, recovered memory, or just my mind stepping up to the work of invention. I do know that the only reason I had the part was because I was living with the playwright at the time. He would be the one to encourage me to write plays, and it would be only a few months later—after I'd finished my first one-act—that he'd walk out the door with the exit line: "If you were a bitch, I wouldn't leave you."

If there's a comeback to that, I've never thought of it.

Returning to the present, I ask Gurf, "So why were you guys in New York anyway?"

"Blaze was opening at The Lone Star," he replies.

My heart sinks. "For Kinky?"

Gurf's nod anchors our final meeting to 1980, earlier than I'd suspected, a conclusive date on an elusive timeline. I can't help but wonder where Blaze's fiancée, Fifi Larue, falls on its arc.

At her mention, Gurf's eyes light up. "They met playing pool," he recalls. "Yeah. Fifi was great. Very funny. Very solid."

Fifi Larue was not her real name of course; she, too, had reinvented herself. A Catholic girl from a likeable, well-to-do family, by day Fifi worked as a urine carrier in a local hospital. At night, she sang in close harmony with her sister Mimi, just as Mike Fuller had done with his.

"His relationship with Fifi was stormy," Gurf allows. "But they had chemistry. Naturally he had lots of girls, before and after her. Dep could fall in love. He could see it coming."

His words squeeze through my heart like toothpaste. I tell myself I should be happy Depty had someone there to love him when I no longer could.

Gurf clears his throat. "He cried whenever he sang 'If I Could Only Fly.' Totally real. That said it all. How torn he was."

"He doesn't sound torn." I grab a napkin. "Sorry," I murmur, dabbing my leaking eyes. "This is such a roller coaster ride."

I crumple the paper. "So wait. Was Dep with Fifi when y'all came to New York?"

Gurf thinks a moment. "Yeah. I believe they'd just gotten engaged."

To my surprise, I'm flooded with relief. Gurf's recollection is taking the sting out of that final encounter, providing a reason for its wrenching restraint. We were each with new partners, I can convince myself. And knowing something of Depty Dawg's romantic code, that afternoon now makes almost acceptable sense.

The year 1980 was a turning point for Blaze. For one thing, Ronald Reagan was elected President, ushering in a rise of homelessness and a national disdain for the arts. Reagan's inauguration prompted Blaze to write "Oval Room," a political song with a refrain that, sadly, has rarely gone out of date: *He's the President but I don't care.*

There was the fiasco in New York City with Kinky Friedman at The Lone Star, and the brief unfulfilled meeting with me. In June, Fifi Larue would break off their engagement the day before their wedding. Her family wanted them to marry in a Catholic church—another conversion attempt on Blaze Foley—but he had opted for a bar. Contrary to rumor, she only backed out once, but it was for good.

Zephyr Records would eventually blow away, along with the station wagon and any remaining hopes for a first album. The following year, Gurf himself would leave Texas for California, though the two would stay friends till the end of Dep's life. To this day, Gurf Morlix remains perhaps the closest witness to Blaze Foley's meteoric rise and fall in Houston.

The sun is sinking behind lavender hills when Gurf and I finally say goodbye, promising not to let another twenty-five years slip away. In the span of hours, we've conquered time. Gurf's memory of his friend as young and intact affirms Dep's haunting presence in me, as if he were a flame reflected infinitely between two mirrors.

47

Loma Ranch

A s the keeper of the Blaze Foley timeline, Kevin is my guide to Blaze's last decade in Texas, providing the roadmap to places he frequented. This morning we're on our way to Loma Ranch, where Blaze and Gurf recorded in 1980. Apparently the ranch became a refuge for Blaze in the years that followed, a place he returned to again and again.

Kevin and I drive through countryside Dep and I once traversed, where the Pedernales meanders beside winding back roads and the dark green mesquite trees hold down the dust. The bracing cold at the cemetery has lifted as quickly as it set in, leaving these hills with a warm patina of spring green over their scrabbled surface.

Moving through time as well as space, Kevin and I piece together Blaze's history after Houston. He returned to Austin in '81. Hardly anyone called him Dep any more. He'd landed back in Austin the way he'd intended to in '76—as Blaze Foley, with a reputation for world-class gallivanting and a battered attaché case full of beautiful songs.

Memory merges with myth as I picture him in his early thirties, clean-shaven and handsome with a mournful blue gaze. By all accounts, his drinking binges had accelerated. No longer writing at a furious clip, he was intent on being a character. His pockets were full of trinkets and aluminum-foil "mood" rings to give away, and he'd made duct tape a way of life. For formal occasions, he would bring out the Duxedo, a tuxedo decorated with the shiny stuff, his ultimate antidote to rhinestone lapels.

Soon after his return to Austin, Blaze fell for Mandy Mercier, an aspiring singer/songwriter and musician. They would live together on and off for two years. After their break-up, Blaze perfected his run on the couch circuit, flopping with friends for days or months, unless he was with a lover. Adamant about giving his all to his music, he maintained that a day job would blunt his ambition, not to mention curb his gypsy feet. He'd disappear for weeks. Few in Austin knew he was going back to Georgia in the summers, to help Glyn build the multiplying sheds and decks at Waller.

"Georgia was one of his best-kept secrets," Kevin remarks. "Except in his songs."

By the early '80s Blaze no longer played in public many of the tunes he'd begun in the tree house. The rare nights he performed in Austin, his shows were packed. His appeal stemmed from his honesty, from that deep sorrowful voice and the seamless way he fused with his music. Drunken, unpredictable behavior would cost him many gigs, but the times he got himself there, the room would be filled with songwriters, come to learn from a master.

Kevin didn't have to tell me this. Every musician I've met here so far has mentioned Blaze's legendary artistry.

I turn to Kevin in the car. "Listen. I need to ask you a favor. Would you please—please—stop introducing me as Blaze's wife?"

"Why?" he stammers. "I'm sorry but it's what feels most true. Don't people tell you that he talked about you? That you were the love of his life?"

"Yeah, so?" I reply, trying to conceal the comfort, and confusion, these remarks had caused.

"So," Kevin goes on patiently. "Your lives were entwined. You were soul mates."

"That still doesn't make me his wife."

"What about the broom-jumping?"

"What about it?" I grumble. "You know too much."

Kevin lifts a hand, smiling blandly. "That's what I'm here for."

He knows my lame protest stems from a reluctance to make any claim among these longtime devoted friends of Blaze. No doubt he's also guessed that secretly I don't mind it. The title places me squarely in Blaze's life, lending me identity, even stature, among strangers. I'm still clinging to the faces others draw on me, though the fact that we jumped over a broom does seem to carry a lot of weight around here.

At Loma Ranch, John comes out to greet us. Producer by profession and dreamer by nature, he has lived here with his wife, Laurie, for decades. His eyes swim huge and blue behind wire-rim glasses, and the beaming energy of his long figure reminds me of Blaze.

Before I can protest, Kevin introduces us. "Blaze and Sybil were married in the summer of '76."

Instantly John falls to the ground, throwing his arms around my knees.

I yelp. "Are you worshipping me or consoling me?"

He stands, grinning and brushing the dust from his shins. "Had him for a little while, did you?"

John gestures for us to come take a look. The ranch house has a generous patio skirting the side and back. In a grove of trees a hundred yards beyond, a steel barn contains the infamous recording studio. A third outbuilding catches my eye, one John calls the tank house. A round stonemason-base once supported a second-story water tank. Today the tank is gone, and the bottom now houses the bathroom for the square wooden shack perched on top. The single-room cabin looks as if it sprouted there—very much like the tree house.

"Oh my God." My hand flies to my mouth. "Did Blaze ever stay in that?"

John grins. "Bee-lined to it first time he saw it."

"He ever mention a tree house to you?" I ask.

"Said he used to live in one."

"We lived there together," I tell him.

John opens his mouth and closes it. At the bottom of the stairs he inclines his head and tells me to go on up. The men trail behind slowly, engaged in manly conversation, something about porch railings I think.

I climb the steep steps and enter the cabin. Inside it's like a kid's bedroom; twin beds against opposite walls give it a cozy, playhouse feel.

I picture Dep asleep on one of the beds, his hair falling over the edge.

What did you dream of here, my dear?

In the years since we parted, I couldn't recall a single dream about him. My New York City journals record no nocturnal meetings. It's only in the last few months that I've begun to dream of him, elusive and changeable, lurking in attics, disappearing into crowds.

On the ride out to Loma Ranch this morning, Kevin reminded me that Blaze recorded his song "Misty Garden" here as a segue to "I Should Have Been Home with You."

"Know any reason why he would string the two together?" Kevin had asked me in the car.

I shook my head. "It's news to me."

Since hearing "Misty Garden" for the first time three months ago, I'd thought of the song as the telling of a dream. Learning that Blaze linked it with the earlier tune makes me wonder if he went to sleep then as I do now, hoping to meet in that ethereal realm between presence and absence.

In the misty garden you walked by me yesterday

Didn't have a lot to say but you smiled at me anyway
In the misty garden you walked by me yesterday
Didn't have a lot to say but you smiled at me anyway
In the misty garden you walked by me
Wouldn't even take the time to show me the way

Wanting to be shown the way—what way does he mean? The way out of himself? Or a way back to the elusive "you" in the dream?

In the misty garden I could hardly see your eyes
Teardrops glistenin' in the morning light
In the misty garden I was offerin' you mine
But all you offered was a swiftly flight
In the misty garden you walked by me yesterday
Wouldn't even take the time to show me the way

When the song dissolves into "I Should Have Been Home with You," it
turns urgent, angry, as if he might be saying he knew why I had to leave; what
he couldn't understand is why I hadn't come back.

He hadn't come back either. I wanted him to tell me why I never heard so
many of these songs while he was still alive. In Chicago he had chosen the
only life he thought he could live. We were both naïve; he had his role models,
I had mine. We let love go so we could write about it.

The path he'd envisioned as the way back to each other—Blaze Foley's fame
and fortune—had not materialized. Over time, his choices began to extract
a price. I'd seen evidence of their cost at The Lone Star. After so much time
apart, maybe he couldn't be sure how I'd respond—or if I'd even recognize
him—and frankly, neither could I.

By the time Blaze returned to Austin, I was wearing the tremulous face
of a budding writer, and it required blinders. Like him, nothing and no one
was going to deter me from realizing my heart's desire. The songs had to wait
until I was ready to hear them.

Well, I was taking the time now; life had insisted on it. It undid me each
time I discovered an instance in his work where he may have invoked me, and
I was not there to receive it.

Sinking onto a bed in the tank house, I weep for the young man who never
stopped dreaming—and for the young woman who did. Along the fragile
traceries that remained, he had called to her again, and I wanted to believe
they were both listening now.

48

Brink of Devotion

B y 1983 Blaze was making plans to record his first album in Muscle Shoals, Alabama. On it he would include the song "Where Are You Now My Love" with the poignant last lines:

> I had to let you know
> If that's what's keepin' you away
> I don't want anything
> That don't come from your heart
> If you don't feel love for me
> I don't want your sympathy
> No, I don't want anything
> That don't come from your heart
> Where are you now my love?
> That's what you are to me

Another signal—if intended for me—that I wouldn't receive for at least twenty years.

I was living alone in a fifth-story walk-up in the Village. The coldwater flat had a bathtub in the kitchen, from which I could see my neighbors' laundry hung like medieval banners above a shadowed courtyard. Having discovered the thrill of my words coming alive in the mouths of actors, I was devoting every second I could to writing plays. To pay the rent, I worked as a waitress and later, wrote narration for documentary films, many of them odd and obscure. It didn't matter; someone was paying me to write, if only for pennies.

The sensation of facelessness had hounded me into my thirties. There were times when I couldn't understand how anyone could be talking to me, since I was so obviously not there. I stayed in bed for days sometimes, nailed to the sheets by violent images, like the time I saw myself cut in half by a buzz saw. At the urging of friends, I got into therapy. My shrink was helping me see this agony as a mirror of my mother's illness, though she kept insisting that Momma was far sicker, possibly schizophrenic; small comfort there. When I dreamt of throwing up and defecating ossified pieces of wood, she said the process was working. One way or another, I was getting out old rage.

Chicago was already a distant memory. I'd lost touch with my mentor, the professor, during the course of her long, harrowing divorce from the doctor. James was almost ten. Since my abrupt exit from Westchester four years ago, he'd lived alone with his father in that big, empty house. I got up there to see them as often as I could. The doctor was becoming bitter and isolated, and James' situation was cause for alarm, though I saw no easy solutions.

It had been months, maybe years, since I'd consciously evoked Depty Dawg. Only once in my journals does his name appear. I wrote:

I begin to see that in so many people there is no real core of passionate feeling, no sensitivity. . . . As I think about it now, it may be that Depty—wrong for me as he was and is—was the one man in my life who carried within him a full flowing emotional life and worthiness.

A fitful mention, archly noted and quickly suppressed, yet that word "worthiness" pierces me today.

But when my mind turned to a new work in early '83, Depty Dawg sprang up in it, insistent and alive. I may have buried his heart, but his wit and poetry hovered just below the surface of my imagination, like germinating seeds waiting for light. The play began to gather to itself elements of the Udo era: Sas' warrior-woman example, Margery's late-in-life pregnancy, Ape-shit's rescue of the kittens—all these found their way into the first draft. More pressing than any detail, however, was a lingering confusion over the abortion. I was learning I had a long history of unexpressed grief.

Brink of Devotion is set in the pine forests of west Georgia. The pivotal character, Sass Kaplan, is a forty-one-year-old research scientist, intrigued by spiders and bugs. She lives alone in a ramshackle cabin, nine months pregnant and without a mate. Into her life blow two young hitchhikers: Jodi Johnson, a runaway from Vidalia, Georgia, herself newly pregnant, and a drifting country singer by the name of Lucky Starr. If I didn't recall Glyn's comment about Blaze Foley being the bastard son of Blaze Starr and Red Foley, the name, when it came to me, felt exactly right for the romantic young musician desperate to make real his dreams of family and fame.

Depty Dawg's wit enlivened Lucky Starr. I stole his quip about Red Butler, as well as *If I was a snake, I'd have bit it.* Whole speeches were lifted from memory, like the description of his family from the closet in the Mill: *Daddy's in a nursing home in Dallas. Mother's real fat; she just got a new husband. My younger sister's a Jesus freak and Quaalude addict. Brother sells insurance in Oklahoma, and my older sister's a dyke.*

The young lovers' banter came easily too. Lucky calls Jodi *little onion*, and when she chides him for being a spendthrift, he responds, *I hate to have it rattling 'round my pocket.*

Lucky's need to be anchored in Jodi is threatened when their lives collide with Sass. Emboldened by the older woman's outward self-reliance, Jodi blurts out her fears for their unborn child: she doesn't trust herself, let alone Lucky. Through Jodi, I wanted to write about abortion—not as issue but as crucible—for any woman having to make an impossible decision.

Therapy had revealed the extent of my illness. In the jargon of the time, my clinical diagnosis was "borderline psychosis." Helpful or not, the pronouncement gave my despair an irreducible reality; I would have to live with those words until they no longer frightened me. The pain and anger I was currently unearthing underscored the decision I'd made eight years earlier. Clearly I was too unstable to mother. Relieved that I'd not passed on to another the suffering that was passed to me, at the same time I had to admit the loss had been profound.

Pregnancy had reinvented all notions of autonomy. In a heartbeat, another being had taken root inside me, unable to exist on its own. This intimate dilemma has always belonged solely to women, demanding our deepest compassion for what it means to be imperfect, and impermanent.

Brink of Devotion was meant to be an investigation of life and death, and the responsibility we have to each. Unfortunately, the characters fell into the trap I was trying to avoid: they got up on their soapboxes. As a novice playwright, I lacked the skill to free them from dogma. And they had their own agendas.

In Sass Kaplan, I was reweaving Georgia with Chicago. Intended as a splicing together of the original Sas' verve, Margery's independent thinking, and the professor's deliberate mentorship, over time the character became a foreshadowing of who I feared I'd be at forty: rigid, skeptical, and alone.

Lucky Starr steered his own course too. Depty's charm had brought the character to life; now his sorrow rose to the surface with it. *Always thought I'd just come and go on this earth,* he tells Jodi. *Just kind of blow across it and be gone.*

Dep's forgotten devotion resonated in the moment when Lucky says to her, *Now I got something holding me, keeping me here.*

My head was summoning truths my heart had put aside, and I was unable—or maybe unwilling—to reconnect the two.

As I labored over *Brink of Devotion* in New York, Blaze was on his way to Muscle Shoals to record his first album. He was not alone. He'd called Gurf in California to do the arrangements of the songs, and to play bass on the album. And for moral support, he brought along Townes Van Zandt.

Townes had made a name for himself as the revered author of, among other songs, the country classic "Pancho and Lefty." His hell-bent, roving ways were an alternative lifestyle Blaze understood well. As their paths crossed again and again in Houston, Austin, and New York City, the charismatic duo nurtured a legendary havoc at music festivals, in bars, and in hotel rooms. I can easily see how these two tortured poets would have gravitated toward one another. Townes' friendship had to mean a lot to Blaze, as a young musician trying to make his mark. Blaze's pals in Austin have told me that he idealized Townes; maybe too much, some still maintain.

In any event, the recording session in Muscle Shoals was delayed, and by the time Blaze went into the studio, he and Townes had gone to jail twice. Townes was put on the bus back to Texas. The album was made *under duress*, Blaze would later admit—a possible allusion to the rumor that he had to be physically threatened in order to sing. The records were pressed, but before they could be released, the executive producer was arrested on drug charges and—according to Blaze—the master tapes confiscated by the FBI.

Stacks of unreleased albums were stored in a warehouse in west Georgia where, from time to time, Blaze could get his hands on some. Carrying copies under his arm, he used them to barter for cab rides and beers. At closing time, I've been told, a bar would be littered with his albums, left by the people who bought him drinks, too drunk to remember to take his record home.

Brink of Devotion never received a stage production. Given its controversial subject, New York producers refused to take it on without major changes. The script had to come down either for or against abortion, they insisted, otherwise the critics would kill it. I didn't mean for the play to take a stand; that was never the point. Producers dismissed me as naïve, the play as flawed. Hungry and vulnerable, this was my first foray into commercial theater, and it hurt. Just as Depty had done in Atlanta eight years before, I was groping professionally—and I wasn't any better at it than he was.

Eventually *Brink of Devotion* ended up in a box in my attic. Decades would pass before I dug it out again. Reading through the script today, I can see that the plot's knottiness was tightened by one essential omission from the character of Lucky Starr: alcohol. Lucky didn't drink.

Here was a narrow attempt to clean up the man I'd loved and lost. A throwback to a more innocent self, Lucky was dedicated to his dreams, unswerving in his beliefs, and ultimately capable of unconditional love.

49

Blaze Takes a Request

The task I've given myself here is absurd: to encapsulate a man's life in a few pithy paragraphs. The more I learn about Blaze's years in Austin, the more I'm struck by his mystique. His history tends toward exaggeration and embroidery; I know this for myself. Yet even a distorted truth is accurate from some perspective, and when certain details are mentioned over and over, they earn reality's stamp.

By all accounts, the foiled release of the Muscle Shoals album was a crushing disappointment for Blaze. From that point on, his timeline begins to tailspin out of control, rendered unstable by alcohol, speed, and homelessness. His rage escalated; he was the victim of frequent beatings, often provoked. Confused and vitriolic, he couldn't understand why he hadn't received more recognition as an artist. His talent had not brought him success or happiness or the thing he yearned for most: a lasting love.

There would be one triumph. In 1987, Willie Nelson and Merle Haggard recorded "If I Could Only Fly" on their duet album, *Seashores of Old Mexico*. In a magazine interview Merle called it "the best country song in fifteen years." Blaze carried the article rolled up in his boot for months, showing it around proudly to everyone he encountered. As the album neared release, the single was promoted on Texas radio; for a time it was the number-one request in the state. On the brink of national release, the record company decided to pull the song in favor of another on the album, another reason why I never heard it in New York.

At last Blaze Foley was being paid as a songwriter. By age thirty-eight, he weighed close to three hundred pounds. His teeth were rotting, his beard long and thick. Occasionally he still tried to get sober. During one extended stay on the wagon, he recorded an album at Bee Creek Studio, with his friends backing him for free. This was the session I would read about years later, where he cried while singing "If I Could Only Fly." His voice had roughened, but he was still a riveting singer and a virtuoso on the guitar. The years of commitment to practice had served him well; his fingers never let him down.

Five weeks before his death, he performed with a borrowed guitar at the Austin Outhouse, one of the few venues in town from which he'd not been permanently barred. Fellow musician Lost John Casner recorded Blaze's performances on those two December nights.

Lost John was a baby-faced kid with a honky-tonk bent, one of several greenhorn singer/songwriters in Austin whom Blaze encouraged and promoted. Fourteen years later, Lost John would be responsible for *Live at the Austin Outhouse*, the recording that pried my sleeping memory open.

This afternoon he's invited me up to his studio on a scrubby hillside outside Dripping Springs. The renovated garage is filled with instruments, sound equipment, and country music memorabilia. An entire wall is dedicated to Ezalb Yelof's (Blaze's name backwards) quirkily cheerful portraits of odd ducks. With his songwriting beginning to ebb, Ezalb turned his creative energy to making these collages of birds, teapots, and clouds, intricate patterns painted in bright magic-marker colors.

I gaze up wonderingly at this unknown side of Blaze.

"If you asked Blaze what kind of art he did," Lost John tells me. "He'd answer, 'Thou art.'"

Lost John expresses his love for his late friend without constraint. He shows me several rave reviews of Blaze's live CD, one from an Amsterdam gazette: "Blaze Foley, Ein Bizarr Genie" (A Strange Genius). Dedicated to keeping Blaze's musical legacy alive, Lost John receives three or four emails a week from new fans all over the world, wanting to know where they can hear more of the homeless legend's music.

I've brought mementoes to show him too—love letters and a ponytail— but Lost John has other surprises for me. When I ask if Blaze ever told him about a tree house, he blanches visibly.

"Yes, he did," he replies. "Talked about it at the Outhouse the second night we recorded there."

Lost John's speech has a slight delay, lending him a tenderness belied by the black cowboy hat and studded metal belt. He peers at me curiously, as if examining my features.

"Are you the woman from the tree house?"

My nod causes him to grin like a man who's opened a vault of rubies with his credit card. It turns out he has a recording of all of Blaze's banter from those two nights. With sudden curious reluctance he now plays a cut entitled, "Blaze Takes a Request."

Blaze's voice is slurry and amused; he'd fallen off the wagon again. He asks for requests from the audience, and a guy calls out, "Play the first song you ever wrote."

"I wouldn't even sing that to myself in the dark," Blaze responds.

The audience laughs. The man persists. "What was it about?"

"It was about living in a tree house," Blaze tells him. "And I lived with a half-black Jewish girl. And we was gonna get married till they told us we couldn't. 'Cause I had to convert to Judaism, and that's a drag, man! You have to read all these books that white people with beanies wrote. You know?"

The heckler dismisses the story. Blaze retorts, "It was called 'Livin' in the Woods in a Tree.' I have a picture of the tree house in my pocket. I do!"

The cut ends there. Lost John is looking at me with trepidation; I am laughing. At this point, I don't even care that he said the song was awful, or that called us Jews *white people*. In a few weeks' time, his life would be over, but that night he was talking about the tree house.

"You think he really had a picture in his pocket?" I ask Lost John.

He considers before answering. "I think if he was feeling it, it was there."

That works for me.

I wonder what photo Blaze might have meant. Lost John admires the snapshot of us at the tree house, the one I've carried with me for twenty-six years, hanging it on whatever wall presented itself. How is it possible to be at once faithful and neglectful?

Lost John reads through all of Blaze's letters to me. Encountering familiar lyrics, he leans forward excitedly. He knows how a phrase can float in the mind like a milkweed seed, for years sometimes, before taking root in a song.

Folding the last note into its ragged envelope, Lost John hands the stack of letters back to me. "Thank you," he breathes. "Not everything about Blaze was pretty. I'm so glad to know this about him."

I take out the handkerchief folded around Depty's ponytail. Since coming to Austin, I've learned not to spring it on anyone too fast: it's that eerily alive.

Carefully revealing the slender rope of hair, I say, "Blaze gave this to me before we parted in Chicago."

After a moment, Lost John picks up the glossy coil and lays it on his knee. He closes his eyes, putting one hand over his heart and pressing the other into the ponytail.

"Earlier that spring," I go on, "he came home from Mardi Gras with a new song to play. That's when I first heard 'If I Could Only Fly.'"

Lost John rocks back in his chair, taking in this new chapter of Blaze biography. In one afternoon he's learned more about his old friend than he ever knew when Blaze was alive. Like a child who's forgotten his parents had a history before him, he's letting in the pieces of Blaze's unknown past, converting him back from legend to mortal.

Suddenly he bolts up. "There's something else you need to hear."

Carefully handing back the ponytail, he plays another Outhouse outtake, this one recorded after Blaze sang "If I Could Only Fly."

Across the decades I hear Blaze say, "I always wished I'd called it 'If We Could Only Fly.'" He sounds wistful. "That was selfish of me."

My eyes brim. Despite distance and the long silence, he'd still not forfeited the *we* of us. I had become myth to him, just as he was becoming for me, in the second play I was writing about him the night he spoke those words.

50

Udo Revised

~~~~~

In December of 1988, I was living in a tiny, sky-lit apartment on tree-lined Charles Street in the Village. It had been twelve years since Depty Dawg and I left paradise. In that time we'd each had our share of romance, though the AIDS epidemic had slowed us both down. I still dreamt of finding my heart's home in a man; unfortunately I had a penchant for bad boys, erotic geniuses with the sticking capacity of teflon.

From time to time I tried choosing sensible mates. The last sensible choice turned out to be a cross-dressing playwright who stopped making love to me the minute I moved in with him. Inevitably, some other guy would make a pass at me and I'd go down like a house of cards. And the cross-dresser would say to me when I left him: "I rejected you for a year-and-a-half and then you betrayed me."

No doubt a country song lurks in there somewhere.

Happily I had encountered a soul mate. Michael David Grody was a gospel-singing Jewish carpenter ambling through Greenwich Village, belting his brand of *Yiddishkeit* blues. Never lovers, we were fast friends; we knew the same Hebrew songs from childhood, and we had both migrated to gospel and John Prine. In the years to come, I would watch Mike Grody transform himself into Yukon the monk. There was the curious dual coincidence of his name, but at the time I thought it had more to do with my present circumstances than any hazy Georgia past. I hadn't heard from Blaze Foley in years.

I was consumed elsewhere. Therapy was ongoing. The specter of facelessness had mercifully fallen away; I no longer considered my mother the enemy. Instead I'd come to see her as a person in anguish who'd done the best she could. More than that, we were becoming friends. Plus, her medication had improved. No doubt she still harbored the hope that I'd one day marry someone safe and preferably Jewish, but I'd given up on that one long ago.

The closest I'd ever come to having a Jewish boyfriend would be a gay Zen Buddhist monk.

My young charge from Chicago, James, was a teenager now, with Yeshiva-boy curls and the beginnings of a beard. As life with his father became pervasively unbearable, I encouraged him to leave Westchester and helped him to orchestrate his getaway. Reunited with his mother in New York City, he and I began to explore a new landscape of restaurants, theaters, and museums. With his own aspirations to write, James faithfully attended the public readings of any plays I was working on then.

The pursuit of fame and fortune had proved unwieldy. I was tired of being told how to write and what to write, of going to parties to *shmooze* and suck up. I'd never learned to do the hustle and now no longer cared. It didn't matter that commerce and art might not mix; neither the lack of money or success was going to keep me from writing. I began to dream of moving back to the country. I couldn't have named it then, but I wanted to reclaim the life I'd glimpsed in Udo. I would dig a garden, get a dog, and maybe, finally, write a book for children.

This time it was the tree house that brought Depty Dawg back. It had begun to nag me actually: here was rich, unmapped creative territory waiting to be charted. In the summer of '88 I began work on a new script. *Living in the Woods in a Tree* was intended to be a comedy about hippies in a tree house, but along the way something else happened: it became a whimsical dream-play I would title *Udo*.

The story of a woman caught—literally—between two worlds, the plot was unconcerned with realism. As the play unfolded, it insisted on mirroring myth, taking shape as a homespun recasting of Demeter the corn goddess and her daughter Persephone.

In the original Greek myth, Hades, Lord of the Dead, carries Persephone away to his netherworld, and Demeter's grief for her stolen child causes the earth to wither. She demands the girl's return, but Hades has already persuaded his young bride to eat seven pomegranate seeds, whose magical properties bind her to him. Over time (and with divine intervention), Persephone learns to move between the two worlds. When she is with her mother, the earth blooms as spring and summer; her inevitable return to Hades brings on autumn's decline and winter.

The myth resonated for me in other ways. Persephone is queen of Hades' timeless underworld, and so possesses Aphrodite's beauty box, a legacy from the goddess of love. Sexual love was a kind of death, a slipping of boundaries, a letting-go of self. So what if—like Wanda at the Mill—Persephone had fallen for her captor? She need not live apart from the love she was capable of giving, if only she could learn to travel gracefully between differing realms.

In the fantasy play, our Udo became the setting for Hades' nether region, his palace the wall-less tree house beside a murmuring stream. The Hades character, named Fewell, sprang from Depty Dawg, with a bit of Ben the warlock thrown in. Fewell is an immortal fool with a mythical birth, conceived on a stalled tractor in a freshly plowed field. He describes the moment of his conception: *Mama kept yelling, "More fuel! More fuel!" Daddy was a horned owl; she made hats. I got my affinity for feathers from her.*

Fewell has the mystical ability to move between worlds. His troublesome presence in the human realm is blamed for ills like sour milk, warts and bunions, broken hearts and bounced checks. Now his abduction of Virginia—the daughter of wealthy grain merchant Cornelia Fuller—is wreaking havoc in both worlds. Until her daughter is returned to her, Cornelia has cut off all wheat production and innocent people are beginning to starve.

The opening scene of the play takes place moments after Fewell has kidnapped Virginia from a bus stop in her sensible world. There she lived a conventional life; controlled by her powerful matriarch she often felt invisible. Stolen away to Udo, she insists on being taken back to her mother, her vehemence a smoke screen for her intense attraction to her captor.

Don't you date? she asks Fewell.

Warlocks don't date.

He has bewitched her. Pomegranates keep showing up in Virginia's purse, signifying, Fewell tells her, indissoluble marriage, everlasting bonds. Her capture was not a moment's whim. He had spied on her for months, till one moonlit night when he crept into her yard and stole her footprint.

Here is where it begins to get weird. These are the facts: when I began work on *Udo*, I had had no contact with Blaze for at least eight years. Knowing nothing of his life—least of all that it would soon be over—I modeled Fewell after a Lord of the Dead. I wrote of enduring marriage, unbreakable bonds, of a man who puts a spell on a woman. All this might seem obvious now, but I didn't make the connection then. I was simply following the play where it wanted to go.

Looking at the script in hindsight, even my skepticism begins to feel like empty bravado. What am I to make of this web of happenstance I find us caught in, so that even in death the force of his life holds me still? For years I kept his ponytail hidden away in a box. Despite my emotional amnesia, part of him remained—a talisman like pomegranate seeds—binding me to him, no matter what.

Myth proved an accurate mirror. Last fall, when I pulled *Udo* out for the first time in at least a decade, along with the first act, I discovered notes of other elements I intended to weave into the play. Among them were the names of two pools in Hades' hidden world: the Pool of Lethe or forgetfulness, and the Pool of Memory.

Average souls, it was believed, drank from Lethe, preferring to forget the life they had lived. More enlightened souls chose to drink from Memory and so spent eternity reliving their lives.

Forgetting is less fraught than remembering, but both extract a price. Memory encompasses pain and regret; forgetfulness relinquishes sorrow, as well as beauty, mystery, joy.

51

Lord of the Dead

D elving into Blaze's life has let him back into mine. Delving into his death will make it mine too; I've inherited it belatedly. Like an octoroon of violence, I now carry his fate in my blood.

Kevin drives me past the house in South Austin where his shooting occurred fourteen years ago. The drab, mustard-colored bungalow is shutdown, blinds drawn across every window, the brown untended lawn an advertisement for permanent limbo. We get out of the van and step across the sidewalk into the yard.

A patch of tiny white lilies blossoms in the grass, delicate as smoke. Kevin spreads his hands above the flowers. "Supposedly this is where Blaze lay bleeding after he was wounded."

And yet they came up white.

I crouch to breathe in the lilies. Pushing my palms into the earth, I try to picture the place as it would have looked in early February 1989. A sixty-six-year-old black man named Concho lived here then, an indelible fixture of this rundown neighborhood, except for a brief time in the mid-'40s when he went away to war. In 1949—the same year Mike Fuller was born—Concho would father a boy. Thirty-nine years later, his son Carey would fatally shoot Blaze Foley in the front room of this house.

By now I've read the newspaper accounts, police records, even Blaze's autopsy report. I wish I didn't know how much his brain weighed, or the condition of his heart. In trying to patch together a version of his last night, I don't claim to have a knack for unraveling truth from fiction. Only that you can't begin to know the shape of someone's life unless you try to understand their death.

It would be impossible to pinpoint the moment when Blaze moved inexorably toward his end. For continuity's sake I'll go back a year, to the final months of 1987. With some money in his pocket from the release of "If I Could Only Fly," Blaze rented a room in a house a few blocks down from Concho. The place was a way station for wayward musicians, a raucous hub where he and his friends played music and cavorted at all hours, much like the old days at Waller, with far fewer rules.

Blaze had a home, a little cash, some new possibilities for his career. He was a professional songwriter, with potential albums of his own in the making and a European tour in the works. Two decades of hard living had slowed him down. He no longer wandered as much, especially since his obstreperous behavior damaged longtime ties with friends in Georgia. After a particularly disruptive visit in the summer of '87, some of his Whitesburg pals had driven him down to New Orleans, dropped him off, and told him not to come back. Their last image of their old friend Depty Dawg would be of heavy, bearded Blaze Foley, sitting atop a stack of Muscle Shoals albums, shooting them the finger as they drove away.

In Austin you often hear that there were two Blaze Foleys: the sober, kind-hearted samaritan, and the ranting, vicious drunk. And you had to know them both, I'm told, to know him at all. Despite his rough exterior, he was still gentlemanly to women, kind and considerate to the elderly and the very young. Some say children took his true measure; they trusted him as a gentle clown, a Paul Bunyan-sized hero.

To certain friends, Blaze admitted he was growing weary. The job of creating a legend had proved exhausting and mostly unsatisfying. The Scriptural teachings of generosity, compassion, and tolerance had never deserted him, though they were underscored by a fury that had broken loose in the last years. Like his Pentecostal grandfather, he could breathe fire and brimstone; but whereas Grandpa preached the One Way, his grandson spread the gospel of All Ways. He remained a BAMAPHD, a Doctor of Diversity. Even as he spoke of reaccepting Christ as his personal Savior, he never failed to defend the myriad ways Beauty could be realized.

The inequities of the world had always pained him; now he was obsessed with them. He'd lived so long on the fringes of society, he couldn't bear the suffering of outcasts. Critical of the fortunate and the ruthless, he railed at the divisions between rich and poor, long after his friends begged him to shut up.

Among the street people of South Austin, whose haunts he often shared, Blaze Foley had acquired a mystical cast. The Duct Tape Messiah, it was whispered, was willing to die for others' sins.

Almost every day the old man hobbled up and down the street to buy a bottle of Thunderbird at the corner store. Concho was frail but lively, despite a recently broken hip. His route always took him by a house that had changed hands many times in the years he'd lived on this block. Nowadays a bunch of ragtag musicians often played in the yard. The music was funky and sometimes beautiful. Concho would stop on the sidewalk to listen and tap his foot. One day, a scruffy musician—a big guy with a limp—invited him to join them. After that, Concho started bringing his bottle and hanging out.

On Lost John's Outhouse outtakes, there's a cut of Blaze imitating Concho's gentle accent and addled quirks of speech. Listening to his affectionate mimicry, I can guess the kinship that drew him to the old man. I can see them drinking and laughing; maybe Blaze told Concho about his half-black Jewish girlfriend. He might have even showed him a picture of the tree house where they'd lived thirteen years before, when he was a hippie musician by the name of Depty Dawg.

Then came the day Concho was in the yard with Blaze, listening to music, and was spied there by his son. Carey was a small man, blunted by anger. He didn't like the idea of his daddy hanging out with *peckerwoods*, his word for whites. He made Concho get up and go home. The way the son handled the father disturbed Blaze; he would have to keep an eye on that old man.

Carey had been staying at his father's house on and off for the last three years, ever since his final release from prison. Recently he'd been holding down a job with the Texas Home Health Agency, taking care of his disabled daddy. Carey hadn't spent much time around his old man before this. His mother still lived somewhere in Austin, but he and his younger brother had mostly been raised by their grandparents. And Carey had spent much of his grown years in jail for dealing drugs.

The son would be at the house when Blaze started coming by in a borrowed car, to take Concho to grocery shop or cash a check. The old man's Social Security and veterans' benefits arrived the first of the month. He confided to Blaze that his son was stealing his money, had the bruises to show where Carey hit him if he refused to hand over his checks. Blaze cautioned Carey to leave his father alone; Carey countered that Blaze was trying to steal his job.

Their stand-off erupted in August of '88, when Carey accused Blaze of assault. The police arrived to find Blaze and an unidentified person sitting on Concho's porch, holding axe handles with ends wrapped in black tape. Blaze told the cops that Carey had pulled a knife on him, that he'd responded by hitting Carey with the axe handle. Both men were jailed.

At Carey's trial a year later, a friend of Blaze's would testify that he heard Carey warn Blaze to stop interfering with him and his daddy—or else he would get killed. Blaze didn't seem to give much weight to Carey's threats. The feud continued. Blaze would spend his last Christmas in jail for fighting with Carey, getting out just in time to make the Outhouse tapes.

January 31, 1989, was a day of skirmishes between the sworn enemies. Concho's neighbors heard the commotion in his house, saw the cops arrive to break it up. When the police departed for the last time, Carey would later report, Blaze ran him off again, insisting it was Concho's house and that the son had no business being there.

Blaze left sometime around midnight. Shortly after, Carey snuck back in and loaded a rifle, leaning it against the backroom wall. Blaze returned at five in the morning. He was driving a blue '68 Suburban he'd borrowed without asking from a friend. He'd been drinking and likely doing speed. It was the first of the month and he would be there in the morning when the old man's checks arrived.

Earlier that night he'd played a set at The Hole in the Wall, a rare occurrence those days. Moving on to the Austin Outhouse, he drank at the bar till someone made an anti-Arab slur and Blaze went ballistic. Shown the door, he headed downtown, stopping to buy a chrysanthemum from a vendor on Sixth Street. It's said that he stood on the sidewalk for over an hour, twirling the flower between his fingers, expounding on the nature of the universe, before going on to Concho's.

In the front room that served as the old man's bedroom, Blaze found him in bed with Juanita, a lady friend who sometimes came to call. The three got to drinking and chatting. Blaze had drawn some pictures in a small blue notebook he'd brought to show to Concho.

Carey was trying to sleep in the back bedroom; he, too, had been drinking. The headlights from the Suburban shone in his window, rousing him. The front door opened. Getting up, he went into Concho's room to see who had come in.

Finding Blaze there with his father, Carey began to yell, "Get this pecker-wood out of my house! I ain't ever killed a peckerwood before!" He turned the corner back into his bedroom, grabbed the rifle, and came out with it.

From this point on, accounts diverge. Concho would later testify that Blaze was sitting peacefully beside his bed, showing him the pictures in the blue notebook. Carey would insist that he picked up the gun only after Blaze brandished a broom handle, hit him with it, and kicked him in the leg. He said he fired a warning shot before the fatal one.

Yet another account—this one repeated secondhand—describes the moment when Carey appeared in the room with the gun. Blaze dropped the broom handle and was backing out the door with his hands up when Carey pulled the trigger.

It's not hard to imagine any, or all, of these scenes; they've been woven into the night's mythology. The one indisputable fact is that Blaze had been mortally wounded. Fleeing into the yard, he lay face down in the grass beside the blue Suburban. One version says he chased Carey up and down the street, but given his weight and the hole in his chest, that seems unlikely.

By his own testimony, after the shooting Carey ran out the back door and threw the rifle over the fence into a neighbor's backyard. Then he knocked on her door. "Call the police," he told her. "There's a white guy in my yard who's bleeding."

It was almost dawn by the time the cops arrived. Blaze had always had a contentious relationship with the law; now it would be policemen who accompanied and recorded the events of his last hours. He was still conscious, still clutching the blue notebook. The bullet hole under his left armpit was leaking profusely.

The sky was turning silver. Two ambulances and a fire truck pulled up to the yard, lights and sirens going. The paramedics couldn't find Blaze's pulse or register his blood pressure. He was taken to Brackenridge Hospital, Austin's trauma center.

In the ambulance, rumor has it, he pleaded with the medics, "Please don't let me die."

As Blaze was being rushed to the hospital, two officers went into the house with Carey. Juanita had already fled. There was blood on Concho's mattress. One cop went with Carey to the back room to get some ID, while the other stayed with Concho. The old man told the officer that the two younger men had been arguing, that he'd witnessed Carey shoot Blaze.

Carey was handcuffed and booked. "Can I lock my back door?" he asked repeatedly. "Who's going to lock my back door?"

A Winchester, lever-action, blue-steel .22-caliber rifle was found in the neighbor's yard. Police also discovered a .22 shell casing on the floor by Concho's bed, and another unfired .22 round in Carey's bedroom.

In the Brackenridge emergency room Blaze went into full cardiac arrest. An ER team performed emergency CPR, and he was sent up to surgery. By then Carey was at the police station, having his rights read to him. After making his official confession, he opted not to sign it.

Word of Blaze's death arrived three hours later. Carey was charged with intentional murder, a first-degree felony, and his bail was set at $25,000.

Blaze had not survived the surgery. The bullet had traversed his abdominal aorta and lodged in his liver. The artery was not repaired in time, and he bled out the puncture wounds in it.

He lived fourteen thousand, two hundred, and eighty-nine days.

52

Duct Tape Messiah

T he morning of Blaze Foley's funeral was stinging cold in Austin. Stunned by his dramatic exit, his friends had worked tirelessly to get the money for his coffin, and a plot to bury it in. The coroner released his body to his good friend, drummer Leland Waddell, for $600. Leland knew a woman who ran an escort service, and her girls sold sexual favors, drugs, and T-shirts—anything to get Blaze Foley in the ground.

A benefit was held at the Austin Outhouse where there was talk of duct-taping Blaze to the door so he could attend. His friends needed to raise $1600 in order to carry out the services necessary to make Blaze presentable, much less portable. And right up to the moment the funeral began, total strangers were donating what they could to help pay for Blaze's casket.

In the chapel, the lyrics to "If I Could Only Fly" were duct-taped to his coffin. His beard was trimmed; he was dressed out in his Pope's robe. As variously described, the Pope's robe was either a smoking jacket with flashy lapels, a green Sergeant Pepper-type tunic, or a full-length red cape. Many can recall Blaze sweeping down a South Austin sidewalk wearing a long cape and a Ronald Reagan mask. Whatever its form, his Pope's robe would be just the thing to wear to meet his Maker, minus the mask of course. God forbid Blaze Foley should be mistaken in Heaven for a Republican.

His memorial service was hugely attended, much to the funeral home's surprise. Crowds of mourners stood outside the chapel while inside, bereaved friends spoke out their remembrances of the Duct Tape Messiah: the devoted artist, the political firebrand, the generous and demanding comrade. Before the service ended, Blaze's body was taken out of the home. The joke went around the room like wildfire: kicked out of every bar in Austin, he'd now been bounced from his own funeral.

The procession of cars and trucks started south toward Live Oak Cemetery—except nobody knew where it was. There'd barely been enough money to bury him, let alone hire a police escort, though the thought of cops accompanying Blaze's remains to their final resting place seemed both ironic and apropos. The roads were icy that morning; lost vehicles making U-turns skidded off the highway. While some cars waited at a red light, here came others from the opposite direction, retracing their tracks. The line of vehicles zigged and zagged before finding its way to the old paupers' cemetery at the edge of town.

A plot had been purchased in the open part of the graveyard where there was nothing to stop the wind. At his gravesite, women keened; the service was chaotic with no preacher to lead the rites. Kimmie Rhodes, the young singer who had backed Blaze on his last studio album, began to sing "Amazing Grace." Her strong clear voice rose above the barren field, gathering other voices before the wind carried the notes away.

As the casket was being lowered, someone remembered the duct tape. The mourners converged in a frenzy, sealing the coffin with layers of silver tape. Bibles, picks, and capos were tossed into the grave where Mike Fuller's body was at last laid to rest.

Late that afternoon in New York City, I received a call from LaNelle in Waco; we hadn't spoken in years. I'd just come in from the first public reading of Act 1 of *Udo*, and now here was the phone ringing, and LaNelle's Texas twang on the line.

"I have bad news," she announced. "Depty Dawg is dead."

"What?" I sank into a chair. "Oh my God."

"I don't know much about it," she went on tonelessly. "Only that he was trying to break up a fight in a bar and one of the brawlers pulled out a gun and shot him."

"Oh my God."

LaNelle's voice broke. "Sybil, I am so sorry."

Moments later, I spoke to Billy in Whitesburg; he and I hadn't talked in a long time either. The phone was out at Waller, so Zonko Joe in New Orleans had called Billy with the news. It was late at night, but Billy had gone down immediately to tell Glyn in person. Only two years had passed since Glyn's stepson, Greg, had been killed by a drunk driver, and now here was another tragic blow for the Waller community.

The night Billy and I spoke, he told me that the circumstances of Blaze's death had instantly elevated him to folk-hero status in Austin. It was like we were talking about someone I'd never met, and in a sense I guess that was true. I hadn't known Blaze Foley, not really; I'd been present for his birth, and then he was gone. The first I heard of Willie Nelson and Merle Haggard recording "If I Could Only Fly" was from Billy that night on the phone. But I had known Depty Dawg, and if I knew anything, it was that he had wanted to be a legend. Now, at the very least, he had gotten his wish.

Yet all I could do was repeat, "Billy, he's dead. I can't believe he's dead."

Before he said good-bye, Billy remarked, "I really do think the tree house was the happiest time of his life."

Somewhere in my confusion I wondered how he knew that.

After our conversation, I dug out Depty's letters and his ponytail, and held them to me, pacing the apartment, trying to absorb that this was final, this was the whole of his life. Not even the fact that I was writing about the tree house at the time could pierce the shock. The cap I'd put on my feelings for him was sealed tight by his violent end. I was too compacted for tears, too numbed by forgetting for grief.

Little did I know then his death would not be the end of the story.

53

Fathers and Sons

N ot even the trial of his killer eight months later would be the end of the story. And for many Blaze Foley fans, Carey's verdict of not-guilty remains an unhealed injustice. His trial began on Monday; by Thursday it was over. It took three days of testimony, and less than two hours of deliberation, for the ten-woman, two-man jury to reach a unanimous conclusion: the accused was acquitted in the shooting death of Michael David Fuller, a.k.a. Blaze Foley, on the grounds of self-defense.

When the jury's decision was read in the courtroom, Blaze's friends protested aloud, shocked and outraged. Storming from the room, they blamed the lawyers, the police, the system itself. I lack the expertise or the objectivity to draw conclusions about the outcome, though I can state with some certainty that it's not often a black man gets acquitted for the murder of a white man in Texas.

Of the two eyewitnesses to the shooting, Juanita disappeared the night of the crime, and Concho now is dead. At Carey's trial, he would testify against his son, maintaining that Carey had no reason to shoot Blaze that night. Even so, the prosecution was unable to convict Carey.

On the stand, the father stuck to his story that Blaze's death had been unprovoked, contradicting what he'd told police the night of the shooting, that Blaze and his son had been arguing. Under oath, he reiterated that Blaze was sitting by his bed, peaceably showing him drawings in the blue notebook when Carey came in with the gun. Perhaps it was all the old man could think to do to stand up for the friend who had stood up for him.

The physical evidence supported Concho's story. An autopsy revealed that the bullet had entered Blaze's body at a fifteen-degree, downward angle. Since Carey was a smaller man than Blaze, it would seem that he had to be standing above Blaze when he fired. There were bloodstains on the mattress, and Blaze was still holding the blue notebook when the police found him in the yard.

Yet the prosecution was sunk from the get-go. Asked to point out his son in the courtroom, Concho couldn't do it. He didn't recognize the clean-shaven man in a coat and tie sitting at the defense attorney's table. Carey's lawyer then proceeded to punch holes in all the old man's assertions, and in closing, referred to Concho as "the world's most reliable drunk."

Then Carey was called to the stand. He testified that Blaze had frightened him, that he'd feared for his life. On cross-examination, the prosecution exposed all the different versions of the shooting Carey had given since the night. At one point Carey told the police that he and Blaze had struggled for the gun and that he fired a warning shot before the fatal blast. A spent .22 round was found in the rifle, though the neighbor would claim she heard only one shot. And there was no sign of a struggle in Concho's house, and no second bullet hole.

Canceling out the father and son's testimonies left the stage open for the defense's most persuasive argument: its portrayal of Blaze Foley. He was painted as derelict, and therefore dangerous, an assumption Carey's lawyer dramatized by slamming an axe handle down on the bench, making the jury jump in their seats. Emphasizing Blaze's height and weight, he exhibited a mortuary photo of the victim's body, wider than the gurney that supported it. The women on the jury shuddered. No doubt they harbored the same prophetic fears Blaze had satirized in "Wouldn't That Be Nice?" In his final statement Carey's lawyer mused that Foley's demeanor reminded him of a country song that went, "You don't tug on Superman's cape, you don't spit in the wind, you don't pull the mask off the Lone Ranger, and you don't threaten Blaze Foley."

Well—it *is* Texas.

The prosecution had no comeback for that. Hard-pressed to find any friend or fan of the victim who could honestly say they'd never seen Blaze Foley drunk or out of control, the last thing the D.A. wanted to bring up in court were Blaze's addictions and the legendary belligerence they could foster. With no mention of Blaze's talent or his musical contributions, Carey's lawyer was able to suggest that his life, as portrayed, didn't amount to much. Fame might have lent him stature but to the jurors' minds, his obscurity equaled lack of talent. After all, this was the '80s, when artists' motives were suspect. By the end the jury may have seen Blaze as they saw Carey—poor and of no consequence. In the trial for his life, Carey's color became a non-issue, and Blaze's rants about class distinction became a self-fulfilling prophecy.

I'm not arguing for or against the verdict. It makes a certain bizarre sense that Blaze's death would play out as surprisingly as his life. For some, sending Carey back to prison might have cauterized the wound of Blaze's death, but would it have healed the pain of his life? True or not, the image of him backing out the door with his hands up haunts me still. Did he know in that moment that this time he'd gone too far? His departure illuminates the contradictions he couldn't see in himself: the compassionate guardian misguided by anger and alcohol, the poet-pacifist at war with the world.

I can believe Blaze was huge and terrifying in his Biblical wrath, just as I can imagine Carey self-righteously fueled in his animosity toward whites. They met at that juncture where self-hatred and racial hatred collide, another sad irony for the legend-mongers as Blaze was one of the more colorblind people I ever happened to know.

What I really think is hardest to say. There will be those who disagree, but I believe it possible that Blaze had wanted out of his life for a long time. And if not out of his life, then surely out of the pressures of his mind. In the tree house I had that single, memorable glimpse of his agony. So often I've wished I'd pursued his early remark about Thorazine. Or that moment when he admitted, *Sometimes I think I ain't glued together right.* I scan his letters for clues, and this jumps out: *I'm so glad we talked, I feel like living now.*

And there are lines in his songs where he speaks of dying. Even "Let Me Ride in Your Big Cadillac" tells of a man asking *Take me out of this old world.* In "Cold, Cold World." he had written, *I could find myself thinkin' that I'd rather be dead.*

Most telling for me are these words, found in his belongings after he died, where he links his desolation to his inability to stay still:

> I can't stay no place
> Can't stay anywhere for too long
> Even when I feel good
> I ain't been feelin' good
> Been a feelin' like dyin'
> I believe I'll be goin' away

Enemies can be useful. They can distract you from your own suffering; they can do for you what friends will not. When Blaze entered the fray between Concho and Carey, he encountered territory he already knew well. Concho's house had become a war zone; maybe it had always been one. I know virtually nothing about Concho, even less about Carey, their relationship or the lack of it. Picturing the moment when the son returned to his father's house after being acquitted—despite Concho's damning testimony or his inability to recognize his own child in court—my mind strays to another father-son scene.

This one takes place in 1971, when Edwin Fuller caught up with his youngest son in Memphis. Mike was twenty-one and already drifting. Edwin was fifty and starting to shrivel. His family had dispersed; his wife was divorcing him. Mike was all he had, and who was Mike? A cripple, a fat kid who cried easily, a loser like his old man who'd never amount to anything—

Fathers and sons, mothers and daughters: these bonds can blind us unless we see through them. I imagine a moment in Memphis when Mike finally realized he was bigger than his formidable dad. Did he do something he regretted, or bolt before he could? It may have been just one small crystallizing moment, clear enough to make him able to break away and reinvent his life.

But by then it may already have been too late. In the end Blaze turned out to be more like his father than he'd bargained for; his furies and bitterness, addictions and torments, were a reprise of Edwin's. He condemned Carey's filial rage, even as he may have intuited its power. He brushed off Carey's threats, yet he'd lived too long and hard not to know how quickly a drunken skirmish can turn lethal. Judgment skewered by alcohol and drugs, he told friends he would protect the old man, even if it killed him. This last chance to halt an abuse would offer Mike the final opportunity to be someone's good son.

And at that point maybe he no longer cared. If this was to be his end, so be it. His death would be the detail that secured his legend. I doubt that even Blaze's creative mind could have dreamed up the twist of Carey going free, but I can't say for sure.

Only that in dying, he accomplished his aims. The prophecy had come true: the Duct Tape Messiah had attained his immortality. As for protecting Concho, after his acquittal Carey received a slew of death threats and had to leave Austin—and his father—for good. It's rumored that he's living in California, an ordained minister tending to the homeless.

Your essential Greek tragedy with a fundamentalist finale: redemption for the sinner, resurrection for the dead.

54

Meeting Persephone

Jealousy is a tenacious sickness. It chokes this grief like a cancer, eating through these belated declarations of regret. The journey back to Texas was intended to heal us, but my need to claim Blaze's devotion as mine alone is only causing me more heartache. His return has reassured me that I can love and be loved, and my enlightened response to that is to hoard his affection as proof.

Tonight I'm on my way to meet Mandy Mercier, the singer/songwriter who was with Blaze for a time in the early '80s.

"Blaze fell in serious love with Mandy," Lost John had told me, grinning at the memory. "An old flame of hers came back to town and Blaze wanted to convince her not to see him. So he borrowed three bucks from me to buy her a drink."

"Really," I replied, busily arranging my face in that feigned interest I instinctively don for any conversation about Blaze's love life.

Lost John chortled with glee. Blaze had lain down in the street, calling back to Mandy on the sidewalk, "See how much I love you?" A car came along, slowed down, and drove around him. A second car did the same. The third car stopped, and two cops got out and handcuffed Blaze.

"He was still yelling, 'See how much I love you!' when they pushed him into the cop car and drove away," Lost John finished, sending them off with a wave of his hand.

"That's funny," I answered, praying he wouldn't notice how tight my smile was.

Lost John shook his head. "Son-of-a-bitch still owes me three bucks."

That smile remains pasted on my face when I enter Momo's, a funky bar in downtown Austin where Mandy is performing tonight. The upstairs is empty when we greet each other about an hour before her gig is to begin.

Dark-haired, hazel-eyed Mandy is a petite waif, not at all the kick-ass country mama I pictured her to be. In a blue silk suit that shows off her cleavage and hourglass curves, she wears boots, lots of bracelets, and bright lipstick, cherry-red.

"So," she asks right off the bat. "Are you the 'Picture Cards Can't Picture You' girl?"

"No, that was Helen," I tell her matter-of-fact, then dare to add, "I'm the 'If I Could Only Fly' girl."

Mandy closes her eyes, pops them open, and grabs my arm.

"Oh, right!" she exclaims. "Kevin told me about you. I had no idea you existed. None! That Blaze was ever married. Come on!"

She shakes her head. "I heard he had a fiancée in Houston that he wrote all those incredible love songs for. But he rarely mentioned her. He was so formal."

"His romantic code." I nod. "I know."

We stare at each other, intrigued to find this bit of Foley lore corroborated. Mandy shrugs. "I don't think Blaze ever wrote a song about me."

Awed by her lack of possessiveness, I say, "None of us could have loved him enough—"

"No," she counters. "But a lot of us tried!"

Mandy's giggle is an infectious burst that wrinkles her nose. She, too, has arrived in her fifties a single woman, and her past love affairs with several country music legends have inspired original songs like "Wild Dreams of the Shy Boys."

"So many men, so few commitments," she comments blithely.

We sit down at a table. At her request I bring out pictures of the tree house and the broom-jump trip. She gazes at them a long moment.

"I can tell you meant a lot more to Blaze than I did," she murmurs.

"Are you kidding?" I reply. "I've been so jealous of you."

Her nose creases. "I'd have been of you, except who knew you existed?" She sobers. "All I knew about the girl in Houston was that it was a pretty wild time. I always assumed he wrote 'I Should Have Been Home With You' for her."

I shake my head. "That was written in a little apartment on Castle Hill in '76."

Mandy puts her face in her hands. "Then all those love songs are to you."

A thrill of joy shoots through me. Funny how it takes another woman to verify the heart of a man.

"I never heard him sing them," I whisper.

"I did," she states.

Of the two songs Mandy wrote for Blaze after his death, "Love Is a Comet" is an exuberant account of their affair. I ask her to tell me how they met.

Her eyes glimmer. "He was performing at Emmajoe's. Everything he said made me laugh. After his set, he came over to the table and told me, 'I'm going to kidnap you.'"

I close my eyes. *Another Persephone.*

I ask about the second song, "Poison Man." "That's a pretty dark lament," I comment.

Mandy gazes at the stage. "That was about the drugs, you know? It was a thing with him, a badge of courage. You had to take them or you didn't have the nerve to be an artist."

He also got on her case for having a day job. She points to herself. "Look at me. I'm small, I'm a woman. I need a place to live, food to eat. It's a jungle out there, they weren't kidding!"

Blaze preached total commitment to one's art, even as he drove her car and let her pay for his beers. She'd come home from work, take speed, and go out to the bars with him all night.

I nod; that sounds familiar. "You know some people say Blaze was afraid of success—"

Mandy rolls her eyes. "Who isn't?"

"Exactly. So do you think that's why he sabotaged himself?"

"No." She rattles her bracelets. "I think he was going to be a legend, and he was going to do it his way and no other."

"And so what is the legend now?"

She thinks a moment. "The legend is—the legend. That it keeps growing, keeps spreading. It brought you here, didn't it?"

The constriction around my heart begins to loosen. We are what Blaze has become, manifesting him in the way we care for each other.

I take Mandy's hand. "He loved you."

Her eyes tear. "How do you know that?"

"Because. I see you. And I know him."

She exhales sharply. "But I rejected him."

"So? That's a detail. My God! I feel like I have no right to any of him—"

"Except you're the one who's come looking." Mandy picks up the photo of the tree house. "You were his wife," she says. "You are his wife."

55

Funny Valentine

M ichael David Fuller was born on December 18, *a week before Jesus,* Depty Dawg liked to say. And every year now since his death, Blaze Foley's birthday has been celebrated in Austin. Each winter the music community holds a birthday bash, collecting clothes and toys for the homeless, and honoring Blaze through his songs and through those written for and about him.

This past December, clips from the not-yet-completed Blaze Foley documentary were featured at the bash. Culled from three hundred hours of interviews, Kevin's short video looped continuously, a valentine to Mike, Depty, and Blaze. Pictures from the eras of his life were displayed, including the one of us in Udo.

December was too soon for me to leave New York, so instead I sent a potted jasmine to Texas, asking Kevin to present it at the bash however he saw fit. The plant survived the frigid journey, arriving in Austin with no blooms on it yet. The day of the party, in the confusion of preparation, it was left behind in Kevin's office. Afterwards, we agreed, its time had not yet come.

But it would be waiting for me when I arrived here in February. And it would finally bloom on February 1, the fourteenth anniversary of Blaze's death.

I couldn't make that up.

Two weeks later, it's Valentine's Day and I'm returning to Live Oak Cemetery with Kevin, Grody Mike, and the jasmine. The men have come to help me plant the blossoming vine at Blaze's grave. I've decided to surrender to the fate I've been handed and make a little myth myself. The legend continues. While I still insist I can withstand its momentum, in truth I'm Alice tumbling down the rabbit hole—startled, resistant, and fascinated by the fall.

On the way to the cemetery, the jasmine's star-shaped flowers are so heavily fragrant, we have to roll down the windows to breathe. It's warmer at the graveyard than the first time I was here, though still overcast and windy. Beyond the fence, bulls with horns full as chandeliers sit in the brown grass, thoughtfully chewing their cud. A pair of black vultures glides above the far horizon, white wrist cuffs flashing like road signs. In the older, shaded section of the cemetery, an elderly couple stoops over a grave, he tending to the ground, she reading from a Bible.

Kevin carries shovels and a rake; Grody Mike has a ten-pound bag of mulch slung over his shoulder. At Blaze's gravesite they stand with their backs to me, somber sentries pretending to watch the buzzards as I kneel again beside the black stone.

They're calling me your wife now, Dep. We're back together again. Maybe that was your intention all along.

Bending over his headstone, I'm reminded that for years only a simple metal plate marked his grave. But his friends were determined: whatever the price, Blaze Foley's stone would be black granite, the same rock that lines the Vietnam War Memorial in Washington, D.C. "Black Granite" also happens to be the title of a song Blaze sang on the album he was making when he died. Written by his friend the late Jubal Clark—another hard-living Texas troubadour—the song invokes the war memorial with the opening lines: *Black granite/so silent/cries out to us all.*

Maya Ying Lin, the monument's young designer, chose the hard, black stone to embody the impenetrable barrier between life and death. The rock is reflective; you can see your own face reading the names of the thousands of dead and missing, a mute reckoning with the waste of war.

Eight years after Blaze's funeral, his black granite headstone was finally laid in Live Oak Cemetery. Then, Jubal Clark, frail and dying of cancer, stood at Blaze's grave and sang "Black Granite" back to his martyred friend. The stone is eloquent, speaking to Blaze's heartbreaking predicament: the angry peace-lover felled on a battlefield of his own making.

Running my hand along the ebony slab, I see myself mirrored behind the titles of his songs and I know, no matter what, I cannot escape this fate. The surface between living and dying has no edge any more; it's become permeable, passed through by the urgent need to reach beyond death to find him. He lies beneath me in his duct tape cocoon, metamorphosing into a bright, wingéd myth.

Depty, I don't know if I'll ever see your death as heroic, but I'd like to believe your life was. Some say you wasted it—and it's true you never overcame your losses or reversed the madness you had to live out. But the thing is, honey, you could love—and you knew it. You knew how to keep both joy and sorrow alive inside you, something I am learning only now, from you.

In his silence hangs the unanswerable question: has the path I took away from him been worth it? Yes. Maybe. I don't know. I only know that I've become more willing to look at my own life honestly. I've had an encounter with madness; I have limitations and blind spots, selfishness and addictions too. My touted skepticism is really its inverse, a heightened romanticism that acts as a buffer, keeping intimacy at bay. A solitary life may be my nature but it has also been my choice.

Dep, maybe I'll never stop wondering what would have happened if you and I had stayed together. Maybe I'll always want it to come out right. But in the end it doesn't matter. The road I took is the one that brought me here.

I stand and pick up a shovel. Kevin and Grody Mike turn from their patient guard. We decide where to plant the jasmine beside the headstone. But before we can put a spade into the earth, the old man is hurrying through the graveyard, arms flopping like a scarecrow.

"You can't dig in here," he yells, bounding over.

Up close, the skin of his face is taut against the bones, smooth as glass, his eyes a pale, watery blue.

Hands on my hips, I ask him, "And how do you know this?"

The old man pushes his cap off his forehead, panting from his sprint across the grounds. "Because. I run the place. And it's against the rules."

Taking in my tear-stained face, his angles soften. "I'm sorry, ma'am. Can't bury nothing here but bodies."

Well, I'd wondered about that. Surely death has its rules, same as life. Blaze's myth has its rules too. I suspect I'll be learning them for the rest of my life.

Beyond the man's bony shoulder, I see the door of his battered pick-up swung open. His wife sits in the front seat, gazing at the longhorns. It's reassuring to know that someone besides the buzzards is looking after the place.

"All right," I concede and smile. "Thanks for telling us."

"That's okay, that's my job. Bless you for your troubles, ma'am."

He dips his cap, gets in his truck, and drives away. Turning to my friends, I throw up my hands. "So much for legend-making."

Kevin gathers up the tools. Grody takes the bag of mulch back to the car. And I leave the jasmine as I leave my sorrow, beside Blaze's grave to whatever fate awaits it.

Part 4

Small Town Hero

56

True North

~~~~~~

My weeks in Austin have left me with a few answers and still more questions. Like an onion, there are innumerable layers of Blaze to peel back; I realize now there will never be an end to them. Yet someday, anyway, I will have to let go.

Meanwhile I have one last stop in Texas. This morning I'm on a north-bound bus to Athens, where Blaze's younger sister, Marsha, lives. We haven't seen each other since 1976 and frankly, I'm nervous about our visit. The botched attempt at mythmaking in the cemetery was a wry reminder. The fates may be free to pronounce me Blaze's wife, but I've no idea what his evangelical Christian family would have to say about that.

The bus leaves Austin behind. Above the freeway, vultures wheel on tilted wings. Myself, I'm done with scavenging; I just want to go home, wherever that is. To find the past, I had to shed the present. I've given up the house in the Catskills, any means of income, and all certainty about the future. Don't get me wrong: I've been lucky. As I ricocheted between New York, Georgia, and Texas, family and friends have caught me every step of the way. In a world where war clamors, the earth sickens, and hunger abounds, I have had the luxury of dallying with a ghost.

Blaze, too, lived by the generosity of others. Though I've always managed to keep a roof over my head, I, like him, have had trouble staying still. Now, home can no longer be determined by coordinates on a map or shelter or even habit. Instead it can only be found by an internal compass, magnetically drawn to some kind of authenticity, to an innate wildness that can be neither charted nor contained, not even in words. I'll always be tumbleweed so long as I look for anchoring anywhere but within.

Seeking such elusive harbor, I left New York City in 1990, the year after Blaze was killed in Texas. My dog, Larue, became home then; with her I was safe wherever we landed in our meandering life. In the Hudson Valley of upstate New York, she led me unerringly back to the woods. Together we roved the bony cliffs of Shawangunk Mountain, watching the turkey vultures soar above and below us. They flew so close, I could almost feel the updraft of their sailing glide. It was there I became enamored of the huge birds, and was moved to write about them. I'd never seen such enormous wings, nor imagined such effortless flight.

The return to rural life coincided with a wave of good fortune. I brought with me a file of letters from theaters around the country regarding *Brink of Devotion*, rejection notices tempered with praise, the epitome of bittersweet. In a little house on Rondout Creek, I knuckled down for a six-month stint as a writer on a daytime soap opera, an experience I can only compare to having a low-grade fever all the time. There I began a novel for young readers, *Speed of Light*, that contained the refrain, sung by the congregation of an African-American church: *I am going to a city/Where the roses never fade/Here they bloom but for a season/Soon their beauty is decayed/I am going to a city/Where the roses never fade.*

The book's publication would take me into classrooms around the country, talking to kids about writing. Mostly they are intrigued by the process of transmuting life into fiction.

"How does a story happen?" they want to know.

"It's a mystery," I tell them. "You have to trust what arises."

From the bus window I see the vultures climbing higher and higher in the blue Texas sky, naked red heads gleaming in the midday light. Below their black-and-silver lapels, the fringes of the highways are once more in bloom with early spring wildflowers.

The bus pulls off at a wayside gas station, which is also the local stop, and a lanky, gray-haired man gets on, plunking down in the seat beside me. His bag—an ice cooler wrapped with bungee cords—doesn't fit in the overhead rack. Finally he shoves it under his feet, apologizing in a mild, cross-eyed manner each time he jostles me.

The bus turns back onto the interstate. "I been traveling a long while," the man explains, grabbing for the cooler as it slides into the aisle. "All the way from Florida. But I'm going to see my wife in Texarkana now, so that's all right."

He stuffs the cooler back under the seat, then folds his arms over his knees. "I'm just going to sit here and think about her," he adds.

"That sounds like a good plan," I reply, studiously avoiding eye contact.
He cocks his head heavenward. "Any special prayer requests?"
Startled, I shake my head. "What do you pray for, sir?"
He bows his head. "I say, 'Lord, carry me safely home.'"
Leaning back, I smile and close my eyes. "That works for me, thank you."
"Back at you," he says.

57

Christian Ladies

Marsha and I share a similar history with her brother. The last time she saw Mike was in 1978. She was pregnant with her second child, whom she would name for her favorite saint. Today her son, Paul, is twenty-five; he never met his uncle.

I learned all this when Marsha and I spoke on the phone in December, a few weeks before I left New York for Texas. She told me then that after Paul's birth, she'd fallen into a tortured run of addiction and crime, ending up in prison twice. Each time she'd held to the belief that Jesus would one day free her from this self-created hell. She read the New Testament over and over until its message was seared on her heart: *I Am The Way.* There'd be more pain and more backsliding, but eventually her faith would prevail over the familial urge to self-destruct.

Released from prison for the last time in 1991, she called her mother, Louise, only to learn that her older sister, Pat, had committed suicide, and her brother Mike had been murdered. Her sister's death did not surprise her; Pat had a history of harming herself. But the loss of the beloved older brother she never really knew was a vast, unforeseen grief. They'd disappeared from each other's life, but she always expected to see him again. So many times she'd thought to take Paul and go find him. She never did.

After that phone conversation, Louise sent Marsha a video of Blaze singing "If I Could Only Fly," produced in Austin in '88. He looked heavy and inert, so different from the lean, energetic man she'd last seen. And for the longest time, that was all she had of him. Then, one day in the late '90s, a friend called to say that a local songwriter named Ricky Cardwell was going down to Austin to record a tribute CD for Blaze Foley. Marsha called Ricky right away and introduced herself as Blaze's sister. Ricky cried over the phone. He'd known her brother since 1976, when he was still going by the name Depty Dawg. I didn't recall meeting Ricky then, but his friendship with Dep had endured into the '80s; he and Blaze Foley had shared gigs in Austin. Ricky couldn't believe he was talking to Blaze's sister—didn't even know Blaze had a sister.

That was the beginning of Marsha's regathering her brother to her life, an act of synchronicity she ascribes to the Lord. In the years since, the Austin music community has showered her with Blaze mementoes. She now owns a little red Airline acoustic guitar he once played, and in a wooden box keeps the many snapshots and whatnots given to her by his friends and fans. Before arriving in Texas, I'd sent her a picture of Depty and me from the tree house days. Now I'm bringing her a letter, signed by Blaze in October of '76, where he writes: *Keep in touch with Marsha and tell her I love her and some day I will help make it easier for her.*

Marsha and I greet each other shyly. After all, it's been decades, and even then our contact was brief. At forty-eight, she has settled gracefully into her skin. There's a gravity about her now, as if weighted by a sorrow she has long accepted. Her likeness to her brother is unchanged: tall frame, sleek hair, chicory-blue eyes, a diamond-sharp energy. She wears blue jeans and a tie-dye T-shirt, the word *"Redeemed"* tattooed in quotes on her ankle.

Marsha lives outside Athens in a trailer set in scrub-oak woods along a rutted road. An elegant, screened-in wooden porch spills off the front door, a wedding present from her third husband, Tom. Two dogs greet me as I arrive, as do four cats with no tails, hummingbirds thrumming at feeders, and a star jasmine flowering in the yard.

Married for four years, Tom and Marsha appear to be crazy about each other. He's a robust patriarch in his late sixties with the quiet assurance of a happily married man. Tom's a clown too; sticking cotton balls up his nose, he waits for me to notice. Both are active in the local Christian community, and keep a small trailer on their property for any pilgrim with nowhere to be. Marsha is still considered something of a renegade, since she smokes cigarettes and hasn't lost her taste for beer. For a time she conducted a prison ministry for incarcerated and newly released women, many of whom spent their first nights of freedom on Marsha's living room couch.

This afternoon, two of her grandchildren play on the swings in the dusty grass. Carlin Praise and Luke—ages five and three—are Paul's children. Her daughter Stephanie is thirty-four now and the mother of two boys, James and Jacob.

"We'll go see them tomorrow," Marsha promises me. "Stephanie remembers Blaze. She wants to meet you."

The children's mother, Mandy, comes forward with a beatific countenance and long, rippling mermaid's hair. I'm eager to meet Paul too, as everyone in Austin has told me how much he looks and sounds like the uncle he never knew.

Marsha thinks it unlikely he'll come around. Her face crumples. "Paul has lost his way."

Estranged from Mandy and his kids, he's taken to disappearing for long stretches of time. Seems he's inherited the same torments that have plagued the Fuller men for three generations.

"And not just the men," Marsha allows, a cryptic nod to her own regretful record of instability.

We watch her grandbabies race around the yard, their mother in pursuit. The little boy tries to eat a rock and cries when it's taken away.

"They're wild today," Marsha declares. "They're missing their daddy." She sighs. "Come on," she says. "There's someone else for you to meet."

Louise Fuller Hacker is eighty-three years old. I'd written to Depty's mother last fall, but when I didn't hear back from her, I figured maybe she had no desire to meet me. But now here she is—still girlishly pretty with a cumulous cloud of white hair, fleshy arms, and playful blue-green eyes—sitting on Marsha's porch, waiting for us.

As we come in the door, she pushes herself out of her chair to take hold of my hands.

"I'm so glad to meet someone who was so close to Mike," she says, pronouncing it *My-ike,* with a lyrical cadence so familiar, it brings on sudden tears.

Marsha calls her brother Blaze now, and she is so like him in body and in spirit that I never tire of looking at her.

She catches my gaze and winks. "Who do you see now? Me or Blaze?"

"I see both of you."

"And do you see Jesus too?"

Jesus has been Marsha's life for as long as she can remember. Her maternal grandfather was a severe-looking Man of God with a snowy Old Testament beard. Grandpa Underwood was a musician too, playing the fiddle at revivals across Arkansas and Georgia. He and his wife, Grace, bestowed on Louise and her twelve siblings the gift of song, a talent they in turn would pass on to a whole generation of harmonizing cousins.

"All my children could sing like angels," Louise informs me, matter-of-fact. "Mike could blend his voice with anyone, close and just beautiful."

"I know," I tell her. "He even made me sound good."

We've easily found common ground, talking about her son under the ceiling fans in the porch's welcome shade. Soon after her third child, Michael David, arrived in Arkansas, Louise picked up her growing family and moved to San Antonio, Texas. Marsha wasn't born when Mike contracted polio, but she and her mother agree it was the Lord that brought him through.

Louise chuckles at his memory. "Mike always was a chunky little thing. Lying in his crib, grabbing at the milk bottle."

Her brow creases. "Then one day he couldn't hold it no more."

She tried putting the bottle in his hand, but it dropped every time. The doctor diagnosed polio. Seven-month-old Mike was admitted to the hospital for eight weeks.

"That was the hardest thing I ever had to do," Louise quavers. "Leaving him there, naked as the day he was born. In isolation."

"Isolation?" I echo.

This new information falls on me like ice. An infant left alone in a strange place, sick and separated from his mother; he was too young to be so lonely.

Louise's hands play absently with a dry tissue. "Uh-huh. For a week or so at first. The nurses saw him of course. And when I come to visit him—why, he acted like he didn't know me. His own mother."

After a few weeks Mike was deemed no longer contagious and moved to a ward with other polio-stricken kids. There, a teenage patient named Marilee befriended him. She painted the baby's toenails red, and they had their picture taken for the San Antonio paper. Marilee had a feeling this child would grow up to be someone special, and she and Louise wrote to each other for years after he was declared well enough to go home.

"Mike told me he was the first one to be cured in Arkansas," I tell her, unaware that I'm already using his childhood name or that my vowels have just gone flatter than a duck's instep.

Louise's eyes flash with merriment. "Nope. Texas. And he weren't the first."

"Ooh, that rascal!"

"And the only reminder?" A born storyteller, his mother holds tight to the tale. "Was that short left leg. Right, Marsha? Mike was a happy-go-lucky kid, wasn't he? Always playing the clown."

His sister agrees. "We was dirt poor. Never had a lot of toys. My brother could make a game out of nothing but a button and some thread."

For years the family crisscrossed the South in pursuit of Edwin, settling for brief periods in Georgia, Arkansas, and Texas. The one constant in their lives was Jesus. He was with them wherever they went, and His name was spoken in song.

Marsha draws on her cigarette. "It was Mother. She was all the time singing 'round the house. Always had the radio tuned to bluegrass and gospel."

Louise clenches a hand above her heart. "I feel the Lord," she cries. "And He makes me feel music. I can't help it. I'm a Christian lady."

"I hope you'll sing for me sometime," I venture.

Marsha's eyes light up. "Any requests?"

"Really? Now?" I think a moment. "Well—Mike used to sing this song—'Where the Roses Never Fade'?"

"That was my daddy's favorite," his sister remarks without expression.

"Mike sang that to you?" Louise is delighted. "Well, bless his heart."

Marsha stubs out her cigarette, closes her eyes, and begins to croon in a low resonant voice: *I am going to a city where the streets with gold are laid.*

Louise chimes in, braiding her voice with her daughter's: *Where the tree of life is blooming and the roses never fade.*

Their voices blend like blue and yellow making green; you can't tell where one hue starts and the other ends. Listening to them, I realize this is what I lost too: years of rocking on a back porch with family, singing the heartfelt hymns that were among Mike Fuller's first gifts to me.

58

Family Secrets

L ate that same evening Marsha and I sit on the porch in the dark, a thing she likes to do when Tom has gone to bed and she's up by herself. Louise has already said good-night, so it's just the two of us, listening to the wind and the distant cries of nightjars. Mike's presence flutters around us, innocent and elusive, attracted by our efforts to recollect his scattered beginnings.

Louise and Edwin had met young and married young. Edwin declared it love at first sight, though it didn't take long for Louise to fall hard too. A fun-loving, independent girl who never wore make-up, she knew her folks would approve of her charming new beau, since he came from strict Methodists out of north Georgia. Edwin was only eight when his father died, right on the cusp of the Great Depression. The boy had promised his grieving mother he'd become a preacher when he grew up. Only he had a wild streak he couldn't contain, and life, apparently, had other plans for him.

How easy it would be to make Edwin the villain of this saga. If nothing else, the sojourn back to Blaze has taught me that our stories precede our lives. Edwin, too, emerged from conditions that shaped him, and even if I know almost nothing about them, I saw their effects in our one brief encounter in a Dallas nursing home.

"Well," Marsha comments when I remind her of his frailness. "That alcohol will eat you up."

"Blaze hardly ever talked about him," I admit. "It was like he never had a childhood."

"I know I didn't," his sister declares. "Daddy'd get drunk and threaten to kill us. One time he accused me of lying to him. Bent my arms so far back I thought they'd rip out. I got married, had a baby. At fourteen. I thought that'd solve everything."

She raises a palm skyward. "'Course I got Stephanie from that, so I am not complaining, Lord."

My heart begins to thump. The moment I've been dreading has arrived.

"Marsha—" I hesitate. "There's something I need to tell you." I fumble for the right words. "I've already written about it—and I wouldn't want you to hear it from anyone but me."

In her wicker chair Marsha has grown still, intent on listening. I'm reminded she's been a counselor to women fallen on harder times than mine, and no doubt there's nothing she hasn't already heard.

"When Blaze and I were together," I begin, taking a breath and letting the admission flow out on it—"I had an abortion."

Marsha bends slightly, drawing on her cigarette. The ember throws shadows on an inscrutable expression.

I push on. "It was not a careless act. For a long time after I didn't think about it. Now it haunts me again. I know—that child would be your family too."

Marsha jabs out the cigarette, sparks flying in the dark.

"I'm not for abortion myself," she replies. "But I can't judge anyone. Only the Lord can do that."

"I don't think anyone's really for abortion," I reply, hoping to leave the Lord out of it. "We made a decision only we could make."

"And then you lived with it."

"Either way you live with it." I spread my hands helplessly. "I don't think I would have made a very good mother."

Marsha's head snaps up. "You think I did?"

"What about Stephanie?"

We'd visited her daughter that afternoon, and I'd marveled at her, a small, delicate housewife and mother, so sturdy and self-contained.

Marsha fans a hand. "Oh, Stephanie's just Stephanie. She's been that way from the moment she was born."

She puts another cigarette to her lips. I'm guessing she's thinking about Paul, and the fallout of her prison stays on him and the grandchildren who now ache from his absence.

"Blaze didn't have much of a father," she allows. "He was running from my daddy all his life."

The match flame lights up the taut lines of her face. "I went and found Daddy before he died," she sighs. "In a hospital in Wichita Falls. Sybil, he was so alone. I'm telling you, my daddy's Bible was wore out!"

Edwin passed away in 1981. "I was hoping Blaze would come to his funeral," Marsha admits, a catch in her voice. "But he didn't."

We sit in silence for a time.

"Didn't you ever want to have kids?" she asks finally.

"There are so many ways to mother," I murmur.

She nods; she understands this.

"And I have James," I explain. "Blaze met him in Chicago. He was a little boy then. I was part of his growing up, and I consider him a child of mine."

"You think Blaze ever thought about it?" Marsha muses. "Later on, I mean."

"I don't know," I reply. "They say he had an affinity with kids."

Maybe we'd each taken Ape-shit's teaching to heart, learning to mother whoever crossed our paths.

Marsha's eyes glimmer. "I wonder what that child would be like, don't you?"

"All the time," I whisper and begin to cry, remorse and relief vying for mercy.

59

Prodigal Daughters

ouise is awake when I come into the bedroom we're sharing tonight. Six months ago I would never have predicted a slumber-party with Depty Dawg's mom in my future.

Pink plastic curlers fringe her face as she lies under the covers, reading her son's letters to me. The *Outhouse CD* plays on the end table beside her bed.

She holds up a page in greeting. "I know this, he loved you." She frowns. "Wished I'd known you then. You'd have loved Howard."

Howard was Louise's second husband, a musician who sang with her in church. She spent eighteen happy years with him on a farm in Missouri until he died quietly in bed one night. He was a Christian man, good to Louise, but she feared he might not approve of Mike and his ways. She didn't want her son's feelings hurt, so she'd go alone to visit him at Doug's, her eldest boy in Tulsa. There they'd bring out the beloved hymns and make tapes of their singing, a trio again. And they recorded the tunes Mike had taken to writing—lullabies about moonlight and two pillows on a bed. Louise never knew where those songs had come from.

"Wonder why he didn't tell me about you?" she ponders. "He always seemed so lonesome."

I settle in the recliner by her bed. "Well," I concede. "He used to call me his half-black Jewish girlfriend. Maybe he wasn't sure how you'd take that then."

From the look on Louise's face, I'm not sure how she's taking it now, so I quickly add, "He talked to me about you."

She brightens. "He did?"

Louise grasps at any evidence that her son loved her and, more crucially, that he knew she loved him. Her memories of Mike are very clear, but until my visit she had no inkling of Depty Dawg, a tree house, or any hippie wedding. Since the recent surge of interest in Blaze Foley, she's learned more about that facet of him than she ever knew while he was living. That man had been a stranger to her, breezing through Missouri once or twice in the mid-'80s, never staying long.

Louise had put the thirty chaotic years with Edwin behind her. Mike had been only eighteen, and a high school dropout, when he convinced his mother to take Marsha and leave her first husband for good. Later he would write in "Small Town Hero":

> Mommy, Mommy, what went wrong?
> Too late for questions now, you're on your own
> Mommy's broke down and your daddy's gone
> They just couldn't make it work no more

Louise and Marsha's departure left Mike with no one but Edwin to hold him in place. "That's when Mike started drifting," his mother sighs, avoiding my eyes.

Mike helped Louise break free of Edwin, but her son got lost in the process. She never knew what to make of the rough, duct-taped stranger who appeared at her door once in a blue moon. Now she can't remember why that even mattered. Her estrangement from her son gnaws at her still.

She turns up the volume to "Our Little Town":

> I don't know why you went away
> And nothin's all you had to say
> Not a word comes through here about you
> And soon my heart will break in two

"Gives me cold chills ever time I hear his voice," she murmurs, lying on her side.

"Because it makes you sad?"

"No!" she insists. "Because he's so good. Listen to that finger-picking."

She credits herself with teaching Mike the three chords she knew on guitar. That was the only formal musical education her son would receive. The rest he taught himself, listening to records, practicing in his room or in the car. When the trio sang in church, Mike would play an electric guitar, and Pat would strum a "standard." Marsha had described the blend of Louise, Mike, and Pat's voices as celestial.

"I never did know what Pat wanted," Louise blurts out now. "I give her everything she asked for. She was so pretty and all."

I wait for her to say more, but she doesn't. What I know of Pat's life I've gleaned today from Marsha. Blonde, charismatic Pat was arguably the most gifted of the four Fuller kids, very likely the most damaged. The star of the trio, she was hard to please and easy to anger. Everyone catered to Pat. At fifteen, she was growing up fast. When their father stumbled in from the bars at night, Marsha and Mike lay in their beds, listening as he clumped through the dark rooms. In the morning the house would be hushed with secrets.

Louise doesn't mention her daughter's suicide, or the fact that two of her children are in the ground before her. Like Marsha, she's a survivor; her faith has brought her peace. If she carries any guilt about Edwin's impact on her children—or her inability to protect them—it's an unspoken sadness, given over to the Lord. And she knows she's already been forgiven.

"Tell you what though," she declares to the ceiling. "I never knew what grief was till I lost my boy."

Nor does she express any malice toward his killer. "The whole thing's just heartbreaking," she opines, including Carey in her benediction. "Any way you look at it."

She has no quarrel with Carey's acquittal either, nor the possibility that he may have become a preacher. Simply more evidence of the Lord's mysterious ways.

"I'm just glad Mike was saved is all," she remarks, folding his last letter and returning it to its envelope.

"Me too," I reply absently, touched by her lack of rancor.

"Honey?" She catches my eye. "Have you accepted Christ as your Savior yet?"

"Uh—" I take the letters from her. "I'm—Jewish, remember?"

"Jews can love Jesus too," she chirps. Her brow furrows. "Didn't Mike talk to you about this?"

"Not like this."

"Well, he should have."

"I try to live a good life," I offer lamely.

"Oh, I know," she states. "That won't get you into Heaven."

"It won't?"

Her curlers rattle lightly. "No. Only Jesus can do that."

"So—where will I go when I die?"

In answer she points a finger downward.

"I'm going to Hell?" I echo.

"'Fraid so," she replies.

"Does that mean my parents are in Hell?" The notion makes me slightly ill.

Louise flusters. "Oh, I'm not doing this right. Let's call in Marsha."

"No, just tell me. What do you have to do to be saved?"

Truthfully, I've never cared about Heaven one way or the other. Only now that I've been denied access, it's sticking strangely in my craw.

Louise waves a hand. "Oh, getting saved is easy! You just got to let Him into your heart. It don't change nothing. Just makes you a little happier is all."

I wonder what she'd say if she knew that my parents had tried to convert her son to Judaism. By her lights, they were burning in Hell anyway. She is looking at me with such guileless eyes, her intentions sincere. She just wants me to have my ticket for eternity, to be there forever, with Mike, and with her. Why couldn't I just accept Jesus—since it's so easy—and give her that? It's the image of my parents in flames that stops me, as if I were the one consigning them to an infinite stay in Louise's Hell.

"I'm sure your folks wouldn't want you to burn," she ventures, reading my thoughts.

"Then it's my choice," I tell her. "'Honor thy father and mother.' That's what I was raised on."

"Well." Her eyes glisten. She pats my hand. "I didn't mean to upset you, honey. Let's just sleep on it, okay?" And pulling the covers up to her neck, she turns away on her side.

"Okay." I sigh. "Good night, Louise."

Slipping into my bed, I listen to her breathing slow to gentle snores. What was it about families anyway, always wanting to bring you to their God? I'd resisted the strict beliefs that divided death into different Heavens and Hells. Mike Fuller had seen through them too: the paradox of One God and All Ways. The fragmented world had broken his heart.

At dawn I wake to find Louise already up and dressed. When I stretch and say, "Good morning," she hurries to my side, bending over me, smelling of talcum.

"I'm so happy Mike had you," she whispers. "That he had someone to love. And someone who loved him. It makes me feel so much better about his life."

I sit up and put my arms around her.

"I love you," she breathes. "I truly do." She holds me close. "You can call me Mom if you want to."

Part 5

The Moon
Shines On

60

Numbers

Nine months after Billy's letter arrived in New York, I've finally come to a stop in Georgia. The Waller tradition of hospitality endures. At Glyn's invitation, I returned here from Texas, to live in the quarters for a time, collecting my thoughts.

Every morning now since the end of February, I've sat at this desk by a window, watching the green seep up out of the earth. By May, Georgia is spring-steeped, hot already. Leaves no longer shimmer with youth; like gardeners' hands, they've darkened with the serious work of summer: gathering sunlight, making sugar. Against a wall of emerald woods, the flowering privets make a shield of white. The Chattahoochee has disappeared behind the trees again, save for the sound the water makes buckling past the cabin. An armadillo forages in the floodplain, and turkey vultures fly low over the quarters, casting shadows on the ground. Glyn says there's still blackberry winter to come, or maybe not this year; so much rain.

How I came to be at Waller writing about lost love is still a great, unsolicited surprise. One thing is certain: Blaze Foley's legend got me here. So much of his true story unfolded in Georgia, and all of his life in the tree house. Our friends in Whitesburg still maintain they witnessed his happiest time, and everywhere is evidence of him.

Here is where I fell in love with Depty Dawg, and here's where I'm finally coming to terms with his ghost. I got a pretty good glimpse of Mike Fuller while he lived; Blaze Foley I know mostly through his songs and letters, other people's memories, and my own dreams and writing.

This spring marks twenty-eight years since he and I first collided at Banning Mill. Blaze once said, *Weird about words*; I would say, *Numbers too*. Twenty-eight is twice fourteen. We met fourteen years before he died; it's now fourteen years since his death. Fourteen is two times seven.

Somewhere I read that the body replaces its cells every seven years, yet certain elements remain: sensation, identity, memory. Indelible information transfers to new sets of sensual records imprinted on tissue. Aging is selective; the way we remember our lives depends on the abilities of nucleus and synapse. Some memories are lost, others relegated to the mind's archives, access denied unless the heart is pierced through, its contents revealed. What's retained becomes the life you've lived; what's forgotten haunts the halls of dreams you can't remember.

Two-hundred-and-fifty-two days and five thousand miles later, this all still feels like a dream. Dropping suddenly into the past has contorted my sense of time. No longer linear, yesterday and today weave in and around each other, so that what I felt then is threaded through what I see now. And these words are the shuttle on memory's loom, one more enfolded layer.

In the past twenty-six years I've written about Depty Dawg often enough to know I can't always separate reality from poetry. What's true is what's remembered, and how it's remembered shifts with time. Emotion stains memory like a photographic tint, fading the past or imbuing it with a black-and-white clarity so crystalline it remains inalterably present.

Being back at Waller gives remembering an ingrown quality. Everywhere I look, I see Depty or Blaze. Past, present, and future are facing mirrors reflecting timelessly. Holding up only one gives me a kind of karmic vertigo: is the past a result of this moment? Has the future already happened? Or maybe it's just my luck to see time as a prism.

Writing may be a solitary occupation, but this room is full of people. Everyone I've spoken to, laughed or cried with about Blaze—and a few I haven't—are looking over my shoulder, wondering if they're going to like what I have to say next. I'm trying to write Mike Fuller without doing harm, Depty Dawg without romance (fat chance), Blaze Foley without judgment. I'll probably fail at all three.

This present attempt to tell our story joins my words to his myth. Even if it were my intention, not to mention within my means, to demystify his legend, simply by the act of writing I am contributing to it. And the work is its own surprise, each day changeable and new. Every time I encounter a fresh view of the past, what I feel is revised word-by-word. I'm not the girl I was nine months ago; I'm not the girl I was nine days ago. I can no longer hold on to the concreteness of anything, myself included. There is more going on all the time, everywhere, than I can ever hope to know. That used to scare me; now it's a relief. The writing is rewriting me too.

Each week brings new challenges. Recently I've learned more about Blaze's Houston fiancée, Fifi Larue—though that is her story, not mine. It turns out they were engaged earlier than I'd thought, so that topples all my comfortable conclusions about our last meeting in New York City, and it invites more mystery. I'll probably never know why I never heard any of his love songs back then. But that no longer matters as much as the fact that it sometimes feels like we are writing this book together.

And I still haven't figured out where the story should end. Fortunately, art is not like life; in art you get to pick your ending. Writing about Depty once again, it's the same dilemma as always. Telling our history gives it the stamp of reality, the apparition of truth. *This is how it was*, the words seem to insist, as if to justify their own existence.

The truth is, I still don't know. It all happened I guess.

61

Head Over Heels

Two months ago, when I sat down to begin writing, I was still full of self-doubt. With so many versions of the truth afoot, who was I to decide which ones were valid? My own faded memories were evidence of this, elusive and incomplete, so many names and places lost.

For instance, in trying to recreate that first night Depty and I spent together, certain images remained vivid: the little smokehouse behind the main house, the bed against the wall, a record player on a high wooden table. Yet I had no idea where we were exactly, on whose property in the county.

One morning, as I puzzled how to write about it anyway, Glyn comes up to the quarters to say he's just gotten a phone call from Dave.

"You remember Dave?" he asks. "He lives in Ohio now. Used to play with Dep at the Mill."

"Dave?" I reply. "As in Dave and Gail? They had a band called Head Over Heels?"

Glyn nods. "That's right. They lived at the old Gilley Place. Dep crashed there some, I believe."

Memory swerves to consciousness. "Wait—did it have little shacks, little outbuildings?"

Glyn thinks so, but I can ask Dave myself because he's visiting in Carroll County and heard I was in town. He's coming over this afternoon to say hello.

Dave and I greet each other breathlessly. These days he is a white-mustached, smiling Gepetto, his enduring mild manner belying a midlife passion for amateur racecars. We play thirty-year catch-up. He and Gail are still head over heels, now the parents of two grown sons. In turn, I tell him something of my life, and what I've learned about Depty Dawg's.

He shakes his head over his old friend's death. "I loved performing with him," Dave recalls. "We even talked of becoming a trio. But Dep was so self-destructive, I couldn't see how it would work."

He grins. "I do remember the joy between the two of you. Oh." He digs into his pocket. "I have something for you."

Pulling out a small plastic bag, he says, "You gave this to him. I guess it got lost. We found it when we cleaned out the Gilley Place before it was sold."

I am amazed. "And you kept it all these years?"

"You don't throw away something like this."

Dave hands it to me. I turn the bag over in my fingers. The clear plastic reveals a tarnished ID bracelet with a broken chain. *Samuel Rosen 32494930.* On the back is the inscription: *I Love You Always Jeannette.*

I'm at a loss for words. To be honest, I'd forgotten all about the bracelet, and yet here it was anyway, back in my hand.

Some things will not let you forget them. No matter how hard you try to let them go, they insist on staying around.

Hours later, Dave and I say good-bye, still off-balance from the tug of threads holding this moment in place. What am I to make of this ageless gift from old, faithful friends, saying as much about their hearts as ours?

Or this message from my parents: *We are in this story too.*

Or this reminder across the decades from Depty Dawg: *Don't ever doubt.*

62

Udo Revisited

I've found Udo. Or rather I finally located someone who remembers where the tree house used to be. Shirley is a pretty countrywoman in her late twenties; she's lived in Star Point all her life. As a kid, she played in the tumbledown shack back in the woods across the road. Now she has two little boys of her own, and the tree house is part of their mythology.

Shirley's father purchased the land from Zonko Joe in the late '70s. It was he who burned down the unfinished house, and moved the sagging trailer into the woods, closer to the tree house. By the time he sold the property to its present owner, little of the old shelter remained. Shirley shows me the original site of Joe's trailer, more than a quarter mile east of the newly built house. Grody Mike and I were that far off when we came looking last autumn. A rusted refrigerator lies over the hole of the abandoned outhouse, making sure no one stumbles back there and falls in.

Shirley sets me on the footpath to the creek and I start out for Udo alone. The sun is sinking behind the clay hills, long beams of light filtering through a forest of young tuliptree and sweet gum. In early autumn, falling leaves sound like footsteps. September is spider season in Georgia. Delicate anchor lines of silk stretch from tree to tree, brushing my face. Lacework circles in the grasses glint in the slanting sunlight. A half ghost-moon tilts overhead, white as sails. There's no firebreak any more, but the creek runs close by, narrow beaches edged with small sandy cliffs shaped by floods. Where the imprint of a carriage road begins, there stands a great black oak, one of the few old trees left. If Shirley's memory is correct, this is the oak that marked the turn for Dep and me. He always said we'd hang a sign from its branches, one that read *Udo*.

Turning blindly onto the carriage road, I tick off ten, twenty, thirty steps, then face into the woods: here is where the tree house would have stood.

There's the border of the stream, and the swale on the other side, deeper now, cleft by time and runoff. A persistent tangle of grapevine and rhododendron marks the spot; that, and two thick pines that have escaped the pulpwooders' saws. They've got to be at least sixty years old; one might even be the pine that grew up through the house. Sunbeams stripe the trunks with orange bands, ephemeral blazes marking invisible paths.

I walk the imagined perimeter of the platforms, recalling the stove, the windows, and us under blankets gazing up at the winter moon. Pushing over rocks and logs, I look for the slightest remnant, anything—a piece of crockery, a door handle, a plastic guitar pick. I can't find a trace of jasmine.

Sinking into the pine needles, I realize Dep was right: *there are no goodbyes.* Neither of us could have foreseen our homecoming looking like this, him gone to legend, and me the grieving widow, fourteen years late. The hardest thing to throw away is the image of who I think I am: I'm an artist, I'm a gypsy, I'm evolved. I cling to the things that mirror these faces—a toaster, a dog, a spiritual life. Blaze was tethered to an idea of himself too, and in the end that may be what killed him. If we could only embrace an alternative lifestyle where the craving for identity does not obstruct the love we're capable of giving.

I thought I might feel sad coming back here, but what I feel is gratitude, a wondering thankfulness for this place and whatever magic touched us, strong enough to wake me and make me remember this jewel of love I almost misplaced. If I had to sum up what the past year has taught me, it would probably all come down to this: *don't miss what's in front of you.*

And one day soon I may be done with regretting.

63

D earest Blaze,
   It's funny, I don't feel haunted by you any more. Your presence has become lighter, more expanded. Like a house with no
walls, you have no inside or out; nothing is left out of you.

The writing belies that of course. It requires me to shape you
into fragments with names: Mike, Tex, Depty, Blaze. A necessary illusion—helpful I guess—like the notion that there were
two Blaze Foleys. Your anger mirrored the depth of your sensitivity; they were one reality, just as you were one man living one
life, however broken it might appear to others. The deception of
dualities—male, female; black, white; Christian, Jew—obscures
our truest identity. Just as, for the longest time, I thought life and
death occupied separate realms. I mean you're dead, and look how
busy you've been.

I had hoped remembering you might give your wandering
heart a home. I didn't know how much it was my own that needed
mooring. You found me out and comforted me, didn't you? Your
return has made me whole—not because I was unfinished—but
because it's given me a glimpse of how things really are.

A plethora of coincidences pave the way to you, my love. I
suspect all of life is like this, each strand spliced by every other,
though we rarely get to see those intersections where warp meets
woof. The mystery of who we're born to and who we're given to
love is beyond my comprehension, honey. So I keep to the small
surprises, like the moment in Austin when I came upon your

drawing of what I first mistook for vultures—a tender pair of birds with heads together and wings outspread. But why should I be surprised that birds are part of our story? After all, they can fly.

I went back to Udo, you know. And it occurred to me while I was there that maybe this is where the story should end—where it began. Only I was wrong about art, Blaze; it is like life. It has no beginning and no end. For there are your songs now, and wherever they wander, they take us with them—us, and a little house in a tree, waiting for two young lovers to come down the path and fall asleep under an apricot moon, both of them whole and in a perfect world.

Depty, I love you all ways.

Sybil

Acknowledgments

Any appreciation of those essential to this memoir must begin with Kevin Triplett. In undertaking a film about Blaze, Kevin set in motion the circumstances that would bring this work to life. He gave me generous access to his documentary archives so that I might more fully understand the arc of Blaze's life and death, and also helped me to assemble many of the photos included here. My debt to him, artistically and emotionally, is practically beyond words. I also want to thank the Abraxas film crew and production staff—Chris Ohlsen, Kai Mantsch, Andy Harthcock, June Burnum, Kathleen Shaw, Joey Trum, and editor Rita Sanders—for their tender care, and especially Mike Nicholson and his wife Melissa Taylor Nicholson for being the romantics they are.

Family members Jill Silverman Pekar and Joseph Berson kindly offered necessary financial contributions. My brother, Joshua Rosen, was a champ of affection and assistance, going to bat for me in myriad ways. For concern, comfort, and/or lost memories, Susan Castner, Karen Paul Rosen, Jason Castner, and Eugenie, Julien, and Sarajane Sacks were all wonderfully receptive, as were Jessica, Austin, and Jared Heitmann, my ever-ardent cheerleaders. To my newfound clan—Louise Fuller Hacker; Tom Weldon; Paul, Carlin, and Luke Berry; and Stephanie, James, and Jacob Hardin—I offer my love and gratitude for their willingness to share Mike, and to let me write about them. To Blaze's sister, Marsha Weldon, goes my deepest appreciation for her generosity, great faith, and boundless friendship.

Close friends and neighbors helped me navigate the first months of Depty Dawg's return: Mary Davin, Marnie Andrews, Amelia Penland Fuller, Katherine Cortez-Adams, Debra Howes, Linda Gluck, Craig Fuller, Jeff Jacobson, Sarah Chodoff, June Stein, Judy Perrenod, Pril Smiley, and Chuck Perrenod. Among old friends and new in Texas and Georgia who shared memories, or lent encouragement, are Dave and Gail Coppock, Lindsey and Kerry Horton, Jane Freer, LaNelle McNamara, Ricky Cardwell, Leland Waddell, Jon Smith and Ryan Rader (producers of the *Tribute CDs*), John and Laurie Hill, Cathy Hubach, George Ensle, Janice and Elliott Rogers, Tom Smith, Robin Carty, Larry Monroe, Leti de la Vega, Johnny McNamara, Geoffrey Outlaw, Tony Scarano, Happy Jack, Gilbert Cardwell, Kay Cardwell, Danny Cummings, Chuck Lamb, Sylvia Benini, Mike Thomas, Julie Gabel, Dawn Raven, Tim Thomas, Wanda Witt, Claire Baker, Rick Pryor, Gordon Chandler, David Moscovitz, Nancy Gaddy, Fred Richards, Bill Eisenhauer, Carol Williams, Steve Voinche, Cathy Balch, Buzz Duffy, Laura Emory, and Joe Nick Patoski. I want to thank Brende Fuller, Lost John Casner, and Mandy Mercier for their helpful suggestions and insightful conversations on just about everything, and especially Gurf Morlix for keeping Dep and The Beaver Valley Boys alive.

Appreciation goes to the Austin Historical Society, Susan Ciegler of Northwest Georgia Regional Hospital's Department of Records, and the staff of the Staples copy center in Carrollton, Georgia, for their patience and meticulousness.

So many names float through this story that at times, in an effort not to overwhelm the reader, it was necessary to drop those appearing only briefly. Others asked to be left unnamed. To those who can be named or, in some cases, were only half-named—Jo Giraudo; Leo Sauer; Ben Douglas; Beth Passavant; Michael Goodman; Dottie Goodman; Peggy Blow; Rabbi Jerome Fox; Eugenie Moskovitz; Myrna Copeland; Roxanne Diehl; Buddy Carroll; Holly Lorrens; Gabi North; Greg Risse; Hughes Holder III; Tricia Berkman; Punk Patrollers Tony Boatwright, Steve Wells, Raymond Cosby, Roger Dukes; Jim Eckert (original tree house architect); Teddi Locke; Freddy and Deborah Manley; Steve Arledge; Keith and Erin Boyle; Frank Campbell; Cynthia Thibideaux; Jim Duffy; Ira Katz; Scott Nolan; Bill, Martha, Betsey, and Cassie Redhed; Jerry Lee Davidson; David Miller; Terry Hayden; Jackie Brooks; John Kostmayer; Hinda Gerwitz; John Bishop; Greg Land; Ralph Bethay; Floyd "Stony" Woods; Les Smith; Mandy Hanson; Howard Hacker; Shirley, Ethan, and Caleb Milam; and Tom Lewis—I am much obliged to you all for making a cameo. If I've inadvertently left anyone out, the fault is mine alone.

Nine deep bows go to my teacher, John Daido Loori, Roshi, and Geoffrey Shugen Arnold, Sensei, and Konrad Ryushin Marjak, Osho, of Zen Mountain Monastery in Mt. Tremper, New York. Fellow monastery students—Michelle Seigei Spark, Chris Koto Trevalyan, Kirsten Tosei Ainsworth-Vincze, Amy Shoko Brown, Julie Shoju Greenwood, Janice Senju Baker, Vanessa Zuisei Goddard, Shideh Tenkei Lennon, Diana Kosei Hartel, Troy Zuikon Gangle, Bethany Senkyu Saltman, Thayer Kyusan Case, Danica Shoan Ankele, Bear

Gokan Bonebakker, Lisa Kyojo Smith, Adam Starritt, Roxie Keien Newberry, Joel Sansho Benson, Liz E-Kun Potter, and Suzanne Taikyo Gilman—offered ears to listen and shoulders to cry on. Enduring love goes to Michael Yukon Grody for refusing to let me get away with anything.

I'm also grateful to Kathleen Hudson, director and founder of the Texas Music Heritage Foundation, for writing about Blaze and guiding me to the University of North Texas Press. I thank UNT Press' Managing Editor Karen DeVinney for her unflagging optimism, sensible counsel, and help with making the text sing. Marketing Manager Paula Oates and Administrative Assistant Mary Young, both of UNT Press, were tremendously helpful and always cheerful. I'm also beholden to C.P. Vaughn for his beautiful portraits of Blaze, and his tender heart.

Writer friends Chris Manheim and Valerie Meiju Linet offered support at just the right moment. I thank my agent Richard Basch for his apparently bottomless faith in me. Much appreciation also goes to my dear James Luria for finding the beginning and sticking with it to the end. Most of all, I extend my deepest thanks to Laura Buchwald, editor and pal, for teaching me so much about my own writing, and writing in general, and for shaping these pages with her sensitive, elegant hand. Her belief in my and Blaze's story inspired and sustained me in moments of frustration and despair.

Last but not least, endless thank-you's for tree house and Waller memories go to "Zonko" Joe Bucher and his wife Kathy Lichtenburg; Will "Bubba," Pam, and Seth Land; "Grody" Mike and his wife Dee Boyle; Basil Bouris; Sas Thomas; and Gabi North. I'm so glad to have found you all again. I particularly want to acknowledge Margery Bouris for her technical support and ceaseless kindness, and Billy Bouris for finding me in New York and reeling me in. And to Glyn Thomas I give my whole heart, for keeping me directionally correct—and for jumping the broom with me at Waller two days shy of thirty years after he held it for Depty Dawg and me.

Discography

1979 *If I Could Only Fly/Let Me Ride in Your Big Cadillac* [45rpm] (Zephyr Records)

1983? *Blaze Foley* [unreleased Muscle Shoals album] (Vital Records)

1983? *Girl Scout Cookies/Oval Room* [unreleased 45rpm] (Vital Records)

1989 *Live at the Austin Outhouse (…and not there)* [cassette tape] (Outhouse Records)

1999 *Live at the Austin Outhouse* (Lost Art Records)

2004 *Oval Room* (Lost Art Records)

2005 *Wanted More Dead Than Alive* (Waddell Hollow/Deep South Productions)

2006 *Blaze Foley and The Beaver Valley Boys: Cold, Cold World* (Lost Art Records)

2008 *Blaze Foley: Dawg Days 1976–1978* [to be released]

? *Big Cheeseburgers* [to be released]

Tribute Albums

1998 *Volume One: In Tribute and Loving Memory* (Deep South Productions)

1999 *Volume Two: BFI Too—Blaze A Blaze* (Deep South Productions)

2000 *Volume Three: BFI Three—Blaze Foley Inside* (Deep South Productions)

2002 *Volume Four: Songs for Blaze, A Friend of Ours* (Deep South Productions)

2004 *If I Could Only Fly: A Blaze Foley Tribute* [box set] (Borderdreams, Spain)

Index

Emmajoe's, 215
Empire State guitar, 68–69, 70, 105, 126–28, 155, 175
Even Cowgirls Get the Blues, 109

F

"Faded Loves and Memories," 97–98
"Farther Along," 39, 87
FBI, 190
Fewell, 198
Fiddler on the Roof, 133
Fisher, Eddie, 62
Foley, Blaze (Michael David Fuller)
    (affinity for children) 46, 59, 160–61, 165, 201, 231
    (alcoholism) 58, 65, 90–91, 136–37, 143–44, 149, 175–76, 183, 192, 194,
        201, 203, 210–12, 215
    (ambivalence about performing) 125–26, 128, 137–39, 184
    (anger) 65–66, 90–91, 201, 211–12, 217;
    (Arkansas) 18, 177, 227;
    (Atlanta) 94, 138, 140–41,146–48, 150–51, 191
    (attempt to enlist for Vietnam War) 91
    (attempted conversion to Judaism) 129–33, 154, 194, 235
    (Austin) 5, 93–94, 119–133, 136–139, 142–143, 171–173, 177–178,
        183–186, 192–195, 200–218, 225
    (Chicago) 6, 14–15, 104, 146, 151, 153, 154–168, 173, 178, 186, 194–95,
        231
    (childhood) 18, 38, 60, 62, 75, 87–88, 113–115, 118, 127, 134, 181, 212,
        227–31, 233–35
    (commitment to art) 141, 183–84, 193, 215
    (death) x, 171–173, 176, 200–12, 216–18, 234, 245, 246
    (description of) 5, 55, 178, 183–84, 192–93, 201
    (drugs) 58, 69, 111, 138, 154, 162, 192, 203, 215
    (duct tape) 49, 183, 206–7, 217, 233
    (Duct Tape Messiah) 5, 201, 206, 212
    (family) 18, 62, 75, 113–115, 117, 127, 132, 181, 212, 221, 224–235
    (father, relationship to) 72, 88, 109, 113–15, 132, 212, 228–31; 233–34
    (funeral) 206–7
    (gravestone) 172–73, 217–18
    (guitar playing) 61, 123, 178, 193, 233
    (homelessness) 5, 23, 27, 33–34, 77, 121, 139, 144, 149, 163, 183–184,
        192, 221